MONETARY POLICY AND THE DESIGN OF FINANCIAL INSTITUTIONS IN CHINA, 1978–90

Monetary Policy and the Design of Financial Institutions in China, 1978–90

Leroy Jin

M
St. Martin's Press in association with St Antony's College, Oxford

First published in Great Britain 1994 by
MACMILLAN PRESS LTD
Houndmills, Basingstoke, Hampshire RG21 2XS
and London
Companies and representatives
throughout the world

This book is published in the *St Antony's/Macmillan Series*
General Editor: Alex Pravda

A catalogue record for this book is available
from the British Library.

ISBN 0–333–62032–1

10 9 8 7 6 5 4 3 2 1
03 02 01 00 99 98 97 96 95 94

Printed in Great Britain by
Ipswich Book Co Ltd
Ipswich, Suffolk

First published in the United States of America 1994 by
Scholarly and Reference Division,
ST. MARTIN'S PRESS, INC.,
175 Fifth Avenue,
New York, N.Y. 10010

ISBN 0–312–12274–8

Library of Congress Cataloging-in-Publication Data
Jin, Leroy.
Monetary policy and the design of financial institutions in China, 1978–1990 / Leroy Jin.
p. cm.
Includes bibliographical references and index.
ISBN 0–312–12274–8
1. Monetary policy—China. 2. Financial institutions—China.
3. China—Economic policy—1976– I. Title.
HG1285.J56 1994
332.1'0951—dc20 94–19510
CIP

Contents

List of Figures

List of Tables

Preface

China's growth performance has been remarkable since the development strategy was transformed and decentralisation– and market-oriented reform were introduced in the late 1970s. However, there is a wide concern about the stability and sustainability of growth in the future because (i) macro control is becoming less effective, and growth is still subject to stop-go cycles; (ii) improvement in efficiency is slow; and (iii) fragility of banks increases. In relation to these, one of the most controversial subjects on policy debate is the continuing monetary expansion. Despite the large attention it has attracted, sources, processes and underlying mechanisms of monetary expansion as well as its interrelations with other phenomena have not yet been clearly understood. As a result, confusion spreads. This itself has become a destabilising factor, i.e. it contributes to policy swings and the related stop–go cycles.

The central theme of this book is simple: monetary expansion could be attributed to partial economic reform – economic reform without reform of local governments' ownership and development of capital markets. It argues that the monetary expansion was driven by the banks' finance for fixed assets investment combined with lack of channels (other than bank deposit-lending) for financial intermediation in a situation where households have become the dominant savers. Excessive bank credit expansion was necessary in a centre-locality investment game under the decentralised Chinese economic system. In this game, local governments' investment was local border-constrained and biased towards setting up small processing industrial enterprises, causing lack of investment for technical transformation of existing enterprises and for infrastructure. At the same time, the central government was no longer the major saver. Unable to resolve these problems of investment allocation directly, the policy-makers turned to expansion of bank loans for priority investment in order to maintain high growth. Given that extra investment for priority activities was necessary, the underdevelopment of capital markets necessitated such investment to be financed by banks. In consequence, aggregate control had to be loosened, and extensive development and slow improvement of efficiency persisted. These in turn further increased the demand for credit from the inefficient enterprises, leading to growth of non-performing loans and erosion of the banks' capital base. Although Chinese policy-makers have been lucky in generally avoiding unmanageable excessive demand thanks to households' long-term saving behaviour, the accumulated liquidity risk increases uncertainty. The problems could not be solved by tightening monetary control alone, as the latter is easily exaggerated under the Chinese economic system and causes recession in the short term and might be unable to stabilise the economy in the longer term.

However, the build-up of money balances is not a disaster. By contrast, the available money can be utilised to facilitate needed ownership reform. The thesis suggests that monetary policy, financial reform, ownership reform and design of corporate control should be coordinated with a focus on promoting industrial restructuring and competition. In this process, the second-best solution would be to internalise the externality problems at provincial level, and to put fiscal means to a more active use in macroeconomic management.

LEROY JIN

Acknowledgements

My principal debt is to Mr Christopher Allsopp and Dr Cyril Lin for their intellectual guidance, advice, criticism and encouragement over the years of my study. I am grateful to Sir Alec Cairncross who read the whole thesis and gave me strong support, and Mr Yongding Yu, Weiying Zhang and Professor Sylvain Plasschaert for their reading of the drafts of, and valuable suggestions for the thesis. I am also grateful to Professor Wlodzimierz Brus and Professor Robert Cassen for their comments on the original outline of the thesis, and Professor Adrian Wood and Dr E. V. K. Fitzgerald for their valuable comments on the final version. In addition, my thanks go to Dr Shujie Yao, Dr Tru-Gin Liu and Dr Duo Qin for their help in some of the early work, and Professor Jinlian Wu and Madam Meizheng Xu for their discussion with the author about the problems in China's economy. I also want to thank Andrew Churchill, Christopher Ashill and Elizabeth Loft-Simson for their help in removing most of my lapses in English grammar. It goes without saying that the author is fully responsible for any of the remaining errors in the work.

Among the many people who have helped me to collect materials for this study, I am especially indebted to Duo Xie, Fang Zeng and Hong Zeng.

Funding for my study from the World Bank and the British Government's Overseas Research Scholarship is gratefully acknowledged. Finally, I am deeply indebted to my wife Hua who not only provides constant encouragement but also helped to make the study in Oxford financially possible.

LEROY JIN

List of Abbreviations

ABC	Agricultural Bank of China
bn	billion
BOC	Bank of China
Bocom	Bank of Communication
CEE	Central and Eastern Europe
CIS	Commonwealth of Independent States
CITIC	China International Trust and Investment Corporation
COEs	Collectively-owned Enterprises
CPEs	The Centrally Planned Economies
EBFC	Ever Bright Finance Company
FOF	Flow of Funds
GDP	Gross Domestic Product
GDR	German Democratic Republic
GNP	Gross National Product
H	high-powered money
ICBC	Industrial and Commercial Bank of China
ICT	industrial and commercial taxes
LCH	life-cycle hypothesis
m	Month; i.e. 1985m1 means the first month of 1985
MB	monetary base
mn	million
MOF	Ministry of Finance
NICs	Newly industrialised countries
NMP	Net material product
OECD	Organisation for Economic Cooperation and Development
000s	thousands (e.g. ¥000s = thousands of yuans)
PBC	People's Bank of China, i.e. the central bank after 1983
PCBC	People's Construction Bank of China
PDC	Public Dividend Capital
PICC	People's Insurance Company of China
PIH	Permanent income hypothesis
Q	quarter; e.g. 1987Q4 means the fourth quarter of 1987
RCCs	Rural Credit Cooperatives
SBs	Specialised Banks
SEZs	Special Economic Zones
SOEs	State-owned enterprises

SSB	State Statistical Bureau of China
TFP	Total Factor Productivity
TICs	Trust and Investment Companies
TVEs	Township and Village Enterprises
UCCs	Urban Credit Cooperatives
Ventech	China Venturetech Investment Corporation
¥	Renminbi (RMB) yuan, the Chinese money unit. ¥1 billion equals ¥1000 million in this book.

NB. This book uses the Pinyin system for romanising Chinese, with some exceptions for personal names that are familiar in the West (e.g. Sun Yat-sen according to the old Wade-Giles system, rather than Sun Yixian according to the Pinyin system). The Chinese surname appears first, followed by the given name, for instance, Zhao Ziyang, where Zhao is the surname and Ziyang is the given name.

1 Introduction

Since 1979, China's economy has been undergoing major changes under the new development strategy and economic reform programme. The new development strategy emphasises increasing in living standards rather than industrialisation *per se*. It calls for the pattern of development to be transformed from heavy industry-dominated, unbalanced growth to more balanced growth with a considered regard towards agriculture and light industry; from extensive to intensive growth (i.e. from input-based growth to growth based on improvements in efficiency; from promoting inland development to promoting coastal development, and from self-sufficiency to opening up to the outside world.[1]

The reform was initiated to support the transformation of the strategy for economic development. Despite sometimes serious disagreements among top policy-makers on the details and precise type of economic system most suitable to Chinese conditions, there has been and remains a broad consensus on the need to decentralise economic management and to introduce market mechanisms into China's economy to enhance economic efficiency.

The reform process has been gradualistic and experimental – a trial-and-error approach. It has been pursued in four main ways:

(i) by decentralising economic management (e.g. investment control and the management of state-owned enterprises) to local governments;
(ii) by gradually introducing market mechanisms (e.g. price liberalisation);
(iii) by promoting the development of non-state sectors;
(iv) by establishing macroeconomic management system based on indirect control.

Noticeably, the ideology of state ownership has remained virtually unchanged. In practice, successes and failures of the reform experiments have fed back into decisions on the development objectives and reform strategy.

With respect to macroeconomic control, reflecting the much weakened role of central physical planning and of the state budget in the mobilisation and allocation of resources, heavy emphasis has been placed

Table 1.1 Growth of money and national income (1952–90)

Money stock (¥ bn)	*Nominal*			*Deflated*[a]		
	1952	*1978*	*1990*	*1952*	*1978*	*1990*
M0 (currency outside of banks)	2.8	21.2	264.4	2.8	18.8	128.6
M1 (M0 + cheque-related deposits)	9.3	99.4	792.6	9.3	88.2	385.5
M2 (M0 + total bank deposits)	10.1	120.4	1557.0	10.1	106.8	757.3
Growth (% p/a)		*1953–78*	*1979–90*		*1953–78*	*1979–90*
M0		8.2	23.4		7.6	17.4
M1		9.5	18.9		9.0	13.1
M2		10.0	23.8		9.5	17.7
Net material product (NMP)		6.5	14.0		6.0	8.4
NMP deflator		0.5	5.6			

Note: Money stock is the year-end figure. Deposits with the Rural Credit Cooperatives (RCCs) and the Urban Credit Cooperatives are included. Assuming differences between deposits and loans of both the RCCs and UCCs are deposited with the state banks, total deposits are estimated as the deposits with the state banks plus loans extended by both the RCCs and UCCs. The state budget deposits are excluded from the deposits because of their transitory nature and also for international comparability. Nominal GNP grew at 14.2 per cent over 1978–90 (SSB, 1991a: 31). [a] Deflated according to national income deflator.

Source: *Almanac of China's Finance and Banking* (1990: 48, 50, 60, 65; 1991: 42, 48, 52–4, 58); SSB (1991a: 32–3).

on monetary policy, both as an instrument of macroeconomic control and as a method of influencing the allocation of resources in a more indirect and market-oriented way. However, numerous difficulties have emerged.

During the period 1978–90, one of the most striking phenomena in China's economy was the rapid expansion of money stock (see Table 1.1). In nominal terms, compared with the pre-1978 period, growth rate of M0 in the period 1979–90 was nearly three times as rapid, M1 was 203 per cent as fast and M2 was 238 per cent as fast. Despite the policy objective of achieving financial and price stability, rapid expansion of the money stock has continued throughout the entire reform period. There have been attempts to curb monetary expansion from time to time,[2] but all were transitory and had no significant impact on the upward trend of monetary expansion.

Table 1.2 Average outstanding monetary holding (broadly defined) as a percentage of GDP (1989)

Low-income economies excluding China with per capita GNP less than US$500	23.6
Middle-income economies with per capita GNP between US$500–1300	41.9
Upper-middle income economies with per capita GNP between US$1300–6,000	49.8
High income economies with per capita GNP more than US$6000	68.3
China (1989)	66.7
China (1991)	98.8[a]

Note: Monetary holdings are the sum of money (International Financial Statistics: Line 34) and quasi-money (International Financial Statistics: Line 35). Money comprises the economy's means of payment: currency outside banks and demand deposits. Quasi-money comprises time and saving deposits and similar bank accounts that the issuer will readily exchange for money. The ratios for country groups are arithmetic averages.

Source: The World Bank (1991: 228–9).[a] The World Bank, cited by Schmidt-Hebbel (1991: 23).

Since money stock (M2) grew much faster than nominal national income (Table 1.1), the money/GDP ratio (i.e. M2/GDP) rose rapidly in China: from 31 to 99 per cent between 1978 and 1991. From an international perspective, China's economy has become an abnormal economy in terms of the money/GDP ratio. For low-income economies (such as China) with per capita GNP less than US$500, this ratio was on average 23.6 per cent in 1989 (Table 1.2). For China, in the same year, it was 66.7 per cent, almost the same as high-income economies with per capita GNP of over US$7600 (68.3 per cent).

China's economy was also abnormal compared with some of its Asian counterparts. For instance, the money/GDP ratio was 21.1 per cent in the Philippines, 27.3 per cent in Bangladesh, 30.2 per cent in Indonesia and 45.6 per cent in India in 1989.[3] The ratio in China in 1991 even exceeds that of many richer East Asian economies in 1990 (Singapore: 97.1%, Thailand: 74.5%, Malaysia: 66.9%, South Korea: 39.8%).[4]

Many economists view monetary expansion and inflation as two sides of a coin over the long-term. One of the often-cited monetarist dictums is Friedman's statement that a steady and sustained rise in prices is always and everywhere a monetary phenomenon. This argument relies on the presumption that the demand for money is reasonably stable in real terms. An even stronger claim is that inflation is essentially a monetary phenomenon, even if changes in the velocity of money are taken into account '. . . a rise in velocity by itself has never caused or substantially intensified serious inflationary trouble' (Haberler, cited in Tietmeyer, 1990: 5). However, despite the fact that, in China, the money supply has been expanding for more than a decade, the average rise in the price level has been moderate since 1979. In the period 1979–90, the GNP deflator rose only 5.4 per cent per annum, the nominal GNP grew at 14.2 per cent and the real GNP at 8.8 per cent compared with a growth of 23.8 per cent per annum in M2: there has been a considerable discrepancy between monetary expansion and the inflation record.

The continuous monetary expansion and the so-far-manageable price rise have generated a heated policy debate in China. There are two basic questions. One is whether or not the monetary build-up matters? The other is what are its sources and processes? Despite of the large attention these issues have attracted, there seem no general agreements among analysts and policy-makers.

With respect to the first question, monetary expansion and the accumulation of monetary stocks have been viewed as either a 'wild tiger in a cage' or a 'working horse in a field'. The former group of analysts argues that high price inflation could be triggered at any time (such as in 1988 – to be discussed in Chapter 7)[5] and therefore, advocates, among other things, the tightening of monetary and fiscal policies. The opposite camp stresses the view that the rapid monetary expansion is inevitable in an economy where decentralisation- and market-oriented reform is going on. To some extent, however, inflation during economic 'take-off' is regarded as unavoidable. Accordingly, this 'no-worry' camp is against austere monetary and fiscal policies and sees these policies as causing recession. Some of them even suggest the adoption of a mildly inflationary policy during economic take-off.

Related to these two opposite views on the significance of monetary expansion in China are two more analytical issues. One refers to the possibility of monetary overhang or repressed inflation. The other is concerned with possible changes in the demand for money during the process of monetisation (see, for example, Yi, 1991).

The repressed inflation argument often uses the money/GDP ratio as an indicator of monetary overhang in socialist or planned economies where household savings are seen as being largely forced, and inflation as repressed due to price controls. As in recent examples, when price control was lifted in the transition economies in central and east

Europe (CEE), price level shot up and money/GDP ratio dropped.[6] From this perspective, the very high money/GDP ratio in China might indicate a monetary overhang, thus repressed inflation (e.g. Feltenstein and Ha, 1989). For the repressed inflation argument to stand, the key question, however, is whether there were forced savings in China, in the sense that excessive money was being held by households in comparison to the nominal value of transactions.

Although there is some truth in the repressed inflation argument, its major problem is the assertion of forced household savings. It is very difficult to agree with this view because the mounting household savings were voluntary. By and large, there were no shortages in the consumer goods market in the 1980s.[7] Therefore, the build-up of monetary balances in China cannot generally be regarded as indications of a monetary overhang or repressed inflation. (For more discussions on Chinese households' saving behaviour, see Chapter 4, section 4.4.3.)

The repressed inflation argument may, however, make some sense if it refers to the disguised price level, particularly in the producer goods market. This is because actual price level was disguised because of (i) the remaining government control over prices and (ii) increasing subsidies from the state budget. During the economic reform, the scope of price control was diminished but it was still an important element in economic life, particularly in producer-goods markets. It is worth noting that the way by which the government partially liberalised the price control was to introduce the so-called 'two-track' price system which allowed part of the output to be priced according to market forces. The existence of repressed inflation can be indicated by the difference between official and market prices. For producer goods at large, the level of market prices was over 30 per cent higher on average than that of official prices in December 1987, nearly 50 per cent higher in December 1988,[8] 60 per cent higher in December 1989 and 37 per cent higher in December 1990.[9]

The prevalence of the two-track price system, particularly the higher level of market price over official price, might imply a degree of repressed inflation. The costs of price control were covered by price subsidies (or via enterprise loss subsidies[10] and tax reduction and exemptions) from the state budget.[11] It is difficult to estimate precisely how many percentage points of price rise should occur if the remaining price control is liberalised and price subsidies are stopped. What does appear plausible is that this is not the main reason for the large discrepancy between the rates of monetary growth and the observed inflation.[12]

Turning to the monetisation argument, it sees monetary expansion as being driven by monetisation process which increases the demand for money. The demand for money is usually related, one way or another, to prevailing institutions, payment practices and transaction costs. In general, mainstream economics holds that the demand for money (real balances) increases as the level of real income rises, and decreases as the nominal interest rate rises. It is, of course, recognised that the monetisation process would increase demand for money, particularly cash, for a given output. During the Chinese economic reform, many measures such as abolition of the People's Communes, the introduction of the Family Production Contractual Responsibility System, the opening-up of free markets, and the development of the non-state sector, all tended to promote monetisation of the economy and hence go some way towards explaining an increase in the demand for money. Monetisation does not, however, seem to be the major factor accounting for the long-term monetary expansion.

In the first place, since monetisation occurred mainly in the late 1970s and the early 1980s, it cannot explain the high growth of money stock in the mid- and late-1980s. Table 1.3 presents data on M0, M1 and M2 as well as (M2−M1) as the ratios to GDP for the period 1978–90. It shows that after 1984 while the increase in M0/GDP ratio slowed quite significantly and M1/GDP ratio stopped rising, M2/GDP ratio continued to rise. These can be seen more clearly in Figure 1.1.

Second, whilst monetisation may partly explain the expansion of M0 and M1, it cannot explain the expansion of M2.[13] There was a significant difference, 4.9 and 4.5 percentage points, between growth rates of M1 and of M2, and between M0 and M2 during the period 1979–90 (see Table 1.1). Noticeably, although the amount of M0 in proportion to M1 increased from 21.3 per cent in 1978 to 33.4 per cent in 1990, mainly reflecting an increasing demand for cash as medium of exchange – there is no cheque transaction service available to household depositors – the M0/M2 ratio declined slightly from 17.6 per cent to 17.0 per cent in 1990. Average annual growth rates of M2 was slightly higher than that of M0 between 1978 and 1990, 23.8 and 23.4 per cent respectively (see Table 1.1). Since M0 might be more closely related to M2, more attention needs to be drawn to the expansion of M2. In particular, the difference between M1 and M2 (i.e. M2−M1) was the chief factor responsible for the rapid expansion of M2. As a ratio to GDP, this component of M2 increased from 5.9 per cent in 1978 to 43.3 per cent in 1990 (see Table 1.3). As will be discussed in Chapter 3, a major part of the monetary expansion was in the term of house-

Table 1.3 Money/GDP ratios (%) (1978–90)

	1978	*1979*	*1980*	*1981*	*1982*	*1983*	*1984*
M0/GDP	5.9	6.7	7.7	8.3	8.5	9.2	11.4
M1/GDP	27.7	30.6	33.9	36.3	38.6	39.4	43.9
M2/GDP	33.6	37.7	43.1	48.0	52.3	56.0	65.0
(M2–M1)/GDP	5.9	6.9	9.2	11.5	13.7	16.5	21.0
		1985	*1986*	*1987*	*1988*	*1989*	*1990*
M0/GDP		11.6	12.6	12.9	15.1	14.7	15.0
M1/GDP		39.1	43.8	44.5	43.0	40.9	44.9
M2/GDP		62.0	70.7	75.2	73.7	76.7	88.1
(M2–M1)/GDP		22.9	27.0	30.7	30.6	35.3	43.3

Note: Money stock is the year-end figure.

Source: *Almanac of China's Finance and Banking* (1990: 48, 50, 60, 65; 1991: 42, 48, 52–4, 58); SSB (1991a: 31).

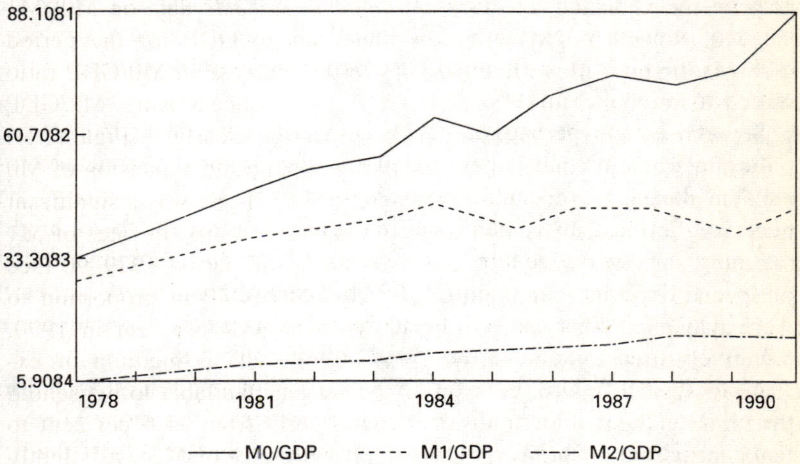

Figure 1.1 Money/GDP ratios (%, 1978–90)

hold deposits. This cannot be explained by monetisation.

In further searching for sources of monetary expansion in the post-reform period, emphases have been put upon either policy failure or system failure. These two strands of the debate are briefly reviewed in turn.

In terms of policy failure, popular criticism usually points to the duality, and possible inconsistency, of monetary policy objectives, i.e. supporting economic growth while maintaining financial stability. According to the typical critique, financial stability was, in actuality, neglected by the policy-makers, who were committed to a quantity drive – the famous objective of quadrupling the gross production of agriculture and industry by the end of this century (e.g. Shao, Q. 1989; Qian, J. 1989; Yu, L. 1989). This criticism implies that monetary expansion was a result of a loose monetary policy, and could have been prevented if the policy had had a clearly defined single objective, i.e. financial stability. More directly, this strand of argument blames the policy-makers for their relaxed attitude towards inflation. In effect, it is argued that the inflationary monetary policy was deliberate (e.g., Yu, R. 1989; Xu, J. 1989; Yu, L. *et al.* 1989).

Despite their prevalence, the above views appear simplistic and not of great use in understanding the problem in depth. First of all, the same quantity drive existed prior to 1978 and yet it did not cause excessive monetary expansion on the systemic overshooting of planned targets (see Table 2.12, Chapter 2). Second, it is unclear as to why the trend of monetary expansion continued even under a policy regime (such as the present one) which genuinely appears to be strongly committed to price stability.

Sometimes and perhaps more plausibly, it is the lack of effective policy instruments that is considered responsible for the monetary expansion during the decentralisation reform. Yet, on the contrary, the necessary policy instruments for monetary control (such as credit rationing, interest rate setting, reserve requirement – including the calling of special deposits – and control over the central bank's lending, etc.) were available. What needs to be addressed is why they were not more effectively used to achieve the stated policy objectives.

As to system failure, monetary expansion is most often attributed to the persistence of some traditional characteristics of the economic system, particularly Kornai's type of 'investment hunger', 'soft credit' and the 'soft budget constraint'[14] (e.g. Feltenstein and Farhadian, 1987; Wulf and Goldsbrough, 1986; Santorum, 1989; Bowles and White, 1989; Wolf, 1990; Blejer and Szapary, 1990). These characteristics are blamed as being the cause of the insatiable demand for money on the one hand and the undisciplined supply of funds on the other. These authors generally go on to argue that, in order to have effective monetary control during transition to a market economy, a major requirement is to harden the budget constraint, i.e. to impose financial discipline on enterprises either before, or simultaneously with, the liberalisation of prices and wages.

It is true that, even today, the 'soft budget constraint' as a characteristic of the SOEs largely survives, and there is a consensus of opinion that financial discipline must indeed be strengthened if the economic reform is be ultimately successful. However, the persistence of 'soft credit' and the 'soft budget constraint' does not necessarily imply monetary expansion. In fact, the money supply has been controlled to some extent, otherwise one would reasonably expect the monetary expansion to have been even more rapid, or even explosive. The key feature that needs to be explained is that money growth in China before and after 1978 was very different, and this difference cannot easily be explained by appeal to the phenomenon of 'soft budget constraint'.

Closely related to the argument of the 'soft budget constraint', the second important explanation with respect to system failure concerns the lack of independence of the central bank. The latter is widely viewed as one of the chief institutional factors responsible for an accommodating monetary policy and, thus, price inflation. For instance, Blejer and Szapary (1990) argue that, although policy instruments have been transformed, the Chinese central bank is still not able to withstand the pressures for an accommodating monetary policy. In fact, it is increasingly accepted in China (as elsewhere) that independence of the central bank is a prerequisite for effective monetary control, and beyond that for the control of inflation.

It is worth noting that empirical findings supporting this hypothesis are neither many nor conclusive. Some international comparative studies confirm that there exists a positive correlation between the degree of independence of the central bank and the inflation rate in the post-war period (e.g. Bade and Parkin, 1980; Alesina, 1988; Burdekin and Willett, 1990). Other studies find no clear-cut, universal link between central bank independence and inflation (e.g. Bodart, 1990). While Bodart finds evidence from developed countries, there are important exceptions, e.g. Japan. More relevant to this study, there is no significant relationship between central bank independence and inflation .to be detected in developing countries. Looking at the problem from an historical perspective and extending the time-span to before the Second World War, Wood, G. (1991) finds no systematic link whatsoever between the degree of independence of the central bank and movements in the price level for either the developed or the developing economies.

More importantly, the central bank independence argument is, at best insufficient, since it does not explain why the government prefers, or at least, tolerates an expansionary monetary policy. In the case of China, given the fact that the central bank has been dependent on the State Council, the explanation of an accommodating monetary policy has to be sought in the behaviour and objectives of the State Council. Yet, it is still not clear why the policy-makers wanted rapid monetary expansion during the economic reform.

In recent years, more developed arguments have emerged that draw attention to the links between monetary expansion and asynchronisation between financial and other aspects of the economic reform. There are two typical views (Zhu and Zhang, 1989a, 1989b). The first sees the cause of ineffective monetary control as residing in the over-rapid progress of financial reform, and especially in the premature decentralisation of financial control. It is suggested that, where market discipline still does not fully apply to enterprises and lower economic agents, financial decentralisation is likely to lead to unjustifiable monetary expansion. The opposite point of view puts the blame on the sluggishness of financial reform as compared with the significant structural and institutional changes in the rest of the economy. It points out that, to date, financial reform has not in fact been fundamental in nature. Thus monetary expansion and its high volatility are attributed to ambiguity in the policy objectives, combined with largely outdated policy methods and instruments. The monetary authorities were thus unable to exercise effective monetary control, let alone any fine-tuning. The undesirably slow progress of the reform in other aspects of the economy only reinforces the urgency of speeding up financial reform and of improving monetary control.

Generally speaking, the argument stressing asynchronisation is insightful because asynchronization is hardly avoidable during the economic transition of the CPEs. However, asynchronization itself cannot reveal the concrete and specific mechanisms of the monetary expansion. In order to understand the underlying mechanisms more systematically and precisely, further studies on this ground are needed.

In summary, although a wide range of insight is shed by the available views and arguments to the problems of monetary expansion in China, the latter has remained insufficiently understood. In practice, this has led to policy swings which themselves became a factor of instability responsible for the 'stop–go' pattern associated with the course of the economic reforms and development in China.[15] The latest swing occurred in 1988–9. Encountering a sharp price rise (the increase in cost of living rose from 8.9 per cent in December 1987 to 26.4 per cent in September 1988), an austere monetary policy was introduced. Although the price increases were brought under control, growth of

GDP decreased by 7 percentage points in 1989. Consequently, the problems of bad debt and the government budget position worsened. In the end, expansionary monetary policy was again resumed. In recognising the dilemma in monetary control, confusion has spread among the Chinese policy-makers and they have become increasingly driven by events. Indeed, recently, Mr Ren Junyin, the Deputy Governor of the People's Bank of China (the central bank) admitted that the monetary authorities do not have a clear set of ideas about financial reform. This fact itself increases the uncertainty about future development of China's economy and reform.[16] It seems essential to develop a clearer and more systematic understanding of the mechanisms and processes that are at work.

This book attempts to study monetary expansion more systematically with a view to identifying its specific sources, processes, mechanisms and links with some other problems. The subject under study is important to the improvement in policy-making because it has been closely related not only to the policy swings, but also to the problems undermining stability and sustainability of growth in the future. It is hoped that the study may also draw lessons from China for other reforming economies in their transition period.

Four main arguments will be developed in the book.

First, monetary expansion was driven by banks' finance for fixed-assets investment combined with lack of alternative channels (other than banks) for financial intermediation in a situation where households had, increasingly, become the dominant savers.

Second, excessive bank-credit expansion (at least in terms of exceeding the planned targets) can be explained as a product of an investment game between the central and local governments. In this game, local governments' investment pattern was locally determined and biased towards setting up new processing industrial enterprises. This caused the investment pattern to deviate from the objectives of the new development strategy intensifying shortage of investment for technical updating and transformation of existing enterprises as well as for infrastructure. At the same time, because of decentralisation, the central government was no longer the major saver with resources for investment. Unable to resolve problems of resource allocation directly, the policy-makers turned to banks to finance the priority investment. In so doing, the investment pattern was adjusted and growth was maintained. However, aggregate control had to be loosened, extensive development and problems of inefficiency persisted. These problems, in turn, further increased the demand for credit from the inefficient enterprises, leading to growth of non-performing loans and erosion of the capital base of banking system.

Third, such a game situation arises from the incompatible incentives, the problem embedded in the Chinese economic system characterised by local governments' property rights. Although decentralisation reform without a fundamental change in the system design alleviated the problem of incentive failure, it exacerbated the problem of incentive incompatibility in resource allocation.

Fourth, as an integral part of the economic system, the banking system facilitated the centre–locality interactions in investment and hence credit expansion. Credit and thus the money supply did not, however, explode because the funds for investment under the control of local governments were, in fact, limited. This set an upper limit to the extra funds necessary for allocative adjustment.

The central theme of this study is that *the monetary expansion can be attributed to the partial nature of the economic reform – economic reform without reform of local government ownership and the related development of capital markets – as well as to the policy-makers' conservative attitude towards alternative financial instruments (e.g. government bonds).* Although Chinese policy-makers have, so far, been lucky in generally avoiding unmanageable excess demand for consumer goods, because of a rise in households' voluntary savings, the accumulated liquidity risk and the lack of risk-bearing capital pose potential problems for the future. The problems cannot be resolved by tight monetary control because monetary expansion *per se* is not the root of the problem. Further, monetary tightening can easily go too far under China's economic system and thus causes recession in the short term without being able to stabilise the economy in the longer-term. From a policy-making point of view, however, the build-up of money balances is not a disaster. By contrast, the available money can be utilised to facilitate needed ownership reform. This book suggests that monetary policy, financial reform, ownership reform and design of corporate control should be coordinated with a focus on promoting industrial restructuring and competition. In this process, the second-best solution would be to internalise the externality problems at provincial level, and put to a more active use fiscal means in macroeconomic management.

In terms of approach, the study tries to avoid the situation where either everything is related to everything else without a focus and a clear analytical understanding or, single links are treated in isolation, e.g. monetary expansion is linked to expansion of high-powered money and thus to a low degree of central bank's independence. The focus is placed upon *interactions between the central and local governments as the dominant agents in markets, and between resource allocation at micro level and monetary control at macro level, during reform.* In such an interactive process, institutional factors deserve to receive central attention. The study first employs the 'flow of funds' framework in combination with sectoral balances to identify the main sources and processes of monetary expansion, and examines the central bank's role in monetary expansion. Then in a game framework (in the light of the Stackelberg duopoly model)[17] it establishes the link between credit expansion and resource allocation. Drawing upon modern theories on incentives and mechanism design, the study further examines incentive compatibility of the system and its unique institutional design. Incentive theories and mechanism design appear to be particularly relevant because attempts to restructure institutions and controls to facilitate economic modernisation have been witnessed throughout the history of PRC. A case study is also conducted to support the argument that tightening monetary control cannot resolve the problems. Finally, based on the findings, the thesis discusses some of the policy implications for future reform of the financial system in China.

One of the major difficulties in studying money and finance in China has been lack of information. Although more and more data are being published, the availability of relevant data is still a problem. Fortunately, this is not a major constraint on this study. Sources of information accessed by the study (many of them unpublished) include:

(a) statistical data on investment, finance and banking published by the authorities;
(b) monthly balance sheets of the state banks (1985–90);
(c) internal reports by the research institutes of banks and non-bank institutions;
(d) documents of the annual conference of the central bank where the monetary policy is made;
(e) interviews with government officials at both central and local levels.

The book is organised into eight chapters. To provide a background against which monetary expansion occurred, Chapter 2 details the successes and problems in economic reform and the implementation of development strategy in China through the period 1978–90. Chapter 3 establishes a framework for monetary analysis within which the major components and counterparts of monetary expansion, as well as the central bank's role in monetary expansion are identified. In so doing, it points to the directions for the following analyses. Chapter 4 explains expansion of bank credit as an outcome of the centre–locality investment game under decentralisation. In this game, in order to adjust resource allocation thus to sustain growth the centre needed to increase investment for priority activities. However, it was unable to solve the allocative problem by alternative means other than expanding bank loans. Expansion of bank loans was also workable because of households' long-term saving behaviour. Chapters 5 and 6 further examine systemic aspects of the investment game. Chapter 5 argues that local governments' ownership and the related fiscal system have a problem of incentive incompatibility. Chapter 6 is a description of the Chinese banking system and its operation. It shows that the banking system was an integrated part of the economic system and therefore subject to the same incentive problem. The banking system facilitated the centre-locality interactions in investment. Chapter 7 is a case study of the austere policy in 1988–9. It confirms that tight monetary control alone could not resolve the underlying problems. Chapter 8 summarises the thesis set forward and discusses policy implications and some issues for further policy research.

2 Economic Reform: Successes and Problems

To provide a background for the study, this chapter summarises the successes and problems of the economic reform in the period 1978–90. It shows that reform was successful in the sense that it contributed to higher and less fluctuating growth, and a substantial improvement in living standards. However, reform was also characterised by problems: macroeconomic control became less effective, leading to stop–go cycles; the improvement of economic inefficiency was slow, and the banking system became fragile.

2.1 THE NEW DEVELOPMENT STRATEGY AND ECONOMIC REFORM

Before considering the post-1978 reform, it is necessary to review briefly the nature of the economic system and the development of the economy in the pre-1978 period.

2.1.1 The pre-1978 economic system and performance

With the ending of the Civil War and the founding of the People's Republic of China in 1949, economic development – and more precisely industrialisation – became the overwhelming objective of the Chinese leadership.[1]

The development strategy adopted in China before 1978 was characterised by:

(a) unbalanced development dominated by heavy industry;
(b) extensive development;
(c) promotion of inland industrialisation and regional self-sufficiency;
(d) self-reliance in technology and finance (particularly after the 1960s when relations between China and the former USSR became hostile and China was more internationally isolated).

To support such a development strategy,[2] China implemented a

Table 2.1 Main economic indicators (1953–78; %)

Annual growth rate of:	*1953–7*	*1958–66*	*1967–78*	1953–78
Net Material Product (NMP)	8.9	4.7	5.8	6.0
Agriculture	3.7	1.0	1.7	1.9
Industry	19.6	10.5	9.0	11.5
(Light)	12.9	8.9	8.1	9.3
(Heavy)	25.4	11.5	10.9	13.8
Construction	19.4	2.9	5.2	7.0
Transportation	12.0	6.0	5.2	6.8
Commerce	8.0	6.9	5.5	4.3
Retail sales of consumer goods	9.2	2.9	5.8	5.4
Urban	11.8	3.6	6.1	6.3
Rural	6.4	2.9	1.6	3.9
Price level[a]	1.9	1.0	0.4	0.9
Investment ratio[b]	24.2	28.1	31.2	29.7
Exports (US$)	14.3	4.5	12.5	10.0

Notes: [a] living cost index of staffs and workers. [b] part of NMP that is used for investment as a proportion to total NMP. Retail sales of consumer goods are deflated by retail price deflators.

Source: SSB (1991a: 31, 33, 40, 55, 230, 591, 615).

particular type of central planning which assigns direct economic management to both central and local governments. The uniqueness of such a system will be discussed in more detail in Chapter 5. Here two features of this system need to be noted. First, the division of economic management powers between the central and the local government was highly variable over time. Centralised management was often followed by decentralised management and vice versa, leading to centralisation-decentralisation cycles. Second, the managerial powers of local governments were very considerable. Even when the economic management system was most centralised (i.e. in 1965), the share of industrial output produced by centrally managed industry did not exceed 43 per cent. On the eve of the reform in 1978, the central government controlled less than 8 per cent of the total industrial output (Xu J. *et al.*, 1984: 160).

Economic performance during this period was very mixed. On one hand, industrialisation progressed rapidly. The share of industry in the 'net material product' (NMP) rose from 19.5 per cent to 49.4 per cent between 1952 and 1978 (SSB, 1990c: 64; 1991a: 32). Mainly because of the rapid industrial expansion, the overall economic growth was quite high. The NMP grew at on average nearly 9 per cent per annum. There

Table 2.2 Manufacturing production as percentage of GDP

China (1981)	*India (1979/80)*	*Normal values for large countries (per capita US$ around 1980/81)*		
		US$300	*US$850*	*US$2500*
24.5	18.1	13	19	25

Source: The World Bank (1985a: 21).

was virtually no inflation and price level was generally very stable. On the other hand, the growth was highly unbalanced (see Table 2.1).

In international comparison, China became an economy in which the manufacturing industry produced a much greater share of the GDP compared with other economies in similar development stage. In 1981, China's manufacturing output accounted for about one quarter of GDP, 35 per cent more than that in India and almost the same as that of large economies with per capita GDP of US$2500 (at that time, China's per capita GDP at producer prices was estimated as around US$250–350) (see Table 2.2).

The rapid industrialisation was achieved by extensive investment on a localised scale. Because of the neglect of technical updating and transformation, the accumulated capital stock was largely technically outdated. At the end of the 1970s, around 60 per cent of machine products were technically equivalent to the international level of the 1950s or pre-1950s; 35 per cent was equivalent to the 1970s level and only 5 per cent reached the 1970s level (Qiu, J. and Huang, J. 1981). On the other hand, rapid industrial growth was achieved at the cost of relatively slow growth in other sectors, great instability and inefficiency and slow improvement in living standards (since 1957).

In contrast to the rapid expansion of the manufacturing sector which took over roughly 40 per cent of the total capital investment,[3] growth of transportation, communications, and particularly of agriculture, were slow. During 1953–78, annual growth rate of heavy industry was 13.8 but that of agriculture was merely 1.9 per cent. Between 1957 and 1978, per capita agricultural output had actually stagnated; per capita grain output remained around 300kg between 1957 and 1978 while per capita cotton output and edible vegetable oil output decreased from 5.2kg and 2.1kg to 4.5kg and 1.6kg respectively (SSB, 1984a: 167; 477). In 1981, China's production of construction, transportation and communications as a share of GDP was small compared with that of India, South Korea and Brazil, and about the same as that of Japan in

Table 2.3 Some indicators of transportation and communications in China and USA

Railway track operated:	China in 1978	48 600 km
	USA in 1860	49 277 km
	USA in 1878	131 531 km
Highway[a] (total):	China in 1978	890 236 km
	USA in 1904	3 462 568 km
Highway (surfaced):	China in 1978	651 068 km
	USA in 1922	662 908 km
Telephone per thousand:	China in 1980	4.3
	USA in 1895	4.8
	USA in 1900	17.6
	World in 1980	11.5

Note: [a] No precisely comparable data was available. Some of the US highway at that time might not have been suitable for motor vehicles. However, the quality of highways in China have been very poor even today (over 80 per cent is of grade four and substandard), the average speed of a vehicle only 30 km/h.

Source: For China: SSB (1989a: 386; 1989b: 54). USA: the US Department of Commerce (1960: 427; 458; 480–1; 1975: 710). For the World: Wang, D. et al (1984: 214).

1965 and Spain in 1972 (The World Bank, 1985a: 22). For instance, transport accounted for 4.4 per cent of GDP in China but 7.6 per cent in both South Korea (1980) and Japan (1965). International comparison is always difficult in value terms because of the price factor. Table 2.3 is a direct comparison of transportation and communications between China and the USA (similar in size to China) in terms of physical indicators. The degree of China's backwardness is remarkable. The seriously underdeveloped infrastructure, especially in transportation and communication, constituted one of China's most crucial problems.[4]

China's economy fluctuated greatly before 1978 because of sectoral imbalances as well as political turmoil. Annual rates of industrial output growth ranged from between nearly 60 per cent up and over 40 per cent down. Table 2.4 lists the standard deviation of annual growth rates in nine economies. The value for China's standard deviation was striking: at 11.34, it was far higher than that of other economies.

China's resource utilisation during this industrialisation period proved to be very inefficient. The World Bank in its country study 'China: Economic Structure in an International Perspective' (1985) finds that China's economy was substantially inefficient in terms of the consumption

Table 2.4 Standard deviation of annual GDP growth

France	2.29	UK	2.30
USA	2.71	USSR	2.93
Taiwan	3.06	W. Germany	3.42
S. Korea	4.15[a]	Japan	4.20
Mainland China	11.34[b]		

Notes: [a] GNP; [b] Net material product. For China, the time period is 1953–78; Korea: 1954–73; other economies: 1953–85.

Source: Chen Y. (1988: 71); SSB (1984a: 30); Council for Economic Planning and Development, Republic of China (1987); The Bank of Korea (1978).

of key materials, capital and the use of intermediate inputs, as well as in terms of total factor productivity. For instance, subject to estimation inaccuracies, the total factor productivity growth over 1952–81 was only 0.5 per cent compared with an average of 2.0 per cent for 19 developing economies and 2.7 for 12 industrialised market economies (The World Bank, 1985b: 31–40). In terms of the utilisation of energy, China's energy consumption increased by 9.6 times between 1953 and 1978, while national income increased by only 3.0 times (SSB, 1991a: 453). For a historical comparison, between 1880 and 1975, the GNP increased by 4.3 times in the UK while energy consumed increased by only 1.5 times. In the USA between 1921 and 1955, the figures were 2.1 and 1.0 respectively (Rong, D. and Huang, R., 1984: 179).

In order to mobilise massive resources for investment, a low wage or incomes policy had been adopted since 1957. The average wage of staff and workers decreased by 13.8 per cent in real terms between 1957 and 1978 against an increase in industrial labour productivity of 98.1 per cent (SSB, 1991a: 130). Although per capita household income of the urban population increased as a result of the increase in the employment participation rate, the decline in average wages held down living standards. According to a survey in 1977, about 40 per cent of the urban population lived below the poverty line.[5] Perhaps one of the most telling indicator of living standards is the housing shortage. Per capita living space (in 182 cities) was only 3.6 square metres in 1978 compared with 4.5 square metres in 1952. In rural areas, food shortages were a serious problem: in 1977–8 there were over 100 million people who had not enough food (Xu, J. et al, 1984).

After the death of Mao in 1976, an ideological crisis ensued. The enthusiasm for building socialism at the expense of a slow improvement in living standards faded. It was in this context that the new development strategy was formulated and economic reform initiated.

2.1.2 The new development strategy and phases of reform

The new development strategy defined the ultimate objective of development as increases in living standards. The target of quadrupling gross industrial and agricultural output between 1980 and 2000 was linked to the quadrupling of per capita income to US$800–1000 over the same period.[6] This required an annual growth rate of 7–8 per cent. The aim was for per capita income to reach the level of the middle income economies by the year 2050.

These objectives demanded a transformation of development strategy:

(i) from heavy industry-centred unbalanced growth to agriculture and light industry-led balanced growth;
(ii) from extensive development to intensive development (i.e. from input-based growth to efficiency-based growth);
(iii) from promoting inland development to promoting coastal development;
(iv) from self-sufficiency to less introvert politics (see, e.g. Liu, G., 1984: 23–7; Dong, F., 1988: 50–8).

In parallel with these changes in development strategy, in late 1978 the economic reform programme was launched. Although debates on reform objectives and strategy are evolutionary in nature, there has been a broad agreement amongst policy-makers on the following:

(i) economic management needs to be decentralised;
(ii) market mechanisms need to be introduced;
(iii) development of the non-state sector needs to be encouraged;
(iv) an effective macroeconomic management system based on indirect control should be established.

There were and are, however, serious disputes over the degree to which the reform should be instituted. The least controversial was the need for decentralisation, based on the recognition that the most serious management problems arise from excessive centralisation and the lack of autonomy of enterprises.[7] On the basis of a broad consensus, as well as political compromises, the Chinese leadership adopted a gradualistic reform strategy characterised by partial experimentation and a trial-and-error approach. The successes and failures of reform experiments fed back into decisions on the future directions of reform policy. Since 1978, the implementation of reform in China may be divided into four phases.

Phase I (1978–83) was dominated by agricultural reform. In the agricultural sector, the measures were rather revolutionary. The people's communes as a command system for agricultural production were abolished. Instead, the 'Household Production Contract Responsibility System' was introduced (i.e. land was leased by the village authorities to peasant households). At the same time, the levels of the agricultural product purchasing prices were raised substantially. For example, government purchasing prices were raised by an average 28.6 per cent in the two years 1979 and 1980. Agricultural taxes were also either removed or reduced in many areas (Zhou, T., 1984: 172). At the same time, price control over agricultural products was gradually liberalised. In 1978, 94.4 per cent of agricultural products sold by farmers was purchased by the state; this ratio declined to 25.2 per cent by 1990. A similar story can be told about the promotion of light industry. It became the priority sector in resource allocation by the government in the early 1980s. Non-agrarian production in the rural areas was strongly promoted, chiefly through the development of TVEs (township and village enterprises) and preferential tax policy.

Meanwhile, reform measures in urban areas progressed in a more gradualistic way. The major reforms were:

(i) the introduction of incentive programmes (e.g. bonus, piece-rate wages);
(ii) the reduction of the degree of central physical planning by cutting both the number and proportion of goods under central government control;
(iii) reduction of the degree of central mobilisation and allocation of financial resources by (a) allowing enterprises to retain an increasing proportion of depreciation funds and profits (profit retention was introduced into various revenue contract schemes after 1981); (b) allowing local governments to retain all revenue after transferring to the central government a fixed amount or proportion of the revenue they collected, and (c) extending the decision-making powers of local governments over investment by increasing their project certification autonomy (to be discussed in Chapter 5);
(iv) extending the autonomy of enterprises in production, trading and

pricing by introducing two-tier systems (e.g. part of production was under the mandatory plan and the other was determined by the enterprises themselves according to market demand);

(v) encouraging development of the non-State sector (i.e. collectively-owned enterprises, privately-owned small businesses, and joint ventures) through a favourable tax policy.

In **phase II (1984–8)**, the reform centred on the urban industrial system: decentralising state-owned enterprises (SOEs)' management at the micro level and attempting to establish an effective indirect control system at the macro level. With the pace of decentralisation- and market-oriented reform in the urban areas speeding up, the problems of enterprise reform along with macroeconomic control became acute.

The invigoration of SOEs was regarded as the key to restructuring the national economy because 'in essence, the drawbacks of our present economic structure are precisely the lack of vitality in our enterprises'.[8] While measures were introduced to continously increase enterprise autonomy in production, sale, pricing, employment, wages, etc., a difficult issue materialised. Given that state ownership was to be retained, some kind of control (associated with property rights) had to be exercised by some government body. The problem was, by whom, and how? According to experience of the pre-1978 situation, decentralisation would cause economic segmentation either between ministries (if greater autonomy was granted to ministries) or between localities (if greater autonomy was granted to local governments). In order to circumvent this dilemma, the focus of autonomy was placed upon the city governments. 'With some exceptions, each ministry of the central government and each province ought to transfer management power of enterprises over to the cities where the enterprises are based . . . To avoid the cities becoming new and fragmented blocks in the economy, the city governments must reduce intervention and extend decision-making power to the enterprises, and separate the enterprises from government' (Zhao Ziyang, 22 April 1985).[9] To strengthen the position of the cities as economic centres, the county governments were made subordinate to the city governments (prior to that, they were subordinated to the provincial governments).

At the macro level, urgent reform measures concerning the establishment of effective macroeconomic management with an increasing reliance on indirect control were initiated. To this end, although administrative methods of control over investment (e.g. investment project had to be certified by the Planning Commission at various levels according to scale), money and credit, were retained, they were decentralised. Meanwhile, an increasing emphasis was placed on the role of banks and monetary policy, in mobilisation and allocation of financial resources.[10] Correspondingly, the monetary sector was considerably reformed. Banks multiplied, specialised and diversified. In order to exercise more effective control over the multiple banking activities, in 1983 the PBC became the central bank, and most of its commercial functions were taken over by the newly established Industrial and Commercial Bank of China (ICBC). As a result, a two-tier financial system took shape. After 1984, the course of pluralisation of financial institutions continued. In terms of monetary policy, use was made of some means of indirect control, such as the rate of interest, the rediscount facility of the central bank and bank reserve requirements. (More detailed discussion of financial reform is in Chapter 6.)

Phase III (1988–91) was characterised by a policy of austerity. Confronted by accelerating inflationary pressures, the policy was shifted to an austere 'economic rectification' in the last quarter of 1988. Bank credit was drastically cut, as were investment projects. As a result, the pace of reform slowed down.

In **phase IV (1992 onwards)**, reform was re-initiated under the slogan of development of the 'socialist market economy'.[11]

Although the reform was gradualistic in nature, the changes they brought to the economic control were nevertheless remarkable. First, allocative control by the central government in the economy was diminished. Between 1980 and 1988, the number of industrial goods under central mandatary planning (by the State Planning Commission) was cut by half – from 120 to 60. The number of centrally allocated capital goods was reduced from 256 to 27. The number of commercial goods controlled by the Ministry of Commerce declined from 188 to 23, and the proportion of capital goods supplied to localities and enterprises by the central government decreased from 70 per cent to 30 per cent (see Table 2.5). Within categories, the proportion of goods centrally allocated was also reduced significantly, as shown in Table 2.6.

Second, the government's (and especially the central government's) direct control over financial resources was substantially weakened. Table 2.7 shows that during the period 1978–89, the total revenues of the state sector as a proportion of the GNP declined by 7 percentage points from 43 per cent to 35 per cent. This reflected the increased importance of the non-state sector in China's economy. State budgetary revenues as a proportion of the GNP, and as a proportion of the total revenues of the state sector, declined far more significantly: by 15 percentage

Table 2.5 Central allocation of resources

	1980	1988
Number of industrial goods involving the central mandatory planning	120	60
Number of the central allocation of capital goods	256	27
Number of consumer goods controlled by the Ministry of Commerce	188	23
Proportion of capital goods supplied to localities and enterprises by the central government (%)	70	30

Source: Gao, S. (1991: Chart 5).

Table 2.6 Proportion of key materials allocated by the State Planning Commission (%)

	Steel	*Coal*	*Timber*	*Cement*
1979	77.0	58.9	85.0	35.7
1984	66.0	50.0	40.0	25.0
1988	46.8	43.5	25.9	13.6
1990	44.0	40.0	22.0	12.0

Source: State Planning Commission; Yuan, B. (1992).

points from 31 per cent to 16 per cent and by 26 percentage points from 72 per cent to 46 per cent, respectively.

In 1981, the central government spent 54.0 per cent of total state budgetary expenditures. This proportion decreased to 45.3 per cent in 1985 and to 39.8 per cent in 1990. Furthermore, the revenues of the state sector collected outside the state budget, namely the 'state extra-budgetary revenues',[12] increased sharply. In proportion to the state budgetary revenues (including domestic debt revenues), the extra-budgetary revenues were only 31 per cent in 1978 but 80 per cent in 1983, and nearly 95 per cent in 1989 (98 per cent if the domestic debt income was excluded) (SSB, 1991a: 221–2).

Third, the non-state sector, particularly the TVEs, flourished. In the period 1980–90, in nominal terms, the gross output value of TVEs increased 14.4 times, compared with a fourfold increase in the total gross material output value (SSB, 1991a: 229, 378, 47).[13] As a result, the importance of the state sector steadily decreased. For instance, 78 per cent of the gross industrial output was produced by the state sector in 1978, while it fell to 55 per cent in 1990. In commerce, the

Table 2.7 Decentralised control of the revenues of the state sector (1978–89) (unit: ¥ bn unless specified)

	1978	*1979*	*1980*	*1981*	*1982*	*1983*
(1) GNP	358.8	399.8	447.0	477.3	519.3	580.9
(2) The state budgetary revenues[a]	112.1	106.8	104.2	96.7	104.0	117.0
(3) The state extra-budgetary revenues[b]	34.7	45.3	55.7	60.1	80.3	89.0
(4) Total state revenues[c]	156.0	161.4	171.2	166.9	200.1	225.7
(5) Ratio of the state revenues to GNP [(4)/(1)] (%)	43.5	40.4	38.3	35.0	38.5	38.9
(6) The state budgetary revenues as ratio to GNP [(2)/(1)] (%)	31.2	26.7	23.3	20.3	20.0	20.1
(7) The central management ratio of the total state revenues [(2)/(4)] (%)	71.9	66.2	60.9	57.9	52.0	51.8
	1984	*1985*	*1986*	*1987*	*1988*	*1989*
(1) GNP	696.2	855.8	969.6	1130.1	1398.4	1591.6
(2) The state budgetary revenues[a]	142.5	177.7	212.2	219.9	235.7	257.2
(3) The state extra-budgetary revenues[b]	107.7	138.4	158.6	184.5	208.4	247.4
(4) Total state revenues[c]	266.2	336.7	403.7	440.8	492.7	562.5
(5) Ratio of the state revenues to GNP [(4)/(1)] (%)	38.2	39.3	41.6	39.0	35.2	35.2
(6) The state budgetary revenues as ratio to GNP [(2)/(1)] (%)	20.5	20.8	21.9	19.5	16.9	16.2
(7) The central management ratio of the total state revenues [(2)/(4)] (%)	53.5	52.8	52.6	49.9	47.8	45.7

Notes: [a] Excluding debt revenues. [b] Excluding 'key energy and transportation funds' collected into the state budgetary revenue and construction tax paid out from the nominal extra-budgetary revenues. [c] (4) is greater than the sum of (2) and (3) because (2) and (3) exclude the revenues which are used to offset losses made by, or subsidies to the SOEs. In budgetary accounting, these subsidies are directly deducted from the revenues of the state budget and extra-budget. For 1978–85, when data was not available, the subsidies are estimated as 80 per cent of the losses made by the SOEs (about 80 per cent in 1986–88; the rest is covered by bank credit).

Source: (1): SSB (1991a: 31). (2): SSB (1991a: 209, 212). (3): SSB (1991a: 220; 222). (4): Enterprise loss subsidies in 1986–9: SSB (1991a: 212); for losses of the SOEs in 1978–85: General Planning Department of the MOF, 1989: 146.

share of state commerce in retail sales declined from 55 per cent in 1978 to 40 per cent in 1990 (SSB, 1991a: 396; 591–2). In construction, the state's share declined to 31 per cent of the total output (SSB, 1991a: 47, 541). In addition, the agricultural sector was almost entirely non-state owned. Although the state sector was still dominant in transportation, communication, banking and finance, in 1990 it accounted

Table 2.8 Distribution of national income (1979–88) (%)

	1979	*1980*	*1981*	*1982*	*1983*	*1984*	*1985*	*1986*	*1987*	*1988*
Initial										
Government	12.2	11.6	11.9	12.1	11.8	11.9	13.8	13.3	12.3	11.4
Enterprises	37.0	34.1	33.2	32.2	30.7	31.2	27.0	25.9	36.9	27.3
Households	50.8	54.3	54.9	55.7	57.5	56.9	59.2	60.8	60.8	61.3
Ultimate										
Government	23.5	18.7	15.3	14.4	15.1	15.5	15.3	15.7	13.9	11.7
Enterprises	12.1	12.1	13.2	13.6	11.1	11.4	10.8	8.4	9.7	10.8
Households	64.4	69.2	71.6	72.0	73.8	73.1	73.9	75.9	76.4	77.5
(net transfer)	13.6	14.9	16.7	16.3	16.3	16.2	14.7	15.1	15.6	16.2

Source: Guo and Han (1991: Tables 3.4 and 3.14).

for only about half of China's GDP.[14]

Fourth, state control over prices and production diminished and market mechanisms became increasingly significant, especially in the product market. Of agricultural products sold by farmers, the proportion for which prices were fixed by the government dropped from 94.4 per cent in 1978 to 25.2 per cent in 1990. At the enterprise level, in 1991 the share of output subject to fixed, guided and market prices reached 45, 19 and 36 per cent respectively. At retail level, the shares of retail sales subject to fixed, guided and market prices were 26, 17, and 57 per cent in 1991 compared with 97, 0 and 3 per cent respectively in 1978 (Schmidt-Hebbel, 1991: i, 3). Mandatory planning was no longer dominant in industrial production, with only 16.3 per cent of industrial production subject to this at the end of 1991 compared with over 80 per cent at the beginning of the 1980s.[15]

Fifth, as a result of the reform measures discussed above, the pattern of national income distribution changed dramatically in favour of the household sector. Despite a decreasing share of the government and enterprises in initial national income distribution, their net income transfer to households (mainly through subsidies and collective welfare) as a proportion of national income was still maintained – even rising slightly in the 1980s, compared with the late 1970s. In ultimate national income distribution, the household sector gained at the expense of the two other sectors.[16] Between 1979 and 1989, the share of the household sector in national income increased 13.1 percentage points from 64.4 to 77.5 per cent (Table 2.8).

Table 2.9 Main economic indicators (1953–90; %)

Annual growth rate of:	*1953–78*	*1979–90*	*1979–83*	*1984–90*
GDP	n.a.	8.8	7.8	9.5
Net material product (NMP)	6.0	8.4	7.3	9.2
Agriculture	1.9	5.6	6.3	5.1
Industry	11.5	10.1	7.3	12.2
(Light)	9.3	13.9	11.6	15.6
(Heavy)	13.8	10.3	5.5	13.9
Construction	7.0	9.6	13.0	8.8
Transportation	6.8	9.4	6.7	11.4
Commerce	4.3	7.2	8.7	6.2
Retail sales of consumer goods	5.4	8.8	10.9	7.4
Urban	6.3	7.6	6.6	8.3
Rural	3.9	10.4	16.1	6.5
Price level[a]	0.9	6.9	3.2	9.6
Investment ratio[b]	29.7	33.3	30.4	34.2
Exports (US$)	10.0	16.7	17.9	15.8

Notes: [a] living cost index of staffs and workers. [b] part of NMP that is used for investment as a proportion to total NMP. Retail sales of consumer goods are deflated by retail sales price deflators.

Source: SSB (1991a: 31, 33, 40, 55, 230, 591, 615).

2.2 ECONOMIC PERFORMANCE IN 1979–90

2.2.1 Achievements

China's economic performance has been impressive since 1979. As indicated in Table 2.9, the GDP in real terms grew by 8.8 per cent per annum during the period 1979–90. In fact, compared with the pre-reform period, all indicators except for inflation record and the growth rate of heavy industry appear better. The lower growth rate of heavy industry was, however, not necessarily a bad thing because this was the result of a more balanced growth. It is worth noting that, in terms of retail sales of consumer goods, the improvement in living standard of the rural population was more significant than that of the urban population in the period 1979–83 when the reform was concentrated in the rural areas. However, this pattern was reversed after 1984.

At the same time, fluctuations in the growth rate were reduced: the standard deviation of annual growth of NMP fell from 11.34 in 1953–78 to a more normal level of 3.33 in 1979–90. It has been the people's living standards that have showed the greatest change since 1978. As

Table 2.10 Possession of durable consumer goods (per 100 population) 1978, 1990

	Sewing machine	*Wrist-watch*	*Bicycle*	*Electric fan*	*Washing machine*
1978	3.5	8.5	7.7	1.0	. .
1990	9.3	34.1	21.1	6.0	2.9
	Refrig-erator	*Tele-vision*	*Tape Recorder*	*Radio*	*Camera*
1978	. .	0.3	0.2	7.8	0.5
1990	0.4	6.6	3.5	22.8	1.1

Note: '. .' indicates the figure that is smaller than 0.1.

Source: SSB (1989a: 461; 1991a: 274).

said in the Survey of China in the *Economist*, reform 'brought about one of the biggest improvements in human welfare anywhere at anytime'.[17] Per capita income in both rural and urban areas has more than doubled since 1978.[18] In per capita terms, urban housing increased from 3.6 square metres in 1978 to 6.7 square metres in 1990 and from 8.1 to 17.8 square metres respectively in rural areas (SSB, 1991a: 269). The 1990s also witnessed a significant increase in households' possession of durable consumer goods (see Table 2.10).

It is likely that the economic reform in China contributed to this success by introducing market mechanisms into the economy and by decentralising control over resources, whilst at the same time avoiding a state-sector production collapse. It is worth emphasising that promotion of the non-state sector was an important factor behind the high growth. For instance, between 1978 and 1990 the non-state sector provided 52.3 per cent of the total incremental industrial output, 55.3 per cent of incremental construction output and 64.0 per cent of the incremental retail sales (SSB, 1991a: 26, 31, 541, 591–2).

In fact, the contribution made by the reform to the economic achievements is widely appreciated.[19] What is sometimes overlooked is the process of implementation of the new development strategy, by which the reform contributed to the achievements. The heavy-industry-centred unbalanced growth pattern was replaced with agriculture- and light-industry-led balanced growth. Referring to Table 2.9, the difference between the sectoral pattern of growth in the pre- and post-1978 periods is clear. In particular, the average annual growth rates of agriculture

Table 2.11 Regional allocation of capital investment by the state sector (1953–90; %)

	1953–78	*79–80*	*81–85*	*86–90*	*79–90*
Total	100.0	100.0	100.0	100.0	100.0
Eastern region	35.9	43.4	47.7	51.8	49.8
Middle region	30.9	29.5	29.3	24.8	26.5
Western region	24.1	20.5	17.2	16.0	16.8
Non-regional specific	9.1	6.6	5.8	7.4	6.9

Note: Eastern region includes Beijing, Tianjin, Hebei, Liaoning, Shanghai, Jiangsu, Zhejiang, Fujian, Shangdong, Guangdong, Guangxi and Hainan. Middle region includes Shanxi, Inner Mongolia, Jilin, Heilongjiang, Anhui, Jiangxi, Henan, Hubei and Hunan. Western region includes Sichuan, Guizhou, Yunnan, Xizang, Shaanxi, Gansu, Qinhai, Ningxia and Xinjiang.

Source: SSB (1987b: 45–50, 104, 231; 1990d: various pages; 1991a: 143, 145).

and industry in 1979–90 were respectively 5.60 and 10.11 per cent, compared with 1.85 and 11.46 per cent in 1953–78. Within industry, the growth rates of light and heavy industry were 13.90 and 10.32 per cent compared with 9.28 and 13.80 per cent respectively. The more sector-balanced growth directly contributed to both the reduction in fluctuations, and the higher growth rate in the post-1978 period. In particular, the strong growth of agriculture and light industry were the main reasons for availability of consumer goods.

In terms of geographic allocation of resources, the bias towards the inland regions was reversed. Total capital allocated to the Eastern (coastal) region was increased by almost 14 percentage points in 1979–90 compared with that in 1953–78 (see Table 2.11). Since the return on investment was higher in the Eastern regions, where the infrastructure was better and skilled labour more available, the change in regional investment priority was positive for growth.

As part of the Open Door policy, preferential measures were designed for this region alone. This included the establishment of the Special Economic Zones, the opening up of fourteen coastal cities, and fiscal incentives for Guangdong and Fujian. Many other coastal provinces took advantage of the fiscal contract system. The pro-eastern region development strategy was further developed into the Coastal Development Strategy adopted by the Chinese Communist Party in 1988.

In terms of opening up to the outside world, the progress of China's integration into the international economy was remarkable. China attracted a large amount of capital and technology inflow. External debt increased from US$0.6 billion in 1978 to US$54.9 billion in 1991; foreign direct investment amounted to US$19.0 billion in the period 1979–90. The scale of technology imports was unprecedented. In the period 1979–90, about 4000 contracts for technology imports worth US$24 billion were signed, compared with only about 900 contracts worth US$11.4 billion in the 30 years prior to 1978.[20] Total exports increased from 4.9 per cent of GNP in 1979 to 10.3 per cent in 1989.[21] Of total exports in 1989, 71 per cent was of manufactured goods.

China's economic achievements during the reform were in striking contrast to what had been experienced in the CIS and other economies in CEE (Central and Eastern Europe) during their more radical post-socialist transition. Measured GDP fell on average by 8 per cent in 1990 and by another 8 per cent in 1991 in Bulgaria, Czechoslovakia, Hungary, Poland and Romania. Within two years (1990–1), GDP dropped by more than 50 per cent in Albania, the former GDR and former Yugoslavia (*Transition*, vol. 3, no. 7, pp.1–3). In 1991, total exports increased by 8 per cent in Hungary, but fell by 12 per cent, 6 per cent, 35 per cent and 40 per cent in Poland, Czechoslovakia, Bulgaria and Romania respectively (Bruno, 1992: 11). Inflation, in terms of the consumer price level, rose by 166 per cent and 5800 per cent in Hungary and Poland over 1987–91, 76 per cent, 551 per cent and 185 per cent in Czechoslovakia, Bulgaria and Romania in 1990–1 respectively, and 897 per cent in Russia in 1992 (Schmidt-Hebbel, 1991: 8).

However, in evaluating China's economic performance, one has to bear in mind that China is still one of the more underdeveloped economies in the world. The majority of the labour force in China (60.2 per cent) was still employed by the agricultural sector in 1990. The high growth may be seen as stemming in part from the initially small economic base. Also, in comparison with most other reforming economies, China was still in the early stages of economic development.

2.2.2 Problems

Despite China's impressive economic growth performance, there is widespread concern in China about its sustainability of growth. As Chapter 1 indicated, during the post-reform period:

(i) macroeconomic control became less effective, accompanied with 'stop–go' cycles;
(ii) improvement in efficiency was slow;

Table 2.12 Implementation of some planned targets (1979–90; ¥ bn)

	1979	*1980*	*1981*	*1982*	*1983*	*1984*	*1985*
(1) Fixed assets investment$_p$	66.9	39.0	47.5	63.0	74.7	94.0	116.0
(2) Fixed assets investment$_a$	69.9	74.6	66.8	84.5	95.2	118.5	168.1
(3) Currency issuance$_p$	1.0	3.0	3.0	5.0	6.0	8.0	15.0
(4) Currency issuance$_a$	5.6	7.9	5.0	4.3	9.1	26.2	19.6
(5) Bank loans$_p$	17.5	17.9	19.5	30.0	37.9	45.3	74.3
(6) Bank loans$_a$	18.9	37.5	35.0	32.0	40.9	117.6	114.0
(7) =(2)/(1)	1.05	1.91	1.41	1.34	1.27	1.26	1.45
(8) =(4)/(3)	5.57	2.62	1.67	0.86	1.51	3.28	1.31
(9) =(6)/(5)	1.08	2.09	1.79	1.07	1.08	2.60	1.53

	1986	*1987*	*1988*	*1989*	*1990*	*1979–90*
(1) Fixed assets investment$_p$	157.0	195.0	206.0	210.0	251.0	1520.1
(2) Fixed assets investment$_a$	197.9	230.0	271.3	253.5	292.7	1923.0
(3) Currency issuance$_p$	20.0	23.0	20.0	40.0	40.0	184.0
(4) Currency issuance$_a$	23.1	23.6	68.0	21.0	30.0	243.2
(5) Bank loans$_p$	95.0	122.5	157.0	160.0	170.0	946.9
(6) Bank loans$_a$	168.5	144.2	151.9	185.8	275.7	1321.8
(7) =(2)/(1)	1.26	1.18	1.31	1.21	1.17	1.27
(8) =(4)/(3)	1.15	1.03	3.40	0.53	0.75	1.32
(9) =(6)/(5)	1.77	1.18	0.97	1.16	1.62	1.40

Notes: These are year-end figures. The subscript letter '$_p$' denotes planned and '$_a$' denotes actual. The planned figures are the formalised ones at the beginning of the year, not the adjusted ones during the year. Fixed investment is of the state sector. Loans include those to the state budget.

Source: (1): Kim (1990: 15); for 1989 and 1990: *Almanac of China's Finance and Banking* (1990: 9; 1991: 14). (2): SSB (1990a: 157); for 1990: *Almanac of China's Finance and Banking* (1991: 249). (3) and (5): PBC. (4) and (6): *Almanac of China's Finance and Banking* (1989: 62–3); SSB (1991a: 642).

(iii) banks became fragile.

These three problems are each described in turn.

When the mechanisms for the mobilisation and allocation of resources are substantially decentralised, it becomes urgent to establish an effective macroeconomic management system based on indirect control. However, despite the effort, macroeconomic control proved problematic. Table 2.12 indicates that the planned targets for investment, for bank credit and for the money supply were exceeded in most years in the period 1979–90: the planned target for fixed assets investment by the state sector was exceeded by, on average, 27 per cent, the target of cash issuance by 32 per cent, and the credit target by 40 per cent. The extent of lack of control over investment was actually greater than is indicated in Table 2.12, which only covers the state sector. For instance, planned investment in fixed assets was ¥228 and ¥287 billion in 1986 and 1987, but the actual figures were ¥301.9 and ¥351.8 billion, exceeding the plan by 34.2 and 22.6 per cent respectively (Wu, J., 1989a: 58–9; 1989b: 37).

These problems of ineffective macroeconomic control also occurred occasionally prior to 1978, when the decentralisation drives took place (e.g. the 'Great Leap Forward' (1958–60)). Generally, however, prior to reform, the planned macroeconomic variables as a whole were under control; e.g. the average ratios of implementation of the cash plan and the credit plan were 0.93 and 0.98 in 1969–77 respectively. By contrast, after 1978, the control appeared generally ineffective unless urgent measures were taken (e.g. in 1988). The policy-makers seemed to have been powerless to fine-tune the economy. As a result, the economy suffered from periodic stop–go cycles. In the period 1979–91, growth of gross industrial output was still fairly unstable (the highest annual growth was 21.4 per cent and the lowest was 4.3 per cent). When 'overheating' growth was curtailed in 1980, 1985 and 1988, the annual growth declined by 5.0, 9.7 and 12.3 percentage points respectively in the following years.

A second major problem was that improvement in efficiency, particularly industrial efficiency, was slow. In fact, the initial improvement was largely reversed during the second half of the 1980s.

Some earlier studies concluded that the new policies had failed to end the long stagnation of productivity in China's state-sector industry (e.g. The World Bank, 1985c: 111; Tidrick, 1986; McGuckin *et al.*, 1989). For instance, according to official statistics, the rate of return on capital in state industry (net profit and taxes as a ratio of net fixed capital and working capital) increased from 19.3 to 24.8 per cent between 1976 and 1980, but declined steadily to 12.4 per cent in 1990 (SSB, 1991a: 416). This view has been challenged by a series of recent studies pioneered by Chen *et al.* (1988a). Based on reconstructed factor input data, especially of the capital stock, they claim that there was a significant gain in TFP (total factor productivity) in Chinese industry during the reform period (e.g. Chen *et al.*, 1988a, 1988b; Lau and Brada, 1990; Jefferson *et al.*, 1992, The World Bank, 1992: 50–4). The differing conclusions depend largely on the differing exercises of the fixed capital stock.

Table 2.13 Annual growth of output and fixed capital of state industry

	1953–78	79–89	53–57	58–78	79–84	85–89
(1) Value added	11.9	6.4	22.2	9.6	6.0	7.0
(2) Fixed capital	12.6	6.8	18.7	11.2	4.3	10.0
(3) =(2)/(1)	1.059	1.063	0.842	1.167	0.717	1.429

Note: Independently accounted enterprises. (1) = gross output/fixed capital stock ratio times fixed capital stock times value added/gross output ratio.

Source: (1): SSB (1990c: 66–7; 64). (2): For methods of calculation and sources, see Appendix 1.

The reconstruction of the fixed capital stock data by Chen *et al.* can be criticised. Using our improved estimates the fixed capital/output ratio of the state-owned industry improved (that is decreased) significantly in 1979–84 but increased again in 1985–9. As a whole, it showed little difference between the two periods of pre- and post-1978 (1.059 and 1.063 respectively, see Table 2.13). Since it is an important aspect of this thesis, that the investment process did, in fact, remain relatively inefficient during the reform period, the data construction and the issues involved are explained in Appendix 1.

Our estimates are consistent with other indicators, such as changes in the accumulation/national income ratio (the Chinese equivalent of a capital/output ratio, given the absence of GDP data before 1978). This ratio decreased from 5.15 in 1953–78 to 4.44 in 1979–90, mainly because of the enormous gain in agricultural net output growth brought by the reform – 1.85 and 5.60 per cent per annum in periods of 1953–78 and 1979–90 respectively (SSB, 1991a: 33). However, the accumulation/national income ratio again rose from 3.37 in 1981–5 to 5.23 in 1986–90 (SSB, 1991a: 32–3, 40).

In 1989, 76 of the total 129 monitored industrial technical-economic efficiency indicators (most of them indicate efficiency of energy/material consumption, equipment utilisation and product quality in physical terms) were no better than the pre-1978 records. On average, 59.3 per cent of indicators during 1979–89 failed to surpass the pre-1978 records (most of which were achieved in 1957 and 1965) (see Table 2.14).

It appears that the pattern of development during the reform period continued to be extensive, even though imports of modern equipment and technology were unprecedented. In the producer goods market,

Table 2.14 Technical-economic efficiency indicators of the industry (1979–89)

Industry	*A*	*B*	*C*
Coal	12	6	87
Power	6	4	44
Petroleum	10	7	50
Metallurgy	51	26	307
Chemistry	8	4	65
Machine building	4	3	37
Building materials	8	4	56
Forestry	4	4	42
Textiles	15	11	97
Light industries	11	4	57
Total	129 (100.0%)	76 (58.9%)	842 (59.3%)

Notes: *A*: No. of indicators. *B*: No. of indicators no better than the pre-1978 record (1989). *C*: No. of indicator-years no better than the pre-1978 record.

Source: SSB (1990c: 78–96).

the phenomena of both shortages and overstocking persisted. Shortages of energy and some raw materials were not eased. One source estimates that, because of shortage of electricity, at least a quarter of production capacity could not be utilised (Wu, J., 1989: 67). Another source gives a similar picture: during the period 1981–5, the production capacity utilisation ratio (actual level over designed level of output) was about two-thirds because of lack of energy, electricity, raw materials, etc. (Deng, Y. *et al.*, 1990: 248).

At the same time, problems of overstocking worsened. Annual changes in stocks as a proportion of annual GDP have been exceptionally high – from 6.0 to 12.6 per cent in 1978–91 (see Table 2.15). This is in stark contrast to international averages.[22] Surely, there are some problems with the data presented here, because they embody statistical residuals. Nevertheless, it is common knowledge that overstocking has been a problem in China and there is no sign of systematic improvement in this respect. This is confirmed by the above data series.

Problems of poor product quality have also persisted. According to a survey conducted by the State Industrial and Commercial Administration Bureau and the China Consumer Association, only 59.5 per cent of the sample products came up to standard in 1991,[23] compared with 73.7 per cent in the last quarter of 1989.[24] From an economic

Table 2.15 Changes in stocks (1978–91, ¥ bn at 1980 prices)

	1978	*1979*	*1980*	*1981*	*1982*	*1983*	*1984*
GDP	385.4	414.7	446.7	466.9	507.4	558.7	639.7
Changes in stocks	27.7	40.1	36.5	42.3	30.4	31.8	37.7
As a percentage of GDP	7.2	9.7	8.2	9.0	6.0	5.7	5.9
	1985	*1986*	*1987*	*1988*	*1989*	*1990*	*1991*
GDP	722.7	783.6	871.8	969.6	1013.7	1070.2	1144.9
Changes in stocks	75.1	72.5	62.5	72.8	127.2	123.1	102.9
As a percentage of GDP	10.4	9.3	7.2	7.5	12.6	11.5	9.0

Source: The World Bank (1992: 187, 189).

developmental perspective, the economist Liu Guoguang regards this as being probably the single most important problem to be tackled.[25]

It is increasingly recognised that problems of capital accumulation stressed in earlier development literature and in the development practice of the 1950s and 1960s may be far less important than the problems of channelling funds to the most promising opportunities and ensuring that those funds are well-used (e.g. Stiglitz, 1989a). The lesser importance of resource mobilisation compared to resource utilisation is similarly stressed by the World Bank – quoting the conclusion from Chenery and Srinivasan (1988) that 'a major difference between [developing and developed economies] seems to be that growth in the former is largely accounted for by the accumulation of inputs rather than the growing efficiency in their development' (The World Bank, 1991: 45). Slow improvement in the efficiency of utilisation of resources is a very serious problem facing China. Since China is the largest developing country (1.2 billion population), where the level of natural resources endowment per capita is only a half of the world average (Deng, Y., 1987), it is unlikely that growth based on the inefficient use of resources is sustainable. Recently, the Chinese Academy of Sciences in its *Report on the National Situation* (no.2, 1992) urged the transformation of China's economy to one based on economising natural resources. It warned that the Chinese population will be 1.5 billion in the 2020s to 2030s whilst per capita cultivated land will have reduced to only 0.08 of a hectare compared with the world average of 0.269 of a hectare in 1988 (SSB, 1990a: 835; 1991a: 820). Chinese agriculture will then reach its maximum supporting capacity. It predicts that about a half of mineral resources, including petroleum and other key resources, will be in seriously short supply by the end

Table 2.16 Capital/deposit ratio and capital base of the state banks (units: ¥ bn)

	1978	*1979*	*1980*	*1981*	*1982*	*1983*	*1984*
(1) Net capital	42.2	38.1	32.7	45.1	50.4	52.1	51.5
(2) Total deposit	113.5	133.9	166.1	202.7	237.0	278.9	358.4
(3) Total assets	187.7	216.3	262.4	317.1	361.8	412.5	537.0
(4) =(1)/(2) (%)	37.2	28.4	19.7	22.3	21.3	18.7	14.4
(5) =(1)/(3) (%)	22.5	17.6	12.5	14.2	13.9	12.6	9.6

	1985	*1986*	*1987*	*1988*	*1989*	*1990*
(1) Net capital	58.1	58.2	55.9	62.0	63.1	62.5
(2) Total deposit	426.5	535.5	651.7	742.6	901.4	1164.5
(3) Total assets	637.5	811.1	987.0	1148.5	1356.2	1683.8
(4) =(1)/(2) (%)	13.6	10.9	8.6	8.4	7.0	5.4
(5) =(1)/(3) (%)	9.1	7.2	5.7	5.4	4.7	3.7

Note: Net capital equals capital (self-owned funds) minus loans to, and overdrafts by the MOF.

Source: *Almanac of China's Finance and Banking* (1990: 52–3). For 1990: SSB (1991a: 642).

of this century if there is no major breakthrough in exploration.[26] It is, therefore, not surprising that the Central Committee of the Chinese Communist Party, in its 'Suggestions to the Ten-Year Programme (1991–2000) and the Eighth Five-Year Plan (1991–5)' at the end of 1990, urged that 'improvement of economic efficiency must be placed at the heart of all economic work'.[27]

The third main problem of China's economy is that the banking sector as a whole has become fragile because of an increasing scale of non-performing loans and little increase in its capital base. Table 2.16 shows that the capital/deposit ratios of the state banks deteriorated. Both the capital/deposit ratios and capital base declined substantially, from 37.2 and 22.5 per cent respectively in 1978, to merely 5.4 and 3.7 per cent in 1990 (Table 2.16, lines 4 and 5).

These ratios however, were, still overstated. Another official source reports that the specialised banks had the nominal capital fund of ¥54.7 billion (16 per cent of the total outstanding loans) at the end of 1983. But ¥50 billion needs to be deducted, if bad debts and government overdrafts are included (PBC *et al.*, 1984: 7–8). Incorporating the Rural Credit Cooperatives (which are essentially an adjunct of the state banks)

Table 2.17 Estimation of capital/deposit ratio of banks and the Rural Credit Cooperatives (%)

	1985	*1986*	*1987*	*1988*	*1989*	*1990*
(1) No bad debt	8.2	4.2	3.6	4.5	4.8	2.8
(2) 1% bad debt	6.9	2.8	2.2	3.1	3.4	1.5
(3) 3% bad debt	4.2	0.1	−0.4	0.3	0.7	−1.0
(4) 5% bad debt	1.4	−2.7	−3.1	−2.4	−1.9	−3.5

Note: Capital is sum of owned fund and gross profits contracted by taxes and profit paid to the MOF, loans to, and overdraft by the MOF and the acknowledged bad debts to be written off. Bad debt in row 2–4 is the hidden bad debt.

Source: People's Bank of China (PBC).

Table 2.18 Distribution of banks' profits (1984–90; ¥ bn)

	1984	*1985*	*1986*	*1987*	*1988*	*1989*	*1990*	*1984–90*
(1) Profit before tax	12.4	20.8	26.0	29.3	36.3	45.5	37.1	207.4
(2) Tax and profit paid to the state budget	10.6	13.2	17.7	18.3	22.2	27.2	30.4	139.6
(3) State budget's overdraft	6.1	0.4	9.5	14.5	6.2	10.8	11.7	59.2
(4) Bad debt to be written off	1.7	0.1	2.7	0.0	0.0	0.0	0.0	4.5
(5) = (2+3+4)	18.4	13.7	29.9	32.8	28.4	38.0	42.1	203.3
(6) = (5)/(1) (%)	148.4	65.9	115.0	111.9	78.2	83.5	113.5	98.0

Source: PBC.

and also taking into account the hidden bad debt,[28] Table 2.17 shows that the capital/deposit ratios effectively approached zero or even a negative figure if the bad debt was estimated at 3–5 per cent of the outstanding loans. The estimation of 3 to 5 per cent of bad debt is conservative. It is widely accepted that non-performing loans accounted for at least 10 per cent.

The low capital base of the state banks resulted partly from the heavy taxation by the central government. For instance, during the period 1984–9, 98 per cent of profits before tax were paid to the MOF one way or another (Table 2.18).

Although there are no reliable measures against which to judge the banks' capital adequacy, the effectively destroyed capital base of the banking sector in China certainly increases the vulnerability of the financial system, and the potential for financial instability. A financial crisis could be triggered even by, for example, a slow-down in the rising household saving ratio, as actually occurred in 1988 (see Chapter 7).

In summary, the achievements of the reform in China since 1978 have been remarkable. They contributed substantially to high and relatively stable growth. They have, however, created problems for macroeconomic control. Also, reform has been far less successful in supporting a development strategy based on intensive growth. It is against this background that the continuing expansion of the money stock heightens concerns over the stability and sustainability of growth.[29]

3 Sources and Processes of Monetary Expansion

Although the rapid expansion of the money supply and the high ratio of money to the GDP has led to much policy controversy in China, there are, as we have seen, remarkably few systematic studies of the nature of this expansion – surely the essential preliminary to an understanding of its causes and of the likely consequences and policy implications. This chapter argues that the expansion of money stock in China in the post-reform period can be ascribed to three interactive factors:

(i) the expansion of household savings associated with changes in national income distribution favouring the household sector;
(ii) the expansion of the banks' finance for fixed assets investment of the production sector;
(iii) the narrow channel of financial intermediation through bank deposits/lending or, the near absence of alternative channels of financial intermediation apart from the commercial banks.

Within these interactions, the central bank played an important role in supporting credit expansion through its massive lending to the specialised banks.

The approach adopted by this chapter begins as basically descriptive, focusing on both sides of the balance sheets of the banking system, with a view to determining which sector or sectors were – in a mechanical sense – responsible for the expansion of liabilities and which for the expansion of assets. Essentially, this is an accounting approach, making use of the identities which apply, in order to identify the main components and counterparts of monetary expansion in post-reform China. Later sections will go on to consider particularly important components and counterparts of monetary expansion in greater detail, and will also attempt to account in economic terms for the main trends.

The chapter commences with the setting-up of a framework for monetary analysis. Within this framework it identifies key components and counterparts of the monetary expansion. Sections 3.3 and 3.4 explain expansion of household deposits and bank finance for fixed assets investment as two key factors in monetary expansion. The final section examines the role of the central bank in the credit expansion process.

3.1 A FRAMEWORK FOR MONETARY ANALYSIS

Though the focus is on the balance sheet identities, the approach is of course closely related to the 'flow of funds' (FOF) approach, frequently adopted – at least as a starting-point – in the analysis of monetary developments in advanced market economies. Typically, the FOF approach starts with the counterpart identity relating changes in broad money to changes in the credit counterparts. Thus:

$$\Delta M = (PSBR - \Delta Gp) + \Delta BLp + \Delta Ext - \Delta NDL \qquad [3.1]$$

where Δ = increment
M = broad money
PSBR = public sector borrowing requirement;
Gp = the government debt sold to the non-bank private sector (NBPS);
BLp = banks' lending to the non-bank private sectors;
Ext = transactions involving the external sector, such as sales of foreign currency which provide external financing for the PSBR;
NDL = non-deposit liabilities.

Neglecting externals and changes in non-deposit liabilities for simplicity and because in practice these tend to be small, the identity relates changes in the money supply to bank loans, which are classified into two sectors: bank loans to the public sector ($PSBR - \Delta Gp$) and bank loans to the private sector (or more generally, to the non-bank, non-government sector).

This formula arises directly from the balance-sheet identities of the banking sector together with the definition of broad money and the sectoral balance identity for the public-sector (the government budget constraint). The public-sector balance demands that a government budget deficit must, by definition, be financed by currency issue, by borrowing from the public or by borrowing from the banking system, if the external factors are neglected.[1] As an identity, the formula, strictly speaking, has no economic implications whatsoever. Nevertheless, the FOF approach is typically used by those who feel it useful to look at the money supply from the side of credit, i.e. causal hypotheses are soon added which do turn it into an economic approach rather than just the use of accounts. A further justification often put forward is that, as a framework, it brings together fiscal and monetary effects – though here it is necessary to insist rather rigorously that, strictly speaking, no causal links between public borrowing and money are implied despite the presence in the usual formula of the PSBR.

The basic point is that the balance sheet or FOF approach which we apply in the Chinese case is, in the first instance, neutral as far as the economics of monetary expansion goes. We believe, however, that the facts that appear within this framework do suggest causal hypotheses and explanations: they also suggest that other causal hypotheses do not match the facts very well.

The more important reasons for the adoption of this approach, however, are that it is general, and also is suitable as a framework to derive a number of different hypotheses. It is less likely than some, commonly adopted, frameworks of monetary analysis either to drive an analysis in a particular direction, or to favour implicitly particular views of the causalities involved. In particular, it is less constricting than the monetary base framework, which has been extremely influential, not only in the West but in conditioning monetary analysis and policy prescription in China.

3.1.1 The monetary base (MB) framework

One of the most influential theories of the connection between money and the economy is the quantity theory of money or, more broadly, monetarism. Within this tradition, inflation is seen as essentially a monetary phenomenon, and the main causal link runs from the authorities' control (or lack of it) over money supply to the price level. (In strict theory, moreover, the real economy is seen as not being influenced to any great extent by anticipated inflation or monetary expansion.)

We have already seen that there are some difficulties in applying this framework in a Chinese context. The theory is usually held to depend on a stable demand for money function, which is difficult to reconcile with the rapid expansion of the money/GDP ratio. (We have noted that attempts to reconcile the difficulties by appeal to changes in the demand for money during monetisation appear forced.) Further problems arise over the assumed mechanisms of monetary control since, in China as elsewhere, most money is created by the banking system and the authorities directly control only a component of it.

The normal response is to relate total money to the monetary base, or, in Friedman's terms, to high-powered money (*H*). High-powered money is currency plus the (non-central) banks' holdings of reserve money. The bank's creation of deposits through the fractional reserve system is then related to high powered-money. In a simplified situation with just bank reserves but with no currency holdings by the public, total money would be related to high-powered money through a money multiplier which would simply be the reciprocal of the reserve/deposit ratio. In more practical but still simplified cases, the money multiplier would depend not only on the deposit/reserve ratio of the banks, but also on the cash/deposit ratio of the public. The latter would have a negative effect on the total supply of money (given *H*) since, necessarily, that part of high-powered or central bank money held outside the banking system is not available as reserves to the banks. Taking currency holdings into account, determination of money stock can be expressed as the product of the money base *H* (or high-powered money) and the money multiplier [.] in formula [3.2].

$$M = H \cdot [D/R\ (1 + D/C)\ /\ (D/R + D/C)]^2 \qquad [3.2]$$

where H = high-powered money;
D/C = deposit to currency ratio of the public;
D/R = deposit to reserve ratio of the banks.

Within the monetary base approach, changes in money stock are related to changes in both high-powered money and money multiplier. The latter is determined by two ratios, deposit/reserve ratio (*D/R*) and deposit/cash ratio (*D/C*). *D/R* is determined by the banking sector subject to the reserve requirement imposed by the monetary authorities,[3] whereas *D/C* is determined by the general public (Friedman, M. 1987). Clearly, whilst the MB approach is usually associated with a particular view of the instruments of monetary policy (control over *H* and/or *D/R*) and the behaviour of the banks, it need not be. Just as with the FOF approach, the above formula can be treated as an identity, which always applies and does not imply causality.

The MB approach was often used in monetary analyses in the UK during the 1950s and 1960s (e.g. Day, 1957; Sayers, 1964; Newlyn, 1962, 1971; Johnson *et al.*, 1972). The main controversy was centred on which factors were key in the creation of bank deposits and the control of money supply – the cash ratio as opposed to some wider liquid assets ratio. In recent years, many have argued that the framework has the advantage of focusing attention on the relative importance of the behaviour of the banks (via *D/R*), the public (via *D/C*) and of the monetary authorities (via *H*) in the determination of money stock. Since the banking system cannot create cash but is dependent on the central bank as the ultimate source, the supply of cash to the banking system is usually seen as the ultimate determinant of the volume of money stock (Carter and Partington, 1984: 176). In other words, it is argued that the behaviour of the monetary authorities, expressed by the money base, plays the most prominent role in substantial or persistent accelerations of the money stock (Brunner, 1987).

Although the behaviour of monetary authorities is important, one of the most crucial issues is whether the authorities do in fact control *H* or whether, for reasons either of political economy or for other reasons, causality runs the other way, from loans to central bank financing. Indeed, one major criticism of the MB approach is that money is *endogenous* (influential papers include, for example, Tobin, 1963; Goodhart, 1973). Not only are the values of the two ratios determining the multiplier likely to change, but also the process of monetary expansion is likely to feed back on the supply of the monetary base itself. Applying the marginal analysis to the bank assets and liabilities, Tobin (1963) points out that marginal return to the banks on their assets must be equal to the marginal cost to them of deposits. Therefore, there is a natural economic limit to the scale of the commercial banks. Tobin's analysis has come to be known as the portfolio adjustment analysis. The implication is that money is an endogenous variable, reflecting the economic behaviour of banks and other private economic units (Hester and Tobin, 1967). Goodhart (1973) also points out that the determination of money supply should be analysed in terms of a general equilibrium stock adjustment model of the financial system. He stresses that high-powered money, *H*, is not exogenous. *H* is related to the budget deficit, government's operations in marketable debt, redemptions of maturing marketable debt, sales of non-marketable debt and external currency flows. Not all these items are immediately under the control of the monetary authorities. Similarly, the point of endogenous money has been stressed by Dow and Saville (1988). They argued that *H* is not controllable by central banks because (i) the banks must leave bank deposits freely convertible into cash, and (ii) the stock of cash appears insensitive to the level of interest.

Another issue, regarded as crucial in developed financial systems, concerns the behaviour of the banks: do they cut loans to meet reserve requirements (asset management), or do they bid for deposits, affecting the interest rate (liability management)? If banks are liability managers, it is often argued that the process runs from an initial change in interest rates, whether administered by the central bank or determined by market forces, to a subsequent readjustment in monetary aggregate quantities. In reality, central banks have generally sought to set interest rates according to various objectives (Goodhart, 1987) even when they have been targeting money.

However, because of a combination of data and econometric problems and structural change in the financial system, the general equilibrium portfolio adjustment models have failed to be developed up to date. The large models of the UK monetary sector (e.g. the National Institute for Economic and Social Studies, the Treasury, and the Bank of England) effectively view money stock as the sum of the various counterparts, allowing for a range of interactions and linkages between them. More detailed study has a strong emphasis on individual money counterparts.

Though the case of China is obviously very different the argument of endogenous money still holds; neither of the two ratios nor high-powered money are particularly helpful in explaining the monetary expansion process – these issues will be examined in the next section in a wider FOF context. Changes in the interest rate are also insignificant in explaining both deposits and loans (Chapters 4 and 7 will cover this point). Moreover, deposit rates are fixed by the central bank and the level of reserves held by the banks are generally much higher than the reserve requirement.

The MB framework can be seen as a special case of the wider balance sheet approach, where the lending behaviour of the banks is taken as constrained by reserves and the authorities seek to control money by controlling the quantity of reserve assets.

3.1.2 The flow of funds (FOF) framework and the sectoral balances

Particularly in the case of relatively underdeveloped financial systems, it is useful to relate the FOF approach to the sectoral positions of the major sectors – the government, households, and enterprises. (In principle, the foreign sector as well.) The reason is that, with relatively few assets or channels of intermediation, sectoral positions impinge directly on banking flows and vice versa. The approach is familiar in Western practice with respect to the government position. In China, with little reliance on bond finance (to be discussed later), public borrowing impinges directly on bank credit and on money. This is equally important in the FOF framework or in the MB framework – in the latter, government borrowing directly expands high-powered-money.

Less familiar is the extension of such approaches to the other sectors. Nevertheless, in China, where property rights are underdeveloped, nearly all financial intermediation goes through the banking system, so that there is a direct relationship between household savings and the expansion of deposits. Similarly, enterprise deficits are closely related to bank financing. In fact, the key point in understanding the process of monetary expansion in China is to note that high and rising household savings have been recycled through the banks to investing enterprises with inevitable effects on the monetary aggregates. In other words, given (i) an expansion of the household savings, and (ii) the fact that most of households' net savings have to be held in the form of bank deposits and cash, an expansion of household savings must result, *ceteris paribus*, in an expansion of money stock. Likewise, borrowing by enterprises is only possible if it is financed by the banks.

A very simple accounting exercise for a closed economy with three sectors, including a production sector (in China's case, composing the government sector and non-bank enterprise sector), a household sector and a banking sector, illustrates the point more formally. Accounts of each sector are assumed as follows:

The economy: Total output = Consumption expenditure + Investment expenditure

Production sector: Receipts = Consumption expenditure + Investment expenditure

Payments = Wage payment

Household sector: Receipts = Wage payment

Payments = Consumption expenditure

Banking sector: Liabilities = Bank deposits + cash outside banks

= Household savings

= Wage payment − Consumption expenditure

Assets = Bank loans (for investment to production sector)

If consumption expenditure equals the wage payment, no financial wealth can be accumulated. If consumption expenditure continues to be less than wage payment, both sides of the bank balance sheet will accumulate. The more the household sector saves, the larger the expansion will be of the bank liabilities, i.e. money stock. In other words, an expansion of household savings must lead to an expansion of money and, of course, must be balanced by production sector's borrowing and an expansion of loans.

This conclusion would not be valid if the assumption of a single channel of financial intermediation through banks was relaxed. Accumulation of non-money financial assets, such as bonds and shares, would absorb the financial surplus of the household sector and thus reduce the magnitude of monetary expansion. From this point of view, the expansion of bank deposits – and thus money stock in China – is also related to fiscal policy (regarding bond issue) and the government's conservative attitudes towards ownership reform (regarding privatisation and equity issues). In practice, in the period with which we are concerned, households were not allowed to exchange their savings for ownership entitlements other than cash and bank deposits.

3.2 MONETARY EXPANSION AND SECTORAL BALANCES

3.2.1 Main components and counterparts of monetary expansion

Applying the FOF approach with sectoral balances in mind, the first thing to do, in order to identify the main components and counterparts of the monetary expansion, would be to look at details on both sides of the banks' balance sheet. In China, banks do not usually publish their balance sheets. However, the so-called 'Report of Implementation of the Bank Credit Plan' is more or less equivalent to such a balance sheet. Table 3.1 presents the balance sheets of the central bank, the specialised banks (SBs) including the Rural Credit Cooperatives and the entire banking sector, at the end of 1990.

A quick comparison of these two balance sheets reveals some important information. At this stage this is: first, items of cash appear on both the liability and assets sides of the PBC's balance sheet, and other banks have no cash assets – cash outside the central bank and the PBC was of the same quantity (¥264.4 billion). Second, gold and silver reserves as well as foreign currency reserves were all held in the PBC. Third, in addition to the official reserve requirement of 12 per cent of their deposits, other banks held a large quantity of non-reserve deposits with the PBC (equivalent to 115 per cent of the officially required reserves).

Table 3.1 Bank balance sheets
(stock at 31 December 1990; ¥ bn)

Central Bank (PBC)	
Sources of funds (Liabilities)	*700.8*
Total deposits (*Dc*)	261.6
State budget deposits (*Dg*)	42.7
Banks' deposits (*Db*)	159.2
Institutional deposits (*Di*)	59.7
Reserve requirements (*Rb*)	139.0
Cash outside banks (*M0*)	264.4
Capital (*Kc*)	9.8
Unclassified items (*Uc*)	26.0
Uses of funds (Assets)	*700.8*
Total loans (*Lc*)	550.7
Bank loans (*Lb*)	510.9
Other loans (*Loc*)	39.8
Gold and silver reserves (*GS*)	9.5
Foreign currency reserves (*Fc*)	49.5
Budget overdraft and borrowing (*Lg*)	90.8
Cash (*M0c*)	0.3
Specialised Banks including the RCCs	
Sources of funds (Liabilities)	*1927.6*
Total deposits (*Ds*)	1202.0
Enterprise deposits (*De*)	434.0
Household deposits (*Dh*)	703.4
Other deposits (*Do*)	64.6
Bonds issued (*Bi*)	9.2
Banks' own capital (*Ks*)	117.4
PBC's loans (*Lb*)	510.9
Unclassified items (*Us*)	88.1
Uses of funds (Assets)	*1927.6*
Total loans (*Ls*)	1611.3
Working capital loans	1229.4
Agricultural loans	124.4
Fixed assets loans	221.5
Other loans	36.0
Bonds possessed (*Bp*)	18.1
Required reserves held in PBC	139.0
Deposits with PBC	159.2

continued on page 48

Table 3.1 continued

Consolidated Balance Sheet of the PBC, the SBs and the RCCs	
Sources of funds (Liabilities)	*1819.0*
Total deposits (*D*)	1304.4
Enterprise deposits (*De*)	434.0
State budget deposits (*Dg*)	42.7
Institutional deposits (*Di*)	59.7
Household deposits (*Dh*)	703.4
Other deposits (*Do*)	64.6
Bonds issued (*Bi*)	9.2
Currency outside banks (*M0*)	264.4
Banks' own capital (*K*)	127.2
Unclassified items (*U*)	113.8
Uses of funds (Assets)	*1819.0*
Total loans (*L*)	1651.1
Working capital loans	1229.4
Agricultural loans	124.4
Fixed assets loans	221.5
Other loans	75.8
Bonds possessed (*Bp*)	18.1
Gold and silver reserves (*Gs*)	9.5
Foreign currency reserves (*Fc*)	49.5
Budget overdraft and borrowing (*Lg*)	90.8

Note: Item of 'pre-tax profit' under liabilities and 'taxes and profit paid to the MOF' under assets are cancelled out and the remaining difference is added to 'own capital', from which 'bad debt to be written off' is taken away. The SBs' balance sheet is derived from the other two balance sheets.

Source: *The Preliminary Reports of the Implementation of the Bank Credit Plan* by the PBC in Feb. 1991.

These facts reflect some features of China's banking system. Banks other than the PBC are not allowed to keep cash. The PBC has exclusive responsibility for cash management – cash issue into, and withdrawal from, circulation. Other banks must transfer all their surplus cash to the PBC. Cash issue is strictly controlled by the PBC under the 'cash plan'. However, convertibility of household bank deposits into cash is guaranteed by the government via the PBC. Thus, unlike commercial banks in a market economy, the 'commercial banks' in China have no liquidity problem to worry about. The large non-reserve deposits in the PBC reflect both the under-developed clearing system and the quantitative control over banks' lending through imposing credit ceilings. Occasionally, the PBC requires other banks to maintain a certain level of their non-reserve deposits with it (as during 1989–90, for instance).

With respect to money-supply process, the relationship between the central bank and the specialised banks will be discussed later in section 3.3. What we are concerned with here are components and counterparts of broad money appearing in the balance sheet of the entire banks' balance sheet. Within the FOF framework, as it has already be discussed, expansion of M2 can be expressed as expansion of banks' assets and change in banks' capital base. In our case, money stock (M2), according to the definition, is the sum of cash outside banks and total bank deposits excluding the state budgetary deposits (D). The counterparts of M2 include bank loans to the non-government sector (L), fiscal deficits financed by banks, i.e. the difference between the banks' lending to the state budget and the latter's deposits with the banks (Fb; $Fb = Lg - Dg$), reserves of precious metal and hard currencies (GF; $GF = Gs + Fc$), and non-deposit liabilities comprising net issue of bonds, banks' capital funds and the unclassified items ($Bi - Bp$, K and U respectively) (identity 3.3).

$$\Delta M2 \equiv \Delta M0 + \Delta D - \Delta Dg \equiv \Delta L + \Delta Fb + \Delta GF - (\Delta Bi - \Delta Bp + \Delta K + \Delta U) \qquad [3.3]$$

where ΔFb is equivalent to (PSBR $- \Delta Gp$), ΔL equivalent to ΔBlp, ΔGF equivalent to ΔExt, and $(\Delta Bi - \Delta Bp + \Delta K + \Delta U)$ equivalent to NDL in formula [3.1].

It is clear from Table 3.1 that, the dominant component was deposits, especially household deposits and enterprise deposits. The former accounted for 55.8 per cent of total deposits (excluding the state budget deposits). The dominant counterpart of M2 consisted of loans particularly the working capital loans. Taking M2 as 100, total loans were equivalent to 108. Obviously, one bank's balance sheet is not enough to identify main components and counterparts of monetary expansion. In other words, it is necessary to have a series of such balance sheets for the period under study. Fortunately we have a series of the Report of Implementation of the Bank Credit Plan for the state banks (including the central bank), the deposits and lending of the Rural Credit Cooperatives (RCCs) and the balance sheets for the Urban Credit Cooperatives (UCCs). Reconstructing the consolidated balance sheets of the entire banking sector (including the RCCs and the UCCs) for the period 1978–90 produces Table 3.2.

Table 3.2 Changes in the bank balance sheet (stocks, 1978–90; ¥ bn)

	Liabilities	*M2*	*(M1)*	*(M0)*	*(Dh)*	*K*	*U*
1978	173.4	120.4	99.4	21.2	21.1	42.2	10.8
1979	206.1	150.6	122.5	26.8	28.1	47.1	8.5
1980	251.0	192.5	151.5	34.6	40.0	49.7	10.7
1981	298.2	228.3	173.4	39.6	52.4	62.2	7.8
1982	347.3	271.1	199.9	43.9	67.5	67.5	8.8
1983	399.6	323.9	228.3	53.0	89.3	72.1	3.7
1984	543.9	450.1	304.3	79.2	121.5	77.6	16.3
1985	633.6	528.4	333.5	98.8	162.3	85.6	19.6
1986	827.4	685.0	423.9	121.8	223.8	95.2	47.3
1987	1022.5	849.9	503.0	145.5	307.3	107.4	65.2
1988	1210.8	1033.1	603.3	213.4	380.2	119.7	58.0
1989	1427.7	1221.1	650.8	234.4	514.7	131.6	75.0
1990	1793.3	1557.0	792.6	264.4	703.4	148.2	88.1
1978–90	Δ1619.9	Δ1436.6	Δ693.2	Δ243.2	Δ682.3	Δ106.0	Δ77.3

	Assets	*L*	*(Lfk)*	*Fb*	*GF*	*NIA*
1978	173.4	189.5	0.0	−18.7	2.7	0.0
1979	206.1	208.7	0.8	−5.9	3.3	0.0
1980	251.0	246.9	5.6	0.6	0.4	0.4
1981	298.2	295.7	13.3	−6.7	10.2	−0.8
1982	347.3	330.2	23.8	−4.9	23.0	−1.0
1983	399.6	375.4	30.7	−4.4	27.8	0.9
1984	543.9	512.1	45.2	3.1	27.6	1.2
1985	633.6	630.6	70.5	−9.3	10.5	1.9
1986	827.4	817.9	100.6	5.9	5.0	−1.3
1987	1022.5	986.7	128.7	20.8	14.4	0.6
1988	1210.8	1159.4	155.9	30.6	17.0	3.9
1989	1427.7	1370.1	177.6	24.7	27.7	5.3
1990	1793.3	1682.8	224.8	42.0	61.1	7.3
1978–90	Δ1619.9	Δ1493.3	Δ224.6	Δ60.7	Δ58.4	Δ7.3

Note: M2 = M0 + total deposits excluding the state budgetary deposits; M1 = M0 + chequeable deposits; M0 = currency outside the banks; *Dh* = household deposits; *U* = unclassified items; *L* = total loans; *L(fk)* = bank fixed assets investment loans; *Fb* = net loans to the state budget ($Fb = Lg - Bi - Dg$); *GF* = reserves of precious metal and hard currencies; ($GF = Gs + Fc$); *NIA* = net assets in international financial institutions. Liabilities (and assets) include liabilities of the SBs and loans extended by the RCCs and the UCCs – assuming that differences between the deposits and loans of the credit cooperatives are deposited in the PBC. Such an estimation is very close to the reality. For instance, the consolidated liabilities or assets of the SBs and the RCCs were ¥1821.3 billion, compared with ¥1825.1 billion by our estimate (*Almanac of China's Finance and Banking*, 1991: 41–42, 53).

Source: *Almanac of China's Finance and Banking* (1990: 52–3, 65; 1991: 42, 48, 52–3).

It is of note that there are small differences between the liabilities of Table 3.2 and of Table 3.1 for 1990 (¥25.7 billion) due to different coverage and data sources. This small difference does not, however, affect our analysis.

Table 3.2 shows that, between 1978 and 1990, 16.9 per cent of ΔM2 was ΔM0 and 83.1 per cent was Δ*D*. Noticeably, although the importance of bank deposits in money expansion remained unchanged, the importance of household bank deposits (*Dh*) surged. As a proportion to M2, they increased from 17.5 per cent in 1978 to 45.2 per cent in 1990. In other words, 48.2 per cent of the M2 or 57.2 per cent of ΔM2−ΔM0 during this period was Δ*Dh*. Obviously, in order to understand the monetary expansion this fact has to be explained. Furthermore, since 80 per cent of cash in circulation is held by households,[4] the major component of monetary expansion is the accumulation of households' financial wealth in the form of cash and bank deposits.

On the assets side of the balance sheet, significance of each counterpart of ΔM2 between 1978 and 1990 is as follows. Taking ΔM2 as 100.0, Δ*L* was equivalent to 103.9, Δ*Fb* 4.2, Δ*GF* 4.1, Δ*K* 7.3 and Δ*U* 5.4 (Table 3.2). Clearly, expansion of M2 in the period 1979–90 was closely related to the expansion of bank loans. Fiscal factors as well as others, at least on the surface, were much less important in explaining changes in M2.

In summary, the primary examination of both components and counterparts of money points to two main issues that require particular scrutiny. One is the expansion of bank assets, especially of household deposits (and cash holdings); the other is the expansion of bank loans. Since bank loans to the state budget have already been taken into account in *Fb* and loans to households in China were very small, this means that the figures in the table refer largely to loans to enterprises. Within this it is noticeable that bank loans for fixed assets investment increased particularly rapidly. As a proportion of total bank loans, they increased from zero to over 13 per cent. The impact of such loans on total credit expansion will be discussed in section 3.4. These features of the changes in the banks' balance sheet lead us to the issue of sectoral balances and financial intermediation.

3.2.2 Sectoral balances and the explanation of intermediation

Table 3.3 presents the sectoral pattern of savings and investment in China during the period 1979–90.

The most noticeable features of Table 3.3 refer to the rapid increase

Table 3.3 Sectoral pattern of savings and investment (1979–90) (¥ 100 million)

	1979	1980	1981	1982	1983	1984	1985	1986	1987	1988	1989[a]	1990[b]
National												
S	1257	1319	1284	1413	1639	2261	2659	3010	3712	4622	5635	6593
I	1281	1358	1272	1339	1587	2152	3066	3360	3788	4823	5665	5948
External (*I* − *S*)	24	39	−12	−74	−52	−9	407	350	76	201	30	−645
Government												
S	538	423	286	260	332	444	504	567	486	335	474	533
I	592	504	434	430	517	643	715	876	858	866	865	671
Net	−54	−81	−148	−170	−185	−199	−211	−309	−372	−531	−391	−138
Enterprises												
S	423	482	587	665	574	724	825	654	956	1389	1447	1600
I	477	587	598	637	660	989	1659	1653	1987	2704	3547	4077
Net	−54	−105	−11	28	−86	−265	−834	−999	−1031	−1315	−2100	−2477
(as % of GNP)	−1.2	−2.1	−0.2	0.5	−1.3	−3.3	−9.0	−8.9	−7.8	−8.0	−11.1	−11.9
Households												
S	296	414	411	488	733	993	1330	1789	2270	2898	3714	4460
I	212	267	240	272	410	520	692	831	943	1253	1253	1200
Net	84	147	171	216	323	573	638	958	1327	1645	2461	3260
(as % of GNP)	1.9	3.0	3.2	3.7	4.9	7.2	6.9	8.5	10.1	10.0	13.0	15.7
Gross saving (national = 100.0)												
Government	42.8	32.1	22.3	18.4	20.3	20.6	19.0	18.8	13.1	7.3	8.4	8.1
Enterprises	33.7	36.6	45.8	47.1	35.0	33.5	31.0	21.7	25.8	30.1	25.7	24.3
Households	23.6	31.4	32.0	34.5	44.8	46 0	50.0	59.5	61.2	62.7	65.9	67.6

Note: *S* = gross saving; *I* = gross investment; *Net* = Net saving (S − I). (a) For 1989, Guo and Han give a figure for sum of government and enterprises' gross savings of 1921. The remaining figures are estimated by the author according to available information on the state budget revenues and expenditures, households' investment in fixed assets etc. (b) For 1990, figures are estimated by the author according to the available sources.

Source: Guo and Han (1991: tables 3.13, 6.5, 7.5 and 7.9); SSB (1991a: 143, 214-5); the World Bank (1992: 185).

in households' net savings with the parallel increase in the financial deficits of government and, in particular, enterprise sectors. In 1979, 90 per cent of the gross investment of the government and enterprise sectors was financed internally. By contrast, in 1990, only 39 per cent of enterprises' investment was financed by internal funds. Their remaining finance came, effectively, from the household sector.

With respect to the government: on one hand, its gross savings decreased ¥53.8 billion in 1979 to ¥47.4 billion in 1989, due to the declining share of state budgetary revenues in the GNP (this share dropped from 31.2 per cent in 1978 to 16.2 per cent in 1989; see Table 2.7 in

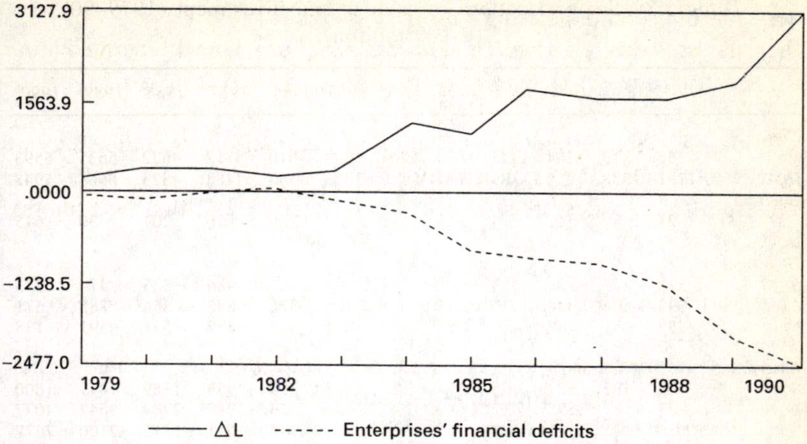

Figure 3.1 Increment in bank loans and enterprises' financial deficits (1979–90)

Chapter 2). On the other hand, the government's investment still increased (though not rapidly) – from ¥592 billion in 1979 to about ¥865 billion in 1989, which resulted in an increase in its financial deficit. Concerning the enterprise sector, under the decentralisation reform, investment of the enterprise sector expanded much more rapidly than that directly undertaken by the state. It increased tremendously from ¥47.7 billion in 1979 to ¥407.7 billion in 1990. As a proportion of the GNP, it increased from 10.9 per cent to 19.6 per cent.[5] *Although the gross savings of the enterprise sector also increased, it increased much less than investment. In consequence, the financial deficits of the enterprise sector mounted.* In relation to bank loans, the dominant counterpart of monetary expansion, it is not difficult to see from Tables 3.2 and 3.3 that these mounting financial deficits during reform were effectively financed by bank loans. This can be seen more clearly in Figure 3.1 which shows that increments in bank loans and enterprises' financial deficits (or their net savings) moved largely in a symmetrical way.

As already noted, the expansion of bank loans was in parallel with the expansion of bank deposits, of which the most important component during reform was households' deposits. The households' deposits expanded because;

(i) distribution of the national income changed in favour of households;

(ii) the households' saving ratio rose fast;
(iii) the banks were virtually the only channel of financial intermediation at the time.

Looking at the ultimate distribution of national income, the share of households increased significantly after 1978 – from 64.4 in 1979 to 77.5 in 1988. As described in Chapter 2, section 2.1, this was mainly because of:

(i) agricultural reform resulting in a increase in rural households' income;
(ii) the income policy in favour of staffs and workers through bonus schemes while maintaining the relative level of net transfers from government and enterprises to households in forms of various subsidies such as housing, health care, price, etc. (around 15 per cent of national income)[6]
(iii) the rapid expansion of non-state sector, especially private sector, in non-agrarian activities.

At the same time as the distribution of national income became in favour of households, the saving ratio of households rose sharply from 2.7 per cent in 1978 to 21.6 in 1990 (see Chapter 4, Figure 4.7, and the related discussions about household saving behaviour). Compared with the government[7] and enterprise sectors, the household sector had become the dominant saver. It provided only 23.6 per cent of total savings in 1979 but over 60 per cent in the late 1980s (see Table 3.3). This ratio is significantly higher than that of some other Asian economies. For instance, it was at around 40 per cent in Thailand (between 1977– 81)[8] and Taiwan (1965–88).[9] It did not exceed 40 per cent in South Korea (1965–1982).[10] Since households' investment grew more slowly than their savings, households' net savings expanded. As a proportion of the GNP, they rose from less than 2 per cent to nearly 16 per cent between 1979 and 1990. As a result, savings flowed out from the household sector into the other two sectors and, in particular, to the enterprise sector.

The changes in households' savings were related to the phases of reform. In the late 1970s and early 1980s, when the reform was concentrated on the agricultural sector, the income of rural households increased relatively faster than that of urban ones. As a result, the rural households' share in total savings increased. After 1984, the reform focused on the urban economy. The urban households' share in

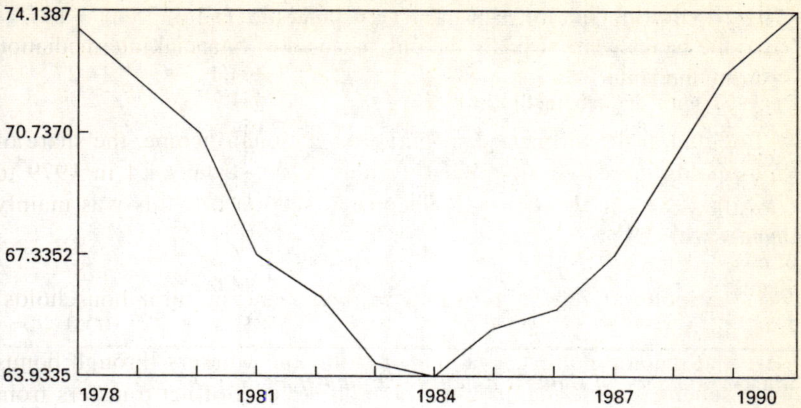

Figure 3.2 Urban households' deposits as a share of total household deposits (1978–90)

Table 3.4 Deposit rate (% p/a) and households' interest revenue (¥ bn)

	1978	*1979*	*1980*	*1981*	*1982*	*1983*	*1984*
Deposit rate	3.24	3.78	5.04	5.40	5.67	5.76	5.76
Interest payment	0.64	0.93	1.71	2.49	3.40	4.52	6.07
Interest received as % of total income	0.35	0.43	0.66	0.89	1.09	1.28	1.38

	1985	*1986*	*1987*	*1988*	*1989*	*1990*
Deposit rate	6.72	7.20	7.20	7.68	11.34	10.02
Interest payment	9.53	13.90	19.15	26.51	51.14	61.70
Interest received as % of total income	1.75	2.15	2.44	2.66	4.51	4.96

Note: Average deposit rate is estimated as equal to the rate for one year term deposits.

Source: *Almanac of China's Finance and Banking* (1989: 152–3; 1990: 171; 1991: 84); Table A5.1.

total savings increased relatively faster than that of the rural ones. So the urban-rural pattern of savings displayed a 'V' shape (see Figure 3.2).

It is worth noting that the policy of increasing interest rate contributed considerably to both the decrease in enterprises' profitability and the expansion of households' income and savings during reform. With respect to the latter, because of both the increasing deposit rate and

Table 3.5 Structure of financial assets (domestic, end of 1990; ¥ bn)

Cash in circulation	264.4	14.2
Deposits with deposit institutions	1351.9	72.7
the state banks	1164.5	62.6
the RCCs	138.4	7.4
UCCs	31.0	1.7
Post Office	18.0	1.0
Deposit with TICs	67.4	3.6
Bonds	170.8	9.2
Shares	4.6	0.2
Total	1859.1	100.0

Source: *Almanac of China's Finance and Banking* (1991: 41, 53–4, 58, 183).

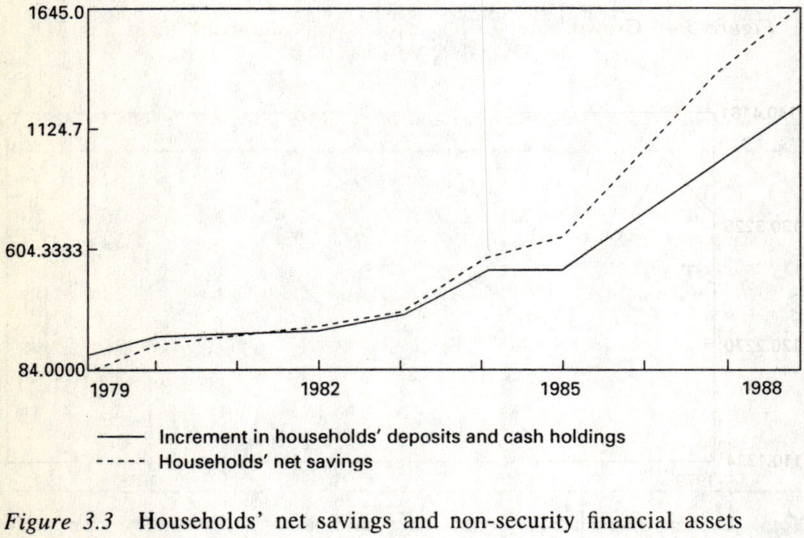

Figure 3.3 Households' net savings and non-security financial assets

the deposits themselves, income from savings increased very considerably. Since Chinese households save for long-term purposes, interest income received was simply added back to their deposits and not spent (to be discussed in Chapter 4). An increase in the deposit rate increases both household income and saving and, therefore, raises the accumulation of household financial assets. Table 3.4 estimates that the interest payments to households expanded from merely ¥0.6 billion in 1978 to nearly ¥62 billion in 1990. As a percentage of household income, it shot up from 0.35 to 4.96.

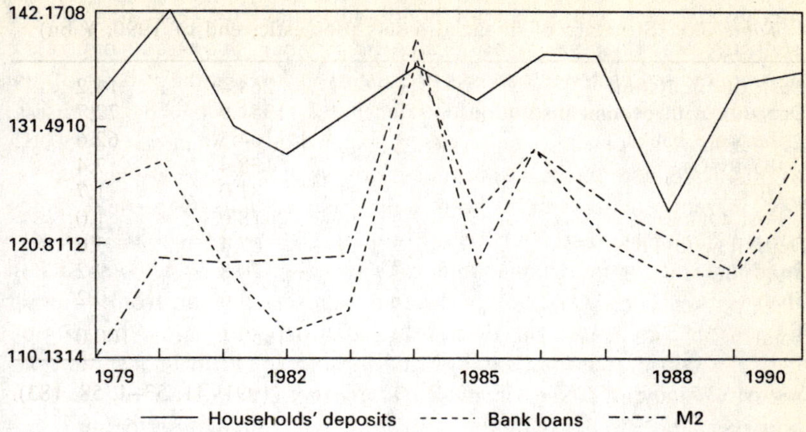

Figure 3.4 Growth rates of households' deposits, bank loans and M2 (Previous year = 100.0)

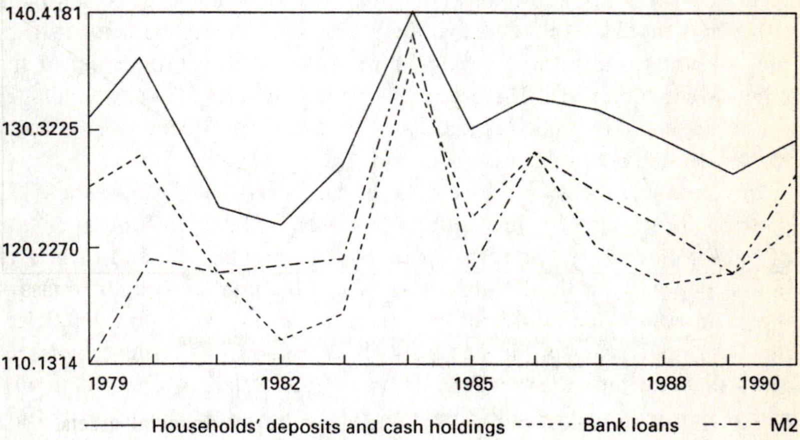

Figure 3.5 Growth rates of households' deposits and cash holdings, bank loans and M2 (Previous year = 100.0)

The parallel expansion of the supply of, and the demand for savings naturally raised the need for financial intermediation. However, while banks as financial intermediaries were encouraged, as a matter of policy, other channels of financial intermediation were restricted: virtually no shares and debentures were allowed to be issued and the issue of government bonds was limited. By the end of 1990, all shares accounted for merely 0.2 per cent,[11] and all bonds accounted for less than 10 per cent, of total financial assets (Table 3.5). Since shares and bonds are not money, but cash and deposits are, the over-domination of banks in the process of financial intermediation contributed to the monetary expansion. From this point of view, the monetary expansion in China can be related, to a considerable extent, to the underdevelopment of capital markets.

Apparently, most of the households' net savings were held in the form of bank deposits and cash. Figure 3.3 plots households' net savings and incremental household cash holdings plus bank deposits in the period 1979–88. Although the two data series come from different sources and are based on different calculations,[12] the close correlation between households' net savings and the increment in household non-security financial assets is clear. The gap between the two curves, however, increased gradually, reflecting both data imperfections and an increase in households' purchases of other financial instruments.

Given the changed patterns in sectoral balances of savings and investment, and the banks as the dominant channels of financial intermediation, it is not at all surprising that the households' deposits, bank loans and money expanded together. This can clearly be seen in Figure 3.4 where these three variables are depicted as a proportion of the GDP. Since a part of the households' savings was kept in cash, changes in the households' deposits and cash holdings were even more closely related to changes in bank loans and M2 (see Figure 3.5).

In summary, the above investigation suggests that the monetary expansion during reform in China was closely related to the expansion of bank loans to the enterprise sector on the assets side, and of households' deposits on the liability side of the bank's balance sheet. With the main component and counterpart of monetary expansion identified, the important issue is the causality. It is argued in the next two sections that the monetary expansion was largely driven by bank loans, and in particular, by banks' finance for fixed assets investment. Furthermore, such an expansion was supported by the central bank.

3.3 CAUSALITY

3.3.1 The loan-driven monetary expansion

With respect to the causality issue, the monetary base approach assumes the money supply process running from the high-powered money (*H*)

Table 3.6 Fluctuation of *D/R*, *D/C* ratios and money multiplier (1985m6–90m12)

	Max.	*Min.*	*Mean*	*SD*
D/R	7.20	4.03	5.35	0.85
D/C	5.43	3.16	4.69	0.54
Money multiplier	3.55	2.71	3.10	0.24

Note: SD is standard deviation.

Source: Monthly data from the PBC.

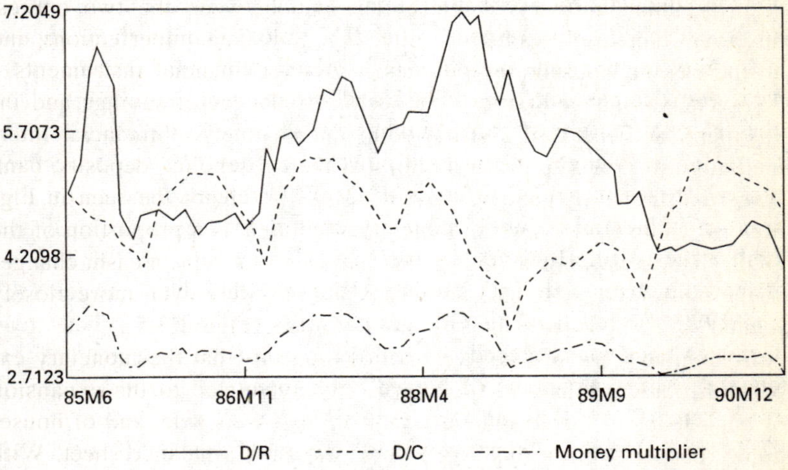

Figure 3.6 Deposit/reserve ratio, deposit/cash ratio, and money multiplier (1985m6–90m12).

to broad money through the money multiplier. Given that both *D/C* and *D/R* ratios are stable, the money supply is a function of *H*. The attention is thus focused on the central bank's control over *H* (discussed in section 3.1). However, as we have already discussed, this depends on whether the *D/C* and *D/R* ratios are stable, and whether *H* is exogenous or controllable by the monetary authorities.

Statistically, the *D/R* ratio (reserves are the sum of the reserve requirement and banks' deposits with the PBC) and the *D/C* ratio were unstable, reflecting changes in both macroeconomic control and the reactions of banks and households. During the period 1985m6–90m12,[13]

D/R moved between 4.03 and 7.20 and *D/C* within 3.16 and 5.43. On the surface, the money multiplier appears less volatile than these two ratios, moving between 2.71 and 3.55. This was due to the fact that changes in *D/R* and *D/C* ratios partly cancelled out – the correlation between the two was −0.26 (see Table 3.6). These ratios are plotted in Figure 3.6.

Under the Chinese banking system where the credit ceiling control was still in presence, banks cannot simply extend loans as they wish, even if they have available funds. Given the quantitative control, the deposit/reserve ratio and deposit/cash ratio (and hence the money multiplier) would depend not only on the banks' behaviour in mobilisation of savings and in lending, but also, largely, on the government's quantitative control over bank credit. A decrease in reserves may reflect the loosening control over bank lending, i.e. allowing bank credit ceilings to be exceeded. With respect to the *D/C* ratio, although there appears a roughly regular time pattern (i.e. it increases in the first half of the year and decreases in the second half of the year, reflecting largely the seasonal feature of corps purchasing), it is nevertheless unstable.

As far as changes in the high-powered money (*H*) are concerned, since changes in banks' reserves in the PBC reflected the credit control, an influential view on monetary control focuses on control over cash issue (M0). However, as we shall see, changes in M0 also reflected the changes in bank lending. Using monthly data between 1985 and 1990, the result of the Granger causality test suggests that movements in bank loans precede cash issue and not the opposite.[14] In explaining M0, coefficients of lagged bank loans (1–3 months) are far from zero (0.5, −0.8 and 0.4 respectively) with significant *T*-ratios (7.7, −8.4 and 4.5 respectively). By contrast, lagged M0 series are powerless in explaining bank loans (the coefficients are −0.1, −0.0 and −0.2 with T-ratios of −0.6, −0.0 and −1.1 respectively, see Table 3.7).

Institutional features of China's banking system will be discussed more fully in Chapter 5 in the light of China's economic system design. What is clear at this stage is that neither money multiplier nor high-powered money explain the process of monetary expansion in the Chinese context. In investigating causality in money supply process, therefore, attention needs to be shifted away from the narrow money (which is the focus of the MB approach) to loans. The very close relationship between M2 and *L* is reflected in their stable correlation (the ratio is 0.999). This can be seen in Figure 3.7 which plots monthly M0, M1 and M2 (vertical axis) against L (horizontal axis). The figure also shows that the correlation between M1 and *L* is fairly stable, but that between M0 and *L* is less so. This is the case because of the time

Table 3.7 Granger causality test of bank loans and cash outside banks

	Explanatory variables						
	Constant	L_{t-1}	L_{t-2}	L_{t-3}	MO_{t-1}	MO_{t-2}	MO_{t-3}
Explained variable							
L_t: Coefficient	−82.0	+1.1	−0.3	+0.2	−0.1	−0.0	−0.2
T-ratio		(8.4)	(−1.2)	(1.4)	(−0.6)	(0.0)	(1.1)
$M0_t$: Coefficient	−33.5	+0.5	−0.8	+0.4	+1.3	−0.4	−0.1
T-ratio		(7.7)	(−8.4)	(4.5)	(11.7)	(−2.7)	(1.1)

Note: Subscript *t* stands for time (end of each calendar month).

Source: The PBC. The time period is 1985m4–1990m12.

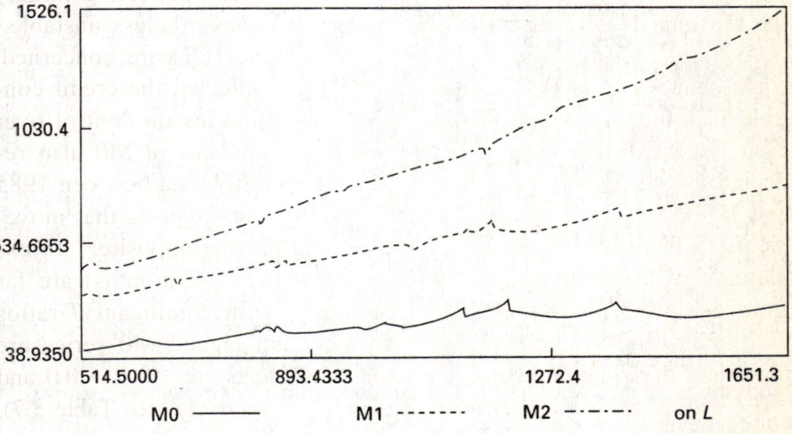

Figure 3.7 Money and bank loans (stock, 1985m1–1990m12)

gap between extension of loans and issue of M0. Correlation between ΔL and $\Delta M0$ suggests that ΔL leads $\Delta M0$ by about one month (Table 3.8), which confirms the result of the Granger causality test of L and M0 (see Table 3.7).

3.3.2 Deposit multiplier vs the PBC's direct control

This section further examines the process of bank credit expansion, with a focus on the relationship between the PBC, the central bank,

Table 3.8 Correlation between ΔL and $\Delta M0$ (1985m1–1990m12)

	ΔL_t	ΔL_{t-1}	ΔL_{t-2}
$\Delta M0_t$	0.28	0.70	−0.08
$\Delta M1_t$	0.66	0.57	−0.12
$\Delta M2_t$	0.72	0.54	0.09

Note: Subscript $t-1$ indicates previous month.

Source: The PBC.

and the SBs. It argues that the SBs would not have been able to expand loans excessively without the PBC lending to them and allowing credit ceilings to be exceeded.

In explaining bank credit expansion, one quite popular view attributes the credit expansion to the policy of 'more deposits, more lending' introduced during the reform period (Balassa, 1982; Byrd 1983; Huang, 1988). It argues that given that the banks were still not subject to financial discipline and liquidity constraints, this policy generated excessive credit expansion through the 'deposit-lending multiplier process'.

Indeed, in the second half of 1979, a policy named 'unified plan, multilevel management, link loans with deposits and controlling the difference' (known as 'more deposits, more lending') was introduced on a trial basis to the province-level bank branches in Shanghai, Fujian, Jiangsu, Hubei, Tianjing and Shaangxi. The essence of this policy was to encourage banks to mobilise more savings by allowing them to extend more loans, subject to the planned difference between deposits collected and loans extended. In 1980, the same policy was extended to all provinces and the centrally administrated municipalities. In order to make the constraints (i.e. the differences between deposits and loans set *ex ante*; the 'differences' can be seen as 'reserves') more credible, 'controlling the differences' was modified to 'contracting the differences' in 1981 (Yang Z. *et al.*, 1985. 56–7). After the establishment of the Central Bank in 1983, this policy remained in place, at least as regards working capital loans, until the last quarter of 1988. Given that the banks extended loans subject only to targets for the differences between deposits and loans in the balance sheet, bank credit could be expanded through the deposit multiplier, if deposits could be attracted.

This hypothesis seems plausible. However, closer examination sug-

Table 3.9 Planned and actual increments of bank loans and deposits (1979–89; ¥ bn)

	1979	*1980*	*1981*	*1982*	*1983*	*1984*	*1985*
(1) D^a-D^p	10.3	24.2	22.9	11.9	13.7	47.7	14.1
(2) L^a-L^p	1.5	19.6	15.5	2.0	5.5	75.3	42.6
(3) L^p-D^p	7.4	9.9	5.0	7.6	7.2	10.5	17.3
(4) L^a-D^a	−1.5	5.3	−2.4	−2.2	−0.9	38.1	45.9

	1986	*1987*	*1988*	*1989*	*1979-83*	*1984-89*
(1) D^a-D^p	44.0	31.2	−34.6	53.8	82.9	108.5
(2) L^a-L^p	73.5	21.7	−4.1	25.8	44.1	234.8
(3) L^p-D^p	30.0	37.5	30.5	55.0	37.0	180.8
(4) L^a-D^a	9.5	28.0	61.0	27.0	−1.8	259.4

Note: *D* stands for increment of deposits. *L* stands for increment of loans excluding that to the state budget; superscript *p* indicates planned and *a* indicates actual. Positive/negative sign indicates over-fulfilment/under-fulfilment of the plan.

Source: The PBC, and *Almanac of China's Finance and Banking* (1990: 52–3).

gests that this process does not explain the credit expansion. There are two reasons. First, nearly one-third of the SBs' sources of funds came from the PBC in the form of the latter's lending. The SBs would not have been able to expand loans excessively without the PBC lending to them. Second, quantitative controls over credit (credit ceilings) remained in place over the period, and continue up to the present. The deposit multiplier process could not be the cause of excessive credit expansion if credit itself is subject to credit ceilings. These two reasons are discussed in more detail below.

To test the extent to which bank credit was expanded through the deposit multiplier, the *ex ante* and *ex post* 'differences' are compared. Table 3.9 examines the planned and actual increments of bank loans and deposits during 1979–89. The hypothesis is that, if the deposit multiplier constitutes the main channel of credit expansion, then banks would extend more credit by using up the allowed 'differences'. In other words, 'more deposits' have to be used up as 'more lending' and this would not cause bank lending plans to be exceeded by more than deposit plans. If bank lending was not sensitive to the planned 'differences', either leaving a large part of 'more deposits' idle or significantly enlarging the 'differences', the credit expansion must be related to other factors.

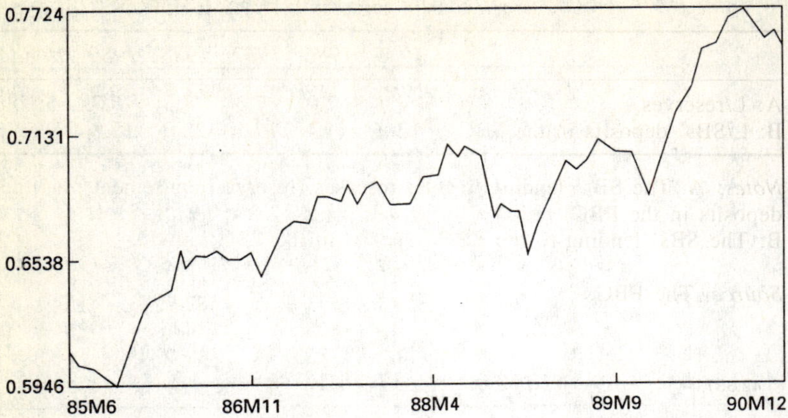

Figure 3.8 The SBs' deposit/lending ratio (1985m6–90m12)

The first row in Table 3.9 shows the difference between planned and actual increments of deposits, whilst the second row shows the difference between the planned and actual increments of loans. Except for 1988, both deposit plans and loan plans were exceeded in the period 1979–89. Comparing the first with the second row, however, there is a noticeable difference. Without exception, during 1979–83 (i.e. before the PBC was transformed into the central bank), 'more deposits' were only partly used as 'more lending'. On average, only 53 per cent of the unplanned increments of deposits were lent out.

In terms of 'difference' control, the results were even more striking: the planned or allowed sum of the differences between the increments of loans and of deposits in the period 1979–83 was ¥37.0 billion, yet the actual one was minus ¥1.8 billion (Table 3.9, rows 3 and 4). Local bank branches apparently failed to take the opportunity of expanding credit to the extent allowed. In contrast to the period 1979–83, for four of the six years between 1984 and 1989 bank lending plans were exceeded more than deposit plans. During the whole sub-period, the unplanned lending was twice that (216 per cent) of the unplanned total deposits. The 'differences' quotas were not only fully used up, but were also exceeded by an average of 43.5 per cent; ¥180.8 and ¥259.4 billion respectively. As a result, the bank credit ceilings (plan quotas) were exceeded by ¥234.8 billion during 1984–9, compared with ¥44.1 billion during 1979–83. Bearing in mind that around 30 per cent of the SBs' lending was financed by the PBC through its lending to the SBs, the deposit multiplier as an explanation of credit expansion seems

Table 3.10 The SBs' lending/reserve ratio (1985–90; %)

	1985	*1986*	*1987*	*1988*	*1989*	*1990*
A: L/reserves	6.7	7.0	7.5	8.3	6.7	5.1
B: L/SBs' deposits in the PBC	12.8	14.4	17.1	22.0	15.3	9.5

Notes: A: The SBs' lending to total reserves (reserve requirement plus their deposits in the PBC) ratio.
B: The SBs' lending to the SBs' deposits in the PBC ratio.

Source: The PBC.

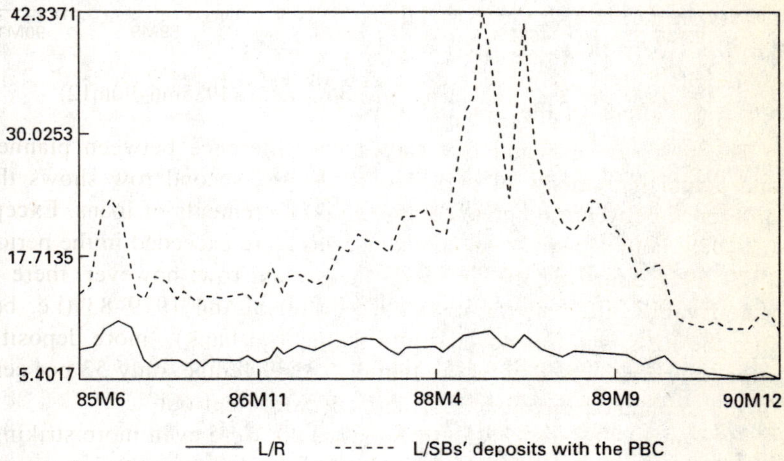

Figure 3.9 Bank lending and reserves (1985m6–90m12)

to have little basis. In fact, the SBs' deposit/lending ratio increased quite considerably over time.[15] In mid-1985, it was around 60 per cent, whereas in late 1990 it rose to around 75 per cent (Figure 3.8). This implies 'more deposits, same lending' rather than 'more deposits,. more lending'.

The simple test above suggests that the claim that the bank credit expansion during the period 1979–83 was due to the deposit multiplier is, at best, of secondary importance. The more important determinants were the credit ceilings when they were still relatively effective. The government allowed the ceilings to be exceeded only to a certain extent. Otherwise, it is difficult to explain why banks did not extend more credit by using up the allowed 'differences'.[16] Similarly, the excessive expansion of bank credit over 1984–9 is better understood as resulting from the failure to maintain the credit ceilings rather than the effect of the deposit multiplier. In fact, the SBs' lending to reserves, in particular, the SBs' deposits with the PBC,[17] ratio, was unstable. These two ratios reached the highest level in 1988 when the actual growth rate of the SBs' lending was the lowest in the period 1985–90 (see Table 3.10). The monthly changes in the SBs' lending to their deposits in the PBC ratio was very volatile (see Figure 3.9). These confirm the view that the SBs' credit expansion depends on the PBC's quantitative control as well as the SBs' lending to them.

The PBC controls the SBs' lending through both the credit ceilings and its direct loans to the SBs. The latter is a very important source of the SBs' loanable funds. For instance, it accounted for 26.5 per cent of the SBs' total liabilities at the end of 1990 (see Table 3.1). The sources of funds of the SBs include:

(i) the disposable deposits, i.e. the sum of enterprise deposits, household deposits and other deposits minus reserves and the SBs' deposits with the PBC;
(ii) the PBC's loans (to the SBs);
(iii) non-deposit liabilities (e.g. capital and net issue of bonds).

In numerical terms, the last source was insignificant. This can be seen in Figure 3.10. On average, the disposable deposits of the SBs provided 56 per cent – or 62 per cent if the SBs' deposits with the PBC is taken into account as part of the disposable deposits – of the loans extended by the SBs, while the PBC provided 30 per cent during 1985–90 (Figure 3.10).

It is interesting that to 'reconcile' the conflict between maintaining credit ceilings and financing the SBs' credit expansion, the PBC's loans to the SBs increasingly took the form of 'temporary loans'. These were defined as loans with a duration of less than 10 days in 1984 (the PBC *et al.*, 1984: 21). In 1987, the temporary loans were redefined. They include:

(i) seasonal loans with a maximum duration of 4 months;
(ii) daily loans with a maximum duration of 20 days (the Fund Management Department of the PBC, 1987: 8).

The 'temporary loans' are not strictly subject to the credit quotas

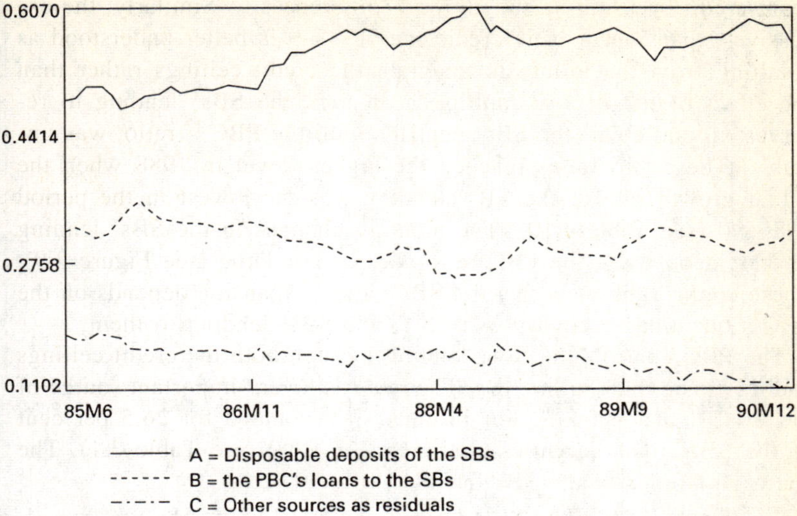

Figure 3.10 Sources of the SBs' lending (per cent of total lending) (1985m6–1990m12)

because they are designed to meet the 'necessary but unpredictable' need in a very short-term. In practice, the temporary loans were *de facto* used as long-term funds. In fact, the PBC directly transmitted them into long-term loans from time to time.

Figure 3.11 illustrates the expansion of the PBC's loans to the SBs and of the SBs' lending. The close relation between the two curves may be interpreted as follows: the credit expansion of the SBs, which was supported by the PBC's lending in the final quarter of the year, continued on afterwards into the following year. In other words, the PBC's loans to the SBs acted as a 'ratchet' in the process of the bank credit expansion.

3.4 KEY FACTORS IN THE SBS' CREDIT EXPANSION

If the deposit multiplier was not the chief mechanism generating bank credit expansion, then what was it? And why did the PBC support (to a degree) the SBs' lending? These questions require further investigation into the assets side of the banks' balance sheet.

Since bank working capital loans accounted for three-quarters of the

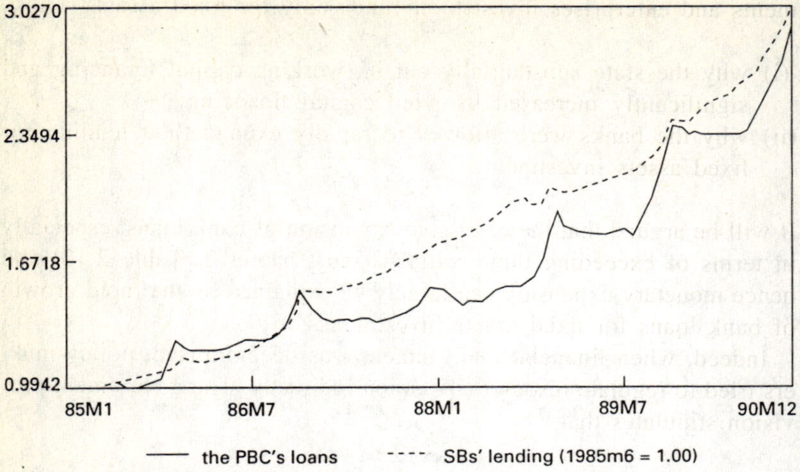

Figure 3.11 The PBC's loans to the SBs and the SBs' lending (1985m6–90m12)

total outstanding bank loans (see Table 3.1), one of the widely accepted views among analysts is that monetary expansion was due to expansion of bank working capital loans. Recently, Wang, Y. (1990, 1991) advanced a model attributing monetary expansion to the expansion of bank loans for working capital investment (in his term, 'circulating funds loans'). He states that, as a consequence of the decentralisation reform, an increasing proportion of funds was put under the control of enterprises. In order to gain additional funds from the banks, enterprises invested their funds in fixed assets only and thus left the burden of working capital financing to the banks. Given this behaviour, the government was forced to provide more funds to satisfy the demand for working capital. Such behaviour was rational – according to Wang – because failure to provide working capital would result in a wastage of newly available production capacity, and hence a loss in total output. This was unacceptable, as the leadership was committed to a quantity drive. Wang's hypothesis appears sensible. The problem is that it cannot stand careful empirical scrutiny. In fact, only a small proportion of the expansion of working capital loans can be explained by this hypothesis. More importantly, the 'working capital loan-led monetary expansion' story overlooks the significance of the bank's finance for fixed assets investment in the process of monetary expansion. This story cannot explain – given that local governments and enterprises invest their funds only for fixed assets –

(i) why the state substantially cut its working capital financing and significantly increased its fixed capital financing;
(ii) why the banks were allowed to rapidly expand their lending for fixed assets investment.

It will be argued that the excessive expansion of bank loans, especially in terms of exceeding their ceilings (see Chapter 2, Table 2.12) and hence monetary expansion can largely be explained by the rapid growth of bank loans for fixed assets investment.

Indeed, when financial management was decentralised, policy-makers tried to regulate resource allocation indirectly. The government provision stipulates that:

(i) the SOEs must use 60 per cent of their retained profits as 'production development funds', after paying the 'energy and transportation funds' collected by the MOF;
(ii) 10 per cent of the production funds should be used as working capital;[18]
(iii) 30 per cent of the quota working capital required by the 'self-financed' fixed investment[19] must be provided by the investors themselves.[20]

In practice, these regulations were not closely adhered to. However, just a small proportion of bank credit can be explained this way. Our investigations suggest that only about 5.3 per cent of the increments in bank loans can be directly attributed to this sort of 'misbehaviour' during the period 1983–8 (for details of estimation, see Appendix 2).

We have seen that fixed assets investment loans were the most rapidly growing component of bank lending. Expansion of bank loans for fixed assets investment was rapid during the reforms. Before 1978, the banks were involved in fixed assets investment on a negligible scale;[21] they were, in general, not allowed to extend loans for fixed investment. There were also no loans to the state budget. This practice was changed in 1979. Instead, banks were allowed to lend for fixed investment. The assignment of increasing quotas in the annual credit plans reflects this policy choice (Table 3.11). On average, the planned increments of bank loans for fixed assets investment (those listed in the state credit plan only) during 1979–89 accounted for 23 per cent of total planned increment of bank loans.

Table 3.11 Quotas for bank loans for fixed assets investment (1979–89; ¥ bn)

	1979	*1980*	*1981*	*1982*	*1983*	*1984*	*1985*	*1986*	*1987*	*1988*	*1989*	*1990*
Quotas	0.0	3.0	4.0	5.8	9.0	10.7	22.6	26.5	31.5	39.0	24.3	n.a.
Actual	0.8	4.8	7.7	10.5	6.9	14.5	25.3	30.1	28.1	27.2	21.7	47.0

Note: The listed loans for fixed assets investment only.

Source: The PBC; *Almanac of China's Finance and Banking* (1990: 52–3; 1991: 43).

In the figure, although fixed assets investment loans appear to account for only 15 per cent of the total increment in bank lending (Table 3.2), there are a number of reasons, however, to think that this understates its true importance very significantly. First, the classification of bank loans has problems. They are classified into the 'working capital loans', the 'agricultural loans', 'fixed assets investment loans', and 'other loans' (i.e. unclassified). The 'agricultural loans' include loans to the state-owned farms and loans to the township and village enterprises (47.3 and 52.7 per cent respectively by the end of 1989). 'Other loans' mainly consist of loans secured by hard currency, loans for purchasing foreign exchange, trust loans and other specially earmarked loans. These loans are used for both working capital and fixed assets investment, but the available data does not classify them separately. In fact, even working capital loans were used to finance fixed assets investment. The scale of the hidden fixed assets investment loans was quite large. For instance, the reported increment in the stock of loans for fixed assets investment was ¥21.7 billion in 1989 – but the actual figure was ¥34.3 billion, 58 per cent more.[22]

Second, a large amount of bank loans were used to finance fixed assets investment in the form of loans to the state budget (the outstanding volume was ¥90.8 billion at the end of 1990, or, it accounted for 6.1 per cent of the increments in total bank loans during 1979–90 (see Tables 3.1 and 3.2). Most of the overdraft and borrowing by the state budget from the banks was used for investment in fixed assets. Table 3.12 shows that the investment financed by the state budget was almost exclusively on fixed assets after 1978 (97.1 per cent during 1978–90). Obviously, there is little difference as to whether the banks finance fixed assets investment directly or via the state budget.

Third, the impact of bank loans for fixed assets investment on bank credit expansion is twofold: they contributed to credit expansion not only directly, but also indirectly. This can be demonstrated as follows.

Table 3.12 The state budgetary investment for fixed assets and working capital (1978–90; ¥ bn)

	1978	*1979*	*1980*	*1981*	*1982*	*1983*	*1984*
(1) Fixed assets[a]	51.5	58.7	50.0	39.6	37.8	46.2	60.1
(2) Working capital	6.7	5.2	3.7	2.3	2.4	1.3	1.0
(3) = (1)/[(1) + (2)](%)	88.5	91.8	93.2	94.6	94.1	97.3	98.4
	1985	*1986*	*1987*	*1988*	*1989*	*1990*	*1979–90*
(1) Fixed assets[a]	68.7	80.2	75.3	78.4	77.2	88.0	760.1
(2) Working capital	1.4	1.0	1.2	1.0	1.2	1.1	22.7
(3) = (1)/[(1) + (2)](%)	98.0	98.8	98.4	98.9	98.7	98.8	97.1

Note: [a] Sum of appropriation for capital construction and for technical updating and transformation.

Source: SSB (1991a: 215).

Total bank loans may be divided into working capital loans (*Lwk*) and fixed assets investment loans (*Lfk*).

$$L = Lwk + Lfk \qquad [3.4]$$

Since *Lfk* requires *Lwk* when the *Lfk*-financed project is completed and put into operation, we divided *Lwk* into two parts, i.e.:

$$Lwk = Lwk1 + Lwk2 \qquad [3.5]$$

where, *Lwk*1 is demanded by the fixed assets investment financed by non-bank loans and *Lwk*2 is demanded by the bank financed fixed assets investment. As a function of *Lfk*, *Lwk* can be expressed as:

$$Lwk2_t = f(Lfk_{t-i}) \qquad [3.6]$$

where, '*t*' stands for time and '*i*' indicates the investment period before working capital is required.

Reorganising (3.4–3.6) and taking time into account, it yields:

$$L_t = Lwk1_t + Lfk_t + f(Lfk_{t-i}) \qquad [3.7]$$

The impact of *Lfk* on credit expansion is via two channels: a direct channel through Lfk_t and an indirect channel through $f(Lfk_{t-i})$. As a direct effect, if bank loans to the state budget and one third of the 'agricultural loans' and 'other loans' are taken into account, *Lfk* would account for 20 per cent of the total outstanding bank loans (including that to the state budget) at the end of 1990 (see Table 3.2).

Indirectly, as argued earlier, bank fixed assets investment loans contribute to bank credit expansion because they require working capital loans to put the completed investment projects into operation – bearing in mind that most incremental working capital was financed by bank loans. Neglecting the time lag 'i' in equation [3.7], the average working capital requirement ratio during the period 1981–90 was 1.03.[23] Taking into account the fact that a part of the working capital loans was used for fixed assets investment, a conservative estimation would be that another 15–20 per cent of the increment of bank loans was related to the expansion of bank fixed assets investment loans.

Taking together bank loans for fixed assets investment and their related demand for working capital, they could explain around 35–40 per cent of the outstanding bank loans in 1990. Bearing in mind that the planned credit ceilings were on average exceeded by 40 per cent, the expansion of banks' lending for fixed assets investment was a key factor responsible for the excessive expansion of bank credit. In particular, banks' finance for fixed assets investment expanded despite the fact that the investment of local governments and enterprises was nearly exclusively in fixed capital formation during reform. Although the quantitative significance of bank fixed assets investment loans in explaining the overall expansion of bank credit is only a crude estimation, it seems certain that bank loans for fixed assets investment was a driving force behind the expansion of credit and hence money supply.

In fact, the policy objective of maintaining the planned variables (e.g. cash, credit and investment) under the ceilings was not compatible with the banks' heavy involvement in fixed assets investment. Interestingly, with respect to fixed investment loans and working capital loans, the policy-makers were aware that the bank credit plan quotas would have to be generally exceeded. The PBC even made known the imbalance in the credit plans. In official Chinese terms, the credit plan often had a 'gap' (*Jihua Quekou*). The 'gap' refers to the amount of bank loans (usually for working capital investment) recognised as necessary but is not included in the planned credit growth. Table 3.13 reports such gaps and their magnitudes.

The magnitude of the gaps was quite large, usually over 10 per cent of the credit plan. Taking the above four years as a whole, the gap was equivalent to 22 per cent of the planned increments of credit ceil-

Table 3.13 'Gaps' of bank credit planning[a]

	1986	*1988*	*1989*	*1990*
(1) The credit gap (¥ billion)	10.0[b]	20.0[c]	30.0[d]	70.0[d]
(2) (1) as % of the planned increment of the total credit	10.5	12.8	18.8	41.2

Note: [a] Excluding loans to the state budget. [b] Over ¥10.0 billion.

Source: Data of the planned credit increments are from the PBC. [b] The Fund Management Department of the PBC, 'Analysis of Receipts and Payments of Money in 1986', January 26, 1987. [c] Cao, F., 'Retrospect of Fund Management in 1987 and Tasks of Fund Management in 1988", January 1988. [d] 'An Opinion about Circulating Fund', the document issued at the PBC's Provincial Governors Meeting 1990.

ings. The gap was usually revealed in the annual meeting of the senior bank officials when the annual credit plan was interpreted. It was expected that additional funds would somehow be generated to finance the gap without breaking the credit ceilings. However, it was often not specified as to how this could be done. What appeared in the credit plan were vague phases, such as through 'reorganising industry', 'control of demand', 'promoting production' etc.[24] One exception was the requirement to speed up the 'turnover' of loans. For instance, it was prescribed that the turnover ratio of working capital should be 3 per cent higher in 1988 (equivalent to a reduction of ¥2 working capital per ¥100 sales of industrial products) and 4 per cent higher in 1989 and 1990 (the PBC). Yet, the actual performance was often the opposite of what was expected. This is not surprising because an increasing proportion of bank loans was used to finance long-term investment, especially fixed assets investment. Thus the credit ceilings were bound to be exceeded with the prevailing 'gaps'. Over time, the expectation that the bank credit plan would turn out to be impracticable rose, and the credibility of the plan (particularly the ceilings) was eroded. The specialised banks were increasingly induced to assume that the PBC would have to allow the credit ceilings to be broken one way or another.

It appears as a paradox that the PBC itself contributed to the failure in maintaining credit ceilings (and hence to monetary expansion). In fact, expansion of bank credit was supported not only by the PBC's lending to the SBs but also by fiscal and income policies. The fiscal policies concerned with here were 'paying the loan before taxation' and even 'paying the loans with taxes'. They allowed enterprises to use the before-tax profit (the enterprise income tax rate was 55 per cent for the SOEs) and even the product taxes (circulating taxes) to repay the fixed investment loans. This implied that the state budget actually paid part of the fixed investment loans for the borrowers. According to the related income policy, where the pre-tax profits were used to repay the fixed investment loans, computation of the 'welfare fund' and 'bonus fund' was permitted to be based not on the retained profit, but on the before-tax profit, so that the repayment of the fixed investment loans would not have a negative impact on these funds (He, Y., 1987).

In summary, given that channels of financial intermediation were limited, monetary expansion was driven by the excessive bank loans for fixed assets investment. Furthermore, the latter was supported by the PBC and the policy-makers. The central question is therefore: why did not or could not the bank fixed-assets investment loans be reduced? This question is taken up in the following two chapters. In a game perspective, Chapter 4 sees credit expansion as an outcome of an investment game between central and local governments. Chapter 5 further examines institutional factors behind the investment behaviour of local governments and policy constraints facing the central policy-makers.

4 Credit Expansion and Centre-Locality Game

Following on from the question raised at the end of Chapter 3, it seems a paradox that expansion of bank fixed-assets investment loans was accommodated by policy-makers in view of the leadership's repeated demands for controlling excessive investment in fixed assets. As shown in previous chapters, both the bank credit ceilings and investment targets were exceeded by large margins, and the banks' capital base was dangerously weakened (see Chapter 2, Tables 2.16–18 and the related discussions).

This chapter examines the mechanisms through which bank credit was expanded. Its focus is on the interactions between local and central governments investment behaviour and the related resource allocation problems which compelled monetary expansion in China. As will be argued in this chapter, loans for fixed-assets investment had to be expanded by the centre as a means of adjusting and rectifying the unbalanced investment pattern of local governments. In a game-theoretic framework, credit expansion by the centre and the investment pattern of local governments can be described as the joint outcomes in a game where central and local governments respond to each other's investment decisions.

This chapter presents two main hypotheses. The first is that (central) policy-makers, confronted with irrational investment patterns of local governments, were compelled to expand bank credit for fixed assets investment in priority areas neglected by local governments. In particular, bank loans had to be expanded to finance vital investments in technical updating and transformation of existing production capacity because these activities were neglected by local governments. Investment in these areas were regarded by the centre as critical to increasing efficiency in utilisation of resources. At the same time, existing bottlenecks in the energy, raw materials, transport and telecommunications sectors caused by an inherited primitive infrastructure and the failure to increase efficiency through industrial restructuring (especially of the manufacturing sector), were exacerbated as economic growth accelerated. Since decentralisation had sharply limited the growth in state budgetary revenues, the banking system had to shoulder an increasing burden of capital construction investment in infrastructure on top of the expanding loans for technical updating investment. The second hypothesis is that because other policies proved ineffective, expansion of bank credit became virtually the only workable instrument available to policy-makers for adjusting the sectoral allocation of investment resources at the time.

This chapter first examines the pattern of investment of local governments and the role of bank loans in adjusting the sectoral allocation of resources. It then constructs a model for analysing why expansion of bank credit for fixed-assets investment was necessary at the cost of allowing credit ceilings to be exceeded. Finally, it analyses why expansion of bank loans for fixed-assets investment was effectively the only workable solution for policy-makers.

4.1 INVESTMENT PATTERN OF LOCAL GOVERNMENTS

Local governments play a very important role in economic activities in China (discussed in more detail in Chapter 5). With respect to the value of fixed assets investment, the local governments controlled over half the total state sector investment. If investment of the collective sector is included, then their control was about two thirds.[1] During the reform period, local governments used their increased financial resources for local extensive development of manufacturing and other activities but neglected investment in technical updating and in infrastructure which in the short term reduced profitability and thus the amount of funds retained by locally controlled SOEs and local authorities.

The new development strategy adopted in the early 1980s gave priority to investment in:

(i) technical updating and transformation of existing enterprises *vis-à-vis* capital construction of new enterprises;
(ii) infrastructure, especially transportation and telecommunication;
(iii) more competitive firms *vis-à-vis* less competitive ones, regardless of their locations.

In practice, these priorities were not adhered to. For example, the Sixth Five-Year-Plan (1981–5) called for the share of state investment in technical updating and transformation sector in total fixed assets investment to be increased from 26 per cent in 1976–80 to 36 per cent in 1981–5. The actual proportion was only 28 per cent.[2] The increase

Table 4.1 Importance of technical updating investment in the state sector (1953–90)

	1953–57	*1958–62*	*1963–65*	*1966–70*
(1) Total fixed assets investment as 100.0	3.8	7.7	15.5	19.3
(2) Change over previous period (%)	–	202.6	201.3	24.5
	1971–75	*1976–80*	*1981–85*	*1986–90*
(1) Total fixed assets investment as 100.0	22.5	26.5	28.1	31.8
(2) Change over previous period (%)	16.6	17.8	6.0	13.2

Source: SSB (1991a: 147).

Table 4.2 Self-financed technical updating investment as percentage of total fixed-assets investment of the state sector (1981–90)

1981	*1982*	*1983*	*1984*	*1985*	*1986*	*1987*	*1988*	*1989*	*1990*
16.9	16.9	18.1	13.8	13.5	16.1	15.9	18.5	17.4	15.6

Source: SSB (1987b: 218; 1989d: 171; 1991a: 147, 175).

of this ratio actually slowed significantly during the reform period compared with the trend since the mid-1960s (see Table 4.1).

The neglect of the centrally determined investment priority was clearly apparent in the pattern of self-financed investment (i.e. locally determined investment financed separately from the state budget, domestic credit and foreign capital). Table 4.2 shows that, as a proportion of total fixed-assets investment, self-financed investment for technical updating not only failed to increase in the 1980s but actually decreased for a number of years.

The primary purpose of technical updating investment was to expand production and increase product variety rather than to economise on energy and raw material consumption for a given output or to improve product quality. In 1980, the policy of 'laying equal stress on increasing output and economising on usage of energy' was proposed. The Energy Conservation Plan for 1981–5 approved by the State Council stipulated that 10–15 per cent of technical updating funds must be invested on energy conservation. Yet even the allocation of technical updating funds within the state sector violated this stipulation. The

Table 4.3 Purposes of technical updating investment of the state sector (1980–90)

	1980	*1981*	*1982*	*1983*	*1984*	*1985*
Productive	88.1	82.3	78.7	78.4	81.6	84.8
(1) Raw material saving[c]	1.8	0.8	0.9	0.9	0.7	0.3
(2) Energy saving	3.4	4.0	4.8	4.5	5.6	3.9
(3) Quality improvement	4.9	3.7	4.6	5.2	5.7	5.9
(4) Environment protection	2.5	1.5	1.6	1.5	2.0	2.0
(5) Increasing product variety			6.3	6.1	7.7	13.7
(6) Production expansion	56.7[a]	47.3[a]	34.7	36.6	34.5	35.7
(7) Others (non-distinguishable)	18.9	24.6	25.8	23.6	25.4	23.3
(8) = (1) + (2) + (3)	10.1	8.5	10.3	10.6	12.0	10.1
Total (¥ billion)	13.7	19.5	25.0	29.1	30.9	44.9
In percentage	100.0	100.0	100.0	100.0	100.0	100.0
Non-productive	11.9	17.1	21.3	21.6	18.4	15.2
(Residential housing)	6.1	9.1	11.5	11.5	7.7	5.6

	1986	*1987*	*1988*	*1989*	*1990*
Productive	83.1	82.1	83.5	83.7	84.6
(1) Raw material saving[c]	0.3	0.3	0.3	0.3	0.3[b]
(2) Energy saving	3.7	3.4	3.1	3.2	3.3
(3) Quality improvement	6.3	5.6	4.9	5.0	6.3
(4) Environment protection	1.9	1.9	1.7	1.9	1.8
(5) Increasing product variety	15.8	14.3	14.3	15.1	15.7
(6) Production expansion	34.1	36.0	40.3	38.4	35.2
(7) Others (non-distinguishable)	20.9	20.5	18.9	19.8	21.8[b]
(8) = (1) + (2) + (3)	10.3	9.3	8.3	8.5	9.9
Total (¥ billion)	61.9	75.9	98.0	78.9	83.0
In percentage	100.0	100.0	100.0	100.0	100.0
Non-productive	16.9	17.9	16.5	16.3	15.4
(Residential housing)	7.0	8.6	9.0	8.0	7.1

Note: [a] Sum of 'increasing product variety' and 'production expansion'. [b] Including for raw material saving. [c] Raw material saving is estimated.

Source: SSB (1987b: 220; 1989a: 358; 1990a: 190; 1991a: 175).

actual ratio was only 4 per cent in 1981–3, 5.6 and 3.6 per cent in 1984 and 1985 respectively (China Social Survey Institute, 1990: 182). Table 4.3 reports the purposes of technical updating investment of the state sector during 1980–90. It can be seen that the proportion of total investment for raw material saving, energy saving and quality improve-

Table 4.4 Capital investment by the state sector in transportation and communication (1952–90; ¥ bn)

	1952–78	*1979*	*1980*	*1981*	*1982*	*1983*
(1) Total capital construction investment	621.6	52.4	55.9	44.3	55.6	59.4
(2) Capital construction investment in transportation & communication	105.5	6.4	6.2	4.1	5.7	7.8
(3) = (2)/(1) (%)	17.0	12.2	11.1	9.2	10.3	13.1

	1984	*1985*	*1986*	*1987*	*1988*	*1989*	*1990*
(1) Total capital construction investment	74.3	107.4	117.6	134.3	152.6	155.2	170.4
(2) Capital construction investment in transportation & communication	10.9	17.1	18.1	19.0	20.8	16.7	20.7
(3) = (2)/(1) (%)	14.6	15.9	15.4	14.1	13.7	10.7	12.2

Source: (1) and (2): SSB (1987b: 73–77; 1990a: 157; 166; 1991a: 150).

ment showed no increase over 1980–90 and even decreased after 1987 (see row 8). As rows 5 and 6 suggest, the dominant purpose of technical updating investment was the expansion of production and increase of product variety.

Because of under-investment in technical updating and transformation, the capital stock of existing enterprises (particularly in the traditional industrial regions) remained largely technically outdated. For instance, in 1985–6, about 70 per cent of industrial equipment in Shanghai dated from the 1950s–60s and 10 per cent from the 1930s–40s. In Tianjin, the majority of industrial equipment was on average 12.5 years old. In Liaoning province, only 1.6 per cent of equipment of enterprises under the Engineering Department was comparable to international quality standards, while 14.3 per cent was advanced and 36.6 per cent technically outdated by domestic standards (Wu, J. 1989a: 50).

Investment in transportation and communication also received little attention from local governments. Table 4.4 indicates that its share of total capital construction investment decreased considerably during the reform period. Initially, a large drop was witnessed during 1979–81. Although it recovered gradually in the period 1982–5, the recovery was reversed in the following years. As a whole, the share was 12.99

per cent in the period 1979–90, or 3.98 per centage points lower than in 1952–78 (16.98 per cent) and 3.33 per centage points lower than in 1971–8 (16.32 per cent).

Underinvestment exacerbated shortages in transport capacity. Railway length increased annually by 988 kilometres (km) during 1952–78, but by only 400 km during 1978–90 (350 km during 1980–90). Highway construction shows a similar contraction. The annual increases in highway length were 29 365 and 11 508 km during 1952–78 and 1978–90 respectively (SSB, 1991a: 494). In 1979, on average 90.7 per cent of the demand for rail freight could be met, but the per centage dropped to 88 per cent in 1980 and to 67.8 per cent in 1988. For some interregional rail freight, the per centage of demand which could be met was only between 10 and 37 per cent (China Social Survey Institute, 1990: 723) compared with about 70 per cent in the early 1980s (Liu, G. 1984: 203).

Instead of investment in technical updating or in transportation and communication, local governments preferred:

(i) to expand their own manufacturing capacity to increase the value added of traditional manufactured products if the localities were 'resource-rich';
(ii) to establish new manufacturing industries to produce new durable consumer goods as a substitute for imports both from other provinces and from abroad.

In consequence, duplication of small-scale investment was enormous and production utilisation ratio generally very low. Thus, extensive development continued. The evidence is shown below.

(a) As a result of massive manufacturing investment, the number of industrial enterprises increased dramatically in the 1980s. The total number of industrial enterprises (excluding village enterprises and the self-employed) increased from 348 400 in 1978 to 1 207 100 in 1985 and 1 223 700 in 1988. If village enterprises are included, this figure was 1 957 500 in 1988 (number of village enterprises was negligible in 1978).[3] Most of the new enterprises were established by local governments at and below the county level,[4] and the number of state-owned industrial enterprises increased by only 15 400 between 1978 and 1988.

(b) While pre-1978 trends in the equalisation of the regional shares of old manufacturing industry persisted during reform, the development of the new manufacturing industries (particularly those producing new durable consumer goods) was also geographically widespread.

Table 4.5 Regional equalisation of industrial output shares (1952–88)

Products	*Standard deviation of provincial shares*				
	1952	*1965*	*1978*	*1984*	*1988*
Steel	12.94	8.38	5.57	4.80	4.59
Steels	11.06	7.90	5.03	4.49	4.23
Metal cutting machine[a]	10.60	6.09	3.37	3.73	3.97
Sulphuric acid	13.13	5.78	3.44	3.13	2.97
Caustic soda	8.16	5.90	3.58	3.34	3.01
Plate glass	13.11	10.10	5.15	4.04	3.57
Car	18.57	15.67	7.57	6.75	5.07
Cloth	6.01	4.53	3.54	3.50	2.87
Bicycle	10.42	10.22	8.31	5.07	4.52
Cigarette	5.92	3.62	3.26	3.36	3.22
TV	n.a.	n.a.	10.46	4.79	4.87
Refrigerator	n.a.	n.a.	11.87[b]	6.69	4.47
Wash machine	n.a.	n.a.	14.50	4.25	4.57
Camera	n.a.	n.a.	11.05	7.37	4.99
Arithmetic mean	–	–	6.91	4.67	4.06

Note: Standard deviation of provincial share is the output share of 29 provinces and the equivalent administrative regions in mainland China. [a] The standard deviation of metal-cutting machine shows a fluctuation. It increased in 1984, decreased to 3.50 in 1985, then rose again to 4.14 in 1987 followed a fall in 1988. [b] 1979.

Source: SSB (1985: 150–81; 1988b: 227; 230; 1989c: 306–17).

The continuing extensive development led to continuing equalisation of regional output shares in manufacturing industries. Table 4.5 reports the standard deviation of selected manufacturing production in 29 regions at provincial level during 1952–88.[5] Almost all declined significantly between 1978 and 1988. As a result of the continuing regional equalisation of industrial output shares after 1978, leading subsectors of manufacturing industry in each locality became more and more identical. In 1987, almost all provinces had four dominant sectors: textile, machinery, food processing and chemical (China Social Survey Institute, 1990: 682).

More importantly, the same trends are seen within a province. A few examples are as follows. In Fujian province, the number of plastics producers increased from about 185 in 1978 to 764 in 1986, causing a severe shortage of raw materials. The number of canned-food manufacturers increased to 572 in 1986, while the rate of capacity utilisation decreased from 88 per cent in 1978 to 74 per cent (Fujian

Table 4.6 Examples of intra-sectoral industrial structure (1991)

	No. of producers	*Utilisation of production capacity*	*Note*
Colour TV	130–50 assembly lines	53%	There are 2 producers in the US, 7 producers in Japan and 4 in S. Korea.
Refrigerator	about 70	32%	The minimum economic scale is 0.2 million. There are only 2 with capacity above 0.2 million.
Washing machine	>80	about 30%	Produced 683 million sets in 1991.
Optical fibre and optical cable	>16	about 10%	
Electric cable (XLPE)	>20 production lines	about 30%	The total capacity is equivalent to over 3 times the market demand.
Aluminium processing	410	40%[b]	One third is newly established and very small.
Plastics processing	4030	58%[b]	One third capacity is excessive.
Car or truck	>120	n.a.	The average output per producer was only 3739 in 1986.
Bearing (1987)	139	n.a.	The average annual output was 59 000 sets compared with 500 000 sets per production line in an advanced economy.
Beer	>813	80%	There are 480 with production capacity of less than 10 000 tonnes per annum.
Cotton spinning	n.a.	about 70%[a]	Present capacity exceeds the demand in 1995 (estimated) by 30%.
Wool spinning	n.a.	60%	Raw materials depend on imports ($900 million in 1988).
Suit	543 production lines	55%[b]	An enormous stock is piling up.

Note: [a] The excessive capacity was 10.0 million spindles. [b] 1990.

Source: *Investment & Construction*, 1992: No.4, p.33; No.5, p.44; No.6, p.45. Wu, J. (1989a: 48). Deng Y. *et al.*, 1990: 170).

Statistical Bureau, 1989). There were 361 truck refit enterprises with a turnover of 15 000 a year in Jiangsu province in 1984–5. The aver-

Table 4.7 Reduction in regional deviation of processing industries (1978–89)

	A		*B*		*C*	
	1978	*1989*	*1978*	*1989*	*1978*	*1989*
Standard deviation of the relative strength of a province	2.86	2.15	5.08	4.29	2.26	1.63
Max. strength	12.16	6.11	13.94	8.27	4.73	4.73
Min. strength	−3.23	−3.37	−14.29	−13.96	−9.51	−5.39

Note: A: manufacturing industry based on agriculture. B: material industry over mining industry. C: processing industry over material industry. Covering 28 regions at province level – provinces, minority nationality autonomous regions and municipalities under the direct administration of the State Council. Output is calculated on value-added basis.

Source: SSB (1990d), various pages.

age production was only 42 a year. There were 45 sets of small thermal power generators installed in 1984–5 in Jiangsu. The total installed capacity was only 518.2 megawatts and the average installed capacity was 11.5 megawatts; the smallest was 1500 kilowatts. In Shanxi province, there emerged over 1000 small furnaces with an average capacity of 30 cubic metres (Zhang, S. *et al.*, 1987). More than 50 small beer producers came into existence in the 1980s in each of seven provinces (Zhejiang, Heilongjiang, Liaoning, Jilin, Hebei, Henan etc.).[6] Table 4.6 shows that for almost every product there were usually a large number of producers (most of them small ones), and the utilisation ratio of production capacity was very low.

(c) Using the data from 28 regions at provincial level, the growth rate of manufacturing output of a locality was closely correlated to its relative output of raw materials. Comparing the output share of a manufacturing industry based on agricultural inputs with the share of the agricultural output of a province, the weaker the relative strength of the former in 1978,[7] the faster the growth of the output of such a manufacturing sector during 1978–89. In other words, in 1978 the relative strength changed negatively in relation to its status (the correlation is −0.67). The same pattern is seen concerning the changes in the relative strength of the material industry over the mining industry and the processing industry over the material industry of a province during this period. (The correlations between the change in strength in the

Table 4.8 Sources of fixed-assets investment of the state sector (1978–90; % of flow)

	1978	*1979*	*1980*	*1981*	*1982*	*1983*	*1984*
State budget[a]	62.2	50.7	34.0	38.6	31.4	32.3	30.1
Domestic bank loans[b]	1.7	15.9	22.4	13.6	13.6	17.4	20.6
Foreign capital	4.2	2.3	7.2	5.4	7.1	6.9	5.9
Self-finance and others	31.9	31.1	36.5	42.4	45.3	43.3	43.4
Total	100.0	100.0	100.0	100.0	100.0	100.0	100.0
	1985	*1986*	*1987*	*1988*	*1989*	*1990*	*1979–90*
State budget[a]	23.0	17.4	14.2	12.5	9.1	9.2	19.2
Domestic bank loans[b]	24.0	27.5	30.9	26.4	25.2	27.6	24.6
Foreign capital	5.3	6.5	7.3	9.0	10.1	9.1	7.6
Self-finance and others	47.7	48.6	47.6	52.2	55.6	54.0	48.6
Total	100.0	100.0	100.0	100.0	100.0	100.0	100.0

Note: For 1978–80, fixed assets investment is the sum of capital construction and technical updating investment. [a] Excluding the increase in borrowing from the banks. [b] Including bank loans extended to the state budget. Sum of items might not equal 100 because of rounding.

Source: For 1978–80: SSB (1984a: 333; 1987b: 59). For 1981–85: SSB (1987b: 14). 1986–90: SSB (1991a: 148). Bank loans to the state budget: *Almanac of China's Finance and Banking* (1989: 62–3); SSB (1991a: 642).

period 1978–89 and its relative strength in 1978 are −0.56 and −0.76 respectively.) In consequence, the standard deviation of relative strength of these three sectors all became significantly smaller over this period (Table 4.7, columns A, B and C).

It is evident that decentralised control over resources generated greater incentives for local governments to promote local industries. But the strategic importance of investment in technical updating and transformation and in transportation and communication was not recognised. Furthermore, the huge number of newly established but for the most part, poorly equipped, local manufacturing enterprises intensified the demand for energy and raw materials which were already in short supply. One source estimates that, because of shortage of electricity, at least one quarter of production capacity could not be utilised (Wu, J. 1989a: 67). Another source gives a similar picture: during 1981–5, the production capacity utilisation ratio was about two-thirds because of lack of energy, electricity, raw materials etc. (Deng, Y. *et al.*, 1990: 248).

Table 4.9 Sources of technical updating investment of the state sector (1978–90)

	1978[a]	*1979*[a]	*1980*	*1981*	*1982*	*1983*	*1984*
Total amount (flow, ¥ bn)	16.8	17.6	18.7	19.5	25.0	29.1	30.9
Of which financed by (%):							
state budget funds	15.8	24.8	17.6	17.9	13.1	12.5	14.8
Domestic loans	6.7	11.3	24.5	20.5	25.6	25.6	29.7
Foreign capital	0.0	0.0	0.0	0.6	1.1	0.9	0.9
'Self-raised' funds	77.5	63.9	57.9	57.9	57.1	59.1	53.0
Others	0.0	0.0	0.0	3.1	3.1	1.9	1.6
Total	100.0	100.0	100.0	100.0	100.0	100.0	100.0
		1985	*1986*	*1987*	*1988*	*1989*	*1990*
Total amount (flow, ¥ bn)		44.9	61.9	75.9	98.1	78.9	83.0
Of which financed by (%):							
state budget funds		4.4	3.3	4.3	2.8	1.8	2.1
Domestic loans		41.6	40.2	40.4	38.6	29.6	32.5
Foreign capital		1.2	1.3	2.3	2.7	3.4	4.1
'Self-raised' funds		50.5	51.3	48.3	51.1	55.9	54.9
Others		2.3	3.8	4.8	4.9	9.4	6.5
Total		100.0	100.0	100.0	100.0	100.0	100.0

Note: 'Self-raised funds' are largely depreciation fund and part of the retained profit. Sum of percentage points might not equal 100 because of rounding.
[a] Estimation is based on SSB (1984a: 333).

Source: SSB (1984a: 333; 1987b: 216, 218; 1989d: 171; 1991a: 147, 175).

4.2 ALLOCATIVE IMPORTANCE OF BANK FIXED ASSETS INVESTMENT LOANS

This section argues that expansion of bank loans for fixed-assets investment was necessary because shortage of investment for technical updating and transformation would otherwise be even greater and sectoral imbalance of investment would be even more severe.

The expansion of bank credit made it a very important financial source for the investment in fixed assets. Almost a quarter of total fixed assets investment of the state sector was financed by bank loans during 1979–90: much more than that financed by state budget appropriations (19.2 per cent) (Table 4.8).[8]

Bank loans for fixed-assets investment in China are classified into two types: loans for technical updating and transformation, and loans

Table 4.10 The role of domestic bank loans in technical updating investment of the state sector (1980–90; ¥ bn)

	1980	*1981*	*1982*	*1983*	*1984*	*1985*
(1) Technical updating investment	13.7	19.5	25.0	29.1	30.9	44.9
(2) Of which financed by domestic bank loans	3.4	4.0	6.4	7.5	9.2	18.7
(3) = (1) − (2)	10.3	15.5	18.6	21.6	21.7	26.2
(4) (1) as % of total fixed investment	18.4	29.3	29.6	30.1	26.1	26.7
(5) (3) as % of total fixed investment excluding (2)	13.8	23.2	22.0	22.7	18.3	15.6
		1986	*1987*	*1988*	*1989*	*1990*
(1) Technical updating investment		61.9	75.9	98.0	78.9	83.0
(2) Of which financed by domestic bank loans		24.9	30.6	37.8	23.3	27.0
(3) = (1) − (2)		37.0	45.3	60.2	55.6	56.0
(4) (1) as % of total fixed investment		31.3	33.0	35.5	31.1	28.4
(5) (3) as % of total fixed investment excluding (2)		18.7	19.7	21.8	21.9	19.2

Source: SSB (1987b: 9, 218; 1991a: 148, 175).

for capital construction. The banks' involvement in fixed-assets investment financing began with technical updating loans in 1978 and this type of loan has expanded rapidly (Table 4.9).[9] Domestic loans provided only about 6.7 per cent of the technical updating investment of the state sector in 1978.[10] The proportion rose to 41.6 per cent in 1985 but dropped to 32.5 per cent in 1990.

Table 4.10 suggests that without the banks' increased lending, technical updating investment as a proportion of total fixed-assets investment of the state sector would have been about 7 per centage points lower in 1981–4 and about 11 per centage points lower in 1985–90.

The expansion of bank loans for technical updating investment led to a commensurate increase in the average scale of technical updating investment during the 1980s. In state industry, technical updating investment as a proportion of the original value of fixed assets was 4.8 per cent in 1980. This ratio rose to 8.1 per cent during 1981–4 and 11.5 per cent during 1985–8 (SSB, 1987b: 225; 1990a: 30; 189). However, despite the heavy involvement of bank lending in financing technical updating investment, the latter as a share of total fixed assets invest-

Table 4.11 Sources of capital construction investment of the state sector (1978–90)

	1978	*1979*	*1980*	*1981*	*1982*	*1983*	*1984*
Total amount (flow, ¥ bn)	50.1	52.3	55.9	44.3	55.6	59.4	74.3
Of which bank loans[a]	0.0	9.5	12.1	4.5	7.3	8.2	14.0
Total (%)	100.0	100.0	100.0	100.0	100.0	100.0	100.0
State budget[b]	77.7	58.7	39.4	50.3	41.9	45.0	40.2
Domestic loans	0.0	18.1	21.7	10.1	13.1	13.8	18.8
Foreign capital	5.6	3.1	9.6	7.8	10.3	10.6	9.0
Self-finance and others	16.7	20.1	29.3	31.8	34.7	30.5	32.0
Total sources	100.0	100.0	100.0	100.0	100.0	100.0	100.0

	1985	*1986*	*1987*	*1988*	*1989*	*1990*
Total amount (flow, ¥ bn)	107.4	117.6	134.3	157.4	155.2	170.4
Of which bank loans[a]	20.2	29.5	40.0	34.7	40.1	49.5
Total (%)	100.0	100.0	100.0	100.0	100.0	100.0
State budget[b]	34.2	27.4	21.8	20.3	13.9	14.4
Domestic loans	18.8	25.1	29.8	22.0	25.8	29.1
Foreign capital	6.8	9.3	10.4	13.9	14.3	13.1
Self-finance and others	40.2	38.2	38.0	43.8	46.0	43.3
Total sources	100.0	100.0	100.0	100.0	100.0	100.0

Note: In the years 1979 and 1980, the increase was mainly due to the bank loans to the state budget. Foreign capital includes both foreign loans and foreign direct investment. Sum of percentage points might not equal 100 because of rounding. [a] Assuming that bank loans to the state budget were all used for capital construction investment. [b] Excluding bank loans to the state budget. Sum of percentage points might not equal 100 because of rounding.

Source: SSB (1987b: 58–9; 1989d: 65; 1991a: 150). Loans to the state budget: *Almanac of China's Finance and Banking* (1989: 62–3); SSB (1991a: 642).

ment showed no increasing trend over 1981–90 (see Table 4.1). It was still too low, accounting for 32 per cent of total fixed investment in 1986–90 in China. For a comparison, the proportion in the USA was 55 per cent in 1947–50 and 77 per cent in 1971–8 (Liu, G. 1984: 115).

Let us turn to bank loans for capital construction investment. The banks began to finance capital construction investment in 1979 (Table 4.11). Bank loans for capital construction investment expanded even more rapidly than loans for technical updating. Although loans for capital construction investment as a proportion of total capital construction investment was generally lower than that for technical updating investment, its absolute amount exceeded the latter most of the time

Table 4.12 Financing capital construction investment in energy and transportation (the state sector) (1978–90; ¥ bn)

		1980	*1981*	*1982*	*1983*	*1984*
(1) Total investment in capital construction of energy and transportation		17.80	13.11	15.94	20.56	27.44
(2) The budgetary appropriation for energy & transportation investment		14.76	9.42	9.77	15.09	21.53
(3) = (1) − (2)		3.16	3.69	6.17	5.47	5.91
	1985	*1986*	*1987*	*1988*	*1989*	*1990*
(1) Total investment in capital construction of energy and transportation	37.63	44.79	52.98	62.37	61.29	76.54
(2) The budgetary appropriation for energy & transportation investment	23.30	26.63	22.71	23.30	n.a.	n.a.
(3) = (1) − (2)	14.27	18.06	30.27	39.07	n.a.	n.a.

Source: (1): General Planning Department of the MOF (1989: 159). (2): SSB (1990a: 166; 1991a: 150).

(compare figures in Tables 4.9 and 4.10). On average, more than half of bank loans for fixed-assets investment went into capital construction (53.7 per cent during 1978–84 and 56.9 per cent during 1985–90). The expansion of bank loans for capital construction merits particular attention, because this was not the initial intention of credit policy.[11]

Data on the scale of the banks' finance for the energy and transport sectors are not available. However, Table 4.12 shows an increasing gap between total actual capital construction investment and state budgetary investment appropriation for these sectors (line 3). Only about half the total investment for energy and transportation was financed by state budgetary appropriation. This suggests that bank finance for investment in energy and transportation sectors was very important.

This is confirmed by other sources of information. According to the PBC, banks were ordered to extend between ¥12 and ¥15 billion fixed investment loans for key energy and transportation projects every year in the late 1980s (Liu, Z. and Liu, R. 1989). The governor of the Bank of China, Mr Wang Deyan, claimed that the BOC extended fixed investment loans of over US$30 billion during 1979–88, of which over 70 per cent was for energy, transportation and other key infrastructure sectors (Wang, D. 1990). Bearing in mind that during 1978–90, ¥90.7 billion of the state budgetary expenditures was actually covered by borrowing and overdraft from banks (see Chapter 3, Table 3.1), it is reasonable to conclude that a major part of capital construction investment in energy and transportation was financed by bank lending.

Given the investment pattern of local governments and the weakened fiscal capability of the state, policy-makers understandably turned to banks for financing investment in priority sectors. In other words, the centre was compelled to increase bank loans for fixed assets investment to:

(i) maintain investment in technical updating and in transportation and communication at levels deemed essential;
(ii) increase investment in energy and materials sectors to adjust the overall investment pattern generally and to rectify the unbalanced investment patterns of local governments in particular.

4.3 CREDIT EXPANSION AS AN OUTCOME OF A CENTRE-LOCALITY GAME

Expansion of bank loans as a means of rectifying investment allocation patterns is a rare case in the Western literature. Traditionally, bank lending is studied in line with portfolio theory. The general assumption is that lending is a function of relative yields and some scale variables (e.g. Parkin, 1970; Courakis, 1974; White, 1975; Bewley, 1981; Spancer, 1986, among others). Outstanding bank loans are usually viewed as a result of a demand function, and there is a lack of explicit specifications of the supply of bank loans. For instance, Moore and Threadgold (1980, 1985) see bank lending to industrial and commercial companies as a function of the latter's demand for working capital. Dow and Saville (1988) argue that as conventional lending criteria are related to borrower's income, bank lending rises with growth of nominal income in rough proportion.

On the supply side, an important conceptual development since the mid-1970s has been to explore the consequences of imperfect and costly information on the functioning of financial markets. Because of asymmetric information (between borrowers and lenders) and adverse selection, credit market 'equilibrium' may be characterised by credit rationing (e.g. Jaffee and Russell, 1976; Stiglitz and Weiss, 1981). Recognition of these market shortcomings, however, does not necessarily lead to a better knowledge of credit supply in quantitative terms. Stiglitz (1989a) makes this point when he writes that 'there is no easy way to represent the supply function for credit'. Since credit is based on information about creditworthiness, there is no simple relationship between the information costs and the amount of credit extended. Changes in economic circumstances can easily destroy the relevance of previously accumulated information.

Using a game theory framework and also applying rational expectation assumptions, efforts were made in the late 1970s and 1980s in the Western literature to study the policy-making mechanisms and forces which may generate inflationary money supply (i.e. the positive analysis of monetary policy). Assuming that policy authorities can control money supply, at least imperfectly, the central question asked is why the policy-makers permit money growth rates that result, on average, in positive inflation (e.g. Kydland and Prescott, 1977; Calvo, 1978; Barro, 1983; Barro and Gordon, 1983a; McCallum, 1990). According to the basic model, the objectives of the monetary authorities are postulated so as to achieve an optimal combination of inflation and unemployment rates. Since there is a trade-off between these two goals, the long-term optimal policy rule is to pre-commit a non-inflationary policy rule and to honour it. However, surprise monetary expansion (compared with the rational expectation of the public, i.e. private firms and households) can reduce unemployment to a level lower than the natural rate without an immediate rise in inflation. The policy-makers therefore have an incentive to initiate a surprise monetary expansion. Since public expectation is rational (i.e. it is correct on average), the excessive money supply generates inflation with no effect on unemployment in the long run. Furthermore, given the expectation of monetary expansion, a lower money growth rate would temporarily result in more unemployment (Kydland and Prescott, 1977; Barro and Gordon, 1983a, 1983b). The main criticism of this explanation of inflationary money growth is its neglect of reputational constraint on the policy-makers (e.g. Backus and Driffill, 1985; Grossman and Van Huyck, 1986). The criticism, however, is not vital, as the preferences of policy-makers may differ and their term of office is not infinite (Barro, 1986; Rogoff, 1987).

Since the discretionary power of monetary authorities is a prerequisite of inflationary money growth, some analysts go further in studying the private motives of policy-makers[12] (e.g. Lombra and Moran, 1980; Kane, 1982; Hetzel, 1986). The effort is generally made to establish the link between the private interest of the monetary policy-makers, such as the image, prestige, pecuniary income, etc., and the discretionary power they obtain. One extreme theory is the 'Leviathan' governments. It claims that since the government is a self-interested institution with objectives distinct from the citizens that they represent, the government *per se* is the *source of inflation.*[13]

Despite many worthwhile efforts, a widely accepted model of monetary policy-making mechanisms is still lacking. This reflects in part the difficulties in generalising the actual motives as well as constraints of policy-makers. Nevertheless, the game perspective is suggestive. Following this line, this study views the expansion of bank loans for fixed-assets investment in China during the reforms as a result of interactions between central policy-makers and local governments in investment behaviour in light of Stackelberg's leader–follower oligopoly theory.

4.3.1 The sequential centre–locality investment game

We divide the total given investment K into two types, K_1 and K_2 ($K = K_1 + K_2$). K_1 is the national-specific investment with positive externalities; K_2 is the local-specific investment without positive externalities. From basic economic theory, we know that the central government has more interest than local governments in K_1. Assume that the revenue is a function of these two types of investment in a Cobb–Douglas form, each level of the government makes its own allocation decision to maximise its revenue (R) subject to its budget constraint as follows.[14]

A local government or local governments:

$$\text{Max } R_L = (K_{1C} + K_{1L})^{\alpha} (K_{2C} + K_{2L})^{\beta}, \qquad [4.1]$$

$$\text{S.T. } K_{1L} + K_{2L} \leq K_L$$

where subscripts C and L denote central and local governments respectively and K_L is the total fund controlled by local governments; α, β, > 0 and $\alpha + \beta \leq 1$.

The central government:

$$\text{Max } R_C = (K_{1C} + K_{1L})^{\tau} (K_{2C} + K_{2L})^{\beta},$$

$$\text{S.T. } K_{1C} + K_{2C} \leq K_C \qquad [4.2]$$

Where K_C is the total fund controlled by the central government: $\tau > \alpha > 0$ because of externalities, and $\tau + \beta \leq 1$.

By the total budget constraint, $K_L + K_C = K_1 + K_2 = K$. Suppose that the game takes a Stackelberg's form, that is, each level of the government makes its decision with the other's given. By a simple mathematical exercise, we can show that the optimal allocation of investment for each level government is a reaction function of the other's, and the overall allocation is an equilibrium solution of the game. However, what we are particularly concerned with is how this equilibrium solution is related to the budget distribution between central and local governments.

Denote by $\theta = K_C/K$ the ratio of the central government's budget to overall budget (accordingly, $(1 - \theta) = K_L/K$ is the ratio of the local budget to overall budget), and by $k_C = K_{1C}/K_C$ and $k_L = K_{1L}/K_L$ the ratio of the central and the local governments' national-specific investment to each total investment respectively (accordingly, $(1 - k_C)$ and $(1 - k_L)$ are the ratios of the local-specific investment to their total investment). The maximising behaviour of local governments will lead to their investment allocation decision being made in correspondence to the central government's allocation decision.[15]

$$k_L = [\frac{\alpha}{(\alpha + \beta)} \frac{1}{(1 - \theta)}] - \frac{\theta}{1 - \theta} k_C \qquad [4.3]$$

Similarly, the central government allocation decision is:

$$k_C = \frac{\tau}{(\tau + \beta)\,\theta} - \frac{1 - \theta}{\theta} k_L \qquad [4.4]$$

[4.3] can be interpreted as follows. First, $\alpha/(\alpha + \beta)$ can be understood as local governments' *preferred* overall allocation of investment which will be chosen if it controls all funds (i.e., $\theta = 0$). Second, for $0 < \theta < 1$, k_L decreases if k_C increases; the slope equals $\theta/(1 - \theta)$. That is, local governments reduce their national-specific to its total investment ratio by $\theta(1 - \theta)$ per cent in reaction to one per centage increase by the central government. Intuitively, the more funds for the national-specific investment from the central government, the less necessary for local governments to finance this type of investment.

[4.4] can be interpreted in a similar way. $\tau/(\tau + \beta)$ is the central government's *preferred* overall allocation of investment which will be chosen if it controls all funds (i.e. $\theta = 1$). The central government's optimal investment ratio is also a decreasing function of the local ratio, with the slope equal to $(1 - \theta)/\theta$.

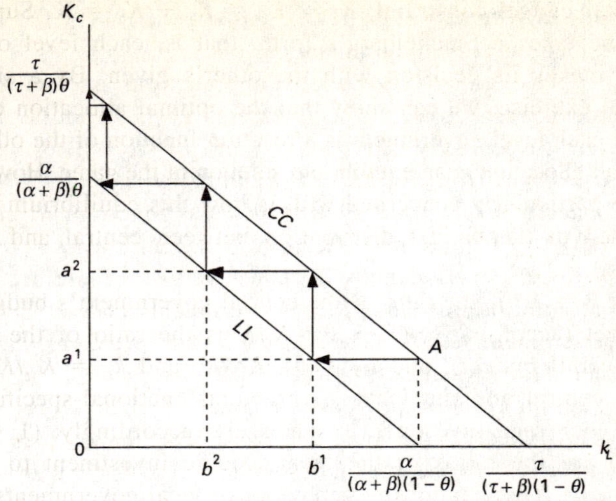

Figure 4.1 Reaction functions of central and local governments

Comparing [4.3] with [4.4] shows that:

(i) the optimal investment allocations are 'strategic substitutes' (Bulow *et al.*, 1985) to both central and local governments;
(ii) two reaction functions are parallel (the slopes are equal);
(iii) local governments' reaction function is always below the central government' (since $\tau > \alpha$) in the term of their allocation ratio with respect to the national-specific investment.

Strong implications of these three characteristics of the reaction functions are that: first, only the corner solution can be at equilibrium; second, the central government cannot be a leader but a follower in allocation of resources. Since $\tau/(\tau + \beta) > \alpha/(\alpha + \beta)$, the central government always has an incentive to fill in the investment gap left by local governments in the national-specific projects – this filling-in behaviour is of course known to local governments. Therefore, it is in the interest of local governments to reduce investment in the national-specific projects as much as possible, and to allocate their funds for the local-specific investment only. It is impossible for the central government to induce local governments to fill in the gap left by itself, unless local governments are sure that the centrally controlled funds are insufficient to meet the local's optimal allocation of funds for the national-specific investment (i.e., $K_C < [\alpha/(\alpha + \beta)]\ K$). The arguments can be made clearer diagrammatically.

In Figure 4.1, *CC* and *LL* are allocation functions of central and local governments respectively. The intercepts of *CC* and *LL* at the vertical axis are respectively $\tau/[(\tau + \beta)\theta]$ and $\alpha/[(\alpha + \beta)\theta]$, and at the horizontal axis are $\tau/[(\tau + \beta)(1 - \theta)]$ and $\alpha/[(\alpha + \beta)(1 - \theta)]$. *LL* is below *CC* since $\tau > \alpha$. Starting with *A*, if local governments choose $k_L = \alpha/[(\alpha + \beta)(1 - \theta)]$, the best choice for the centre is $k_C = a^1$; but given $k_C = a^1$, local governments will reduce k_L to b^1; therefore point *A* cannot be at equilibrium. Once local governments choose $k_L = b^1$, the central government has to raise k_C to a^2. The process continues until the corner point, where $k_C = \tau/(\tau + \beta)\theta$ and $k_L = 0$, has been reached. This action–reaction process is characterised by a process of 'reduce-increase'. Clearly, the central government cannot lead local governments to invest in the national–specific projects. On the other hand, local governments can always do better by choosing $k_L = 0$ (as long as $\theta \leq \alpha/(\alpha + \alpha)$, discussed later).

With the above arguments in mind, we now analyse the relationship between the equilibrium pattern of overall-investment and the budget (or investment funds) distribution. The relationship is implied by the following ratio constraint: $0 \leq k_C, k_L \leq 1$, which we have ignored so far. Denote by *k* the overall ratio of the total national–specific investment to the total budget:

$$k = (K_{1L} + K_{1C})/K = (1 - \theta)k_L + \theta k_C \qquad [4.5]$$

This implies that *k* is a weighted average of k_L and k_C with weights equal to $(1 - \theta)$ and θ. We consider the following three cases:

$$0 \leq \theta \leq \alpha/(\alpha + \beta); \qquad [i]$$

$$\alpha/(\alpha + \beta) < \theta < \tau/(\tau + \beta) \qquad [ii]$$

$$\tau/(\tau + \beta) \leq \theta \leq 1 \qquad [iii]$$

Case [i] is shown in Figure 4.2. Since $\theta \leq \alpha/(\alpha + \beta)$ implies that $\{\tau/(\tau + \beta)\theta\} > \{\alpha/(\alpha + \beta)\theta\} \geq 1$, $k_C = \tau/(\tau + \beta)\theta > 1$ is not feasible. At equilibrium, $k_C^* = 1$, $k_L^* = \{\alpha/(\alpha + \beta) - \theta\}/(1 - \theta)$, and $k^* = \alpha/(\alpha + \beta)$. In other words, if the central government budget ratio is smaller than the investment ratio preferred by the local government, the central government allocates all its funds for the national–

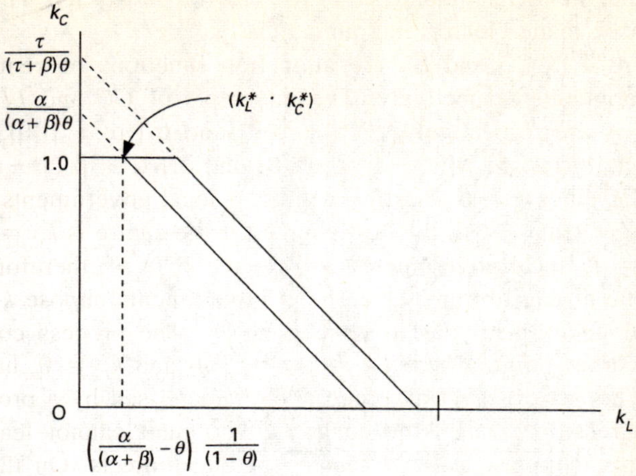

Figure 4.2 Equilibrium solution in case [i]

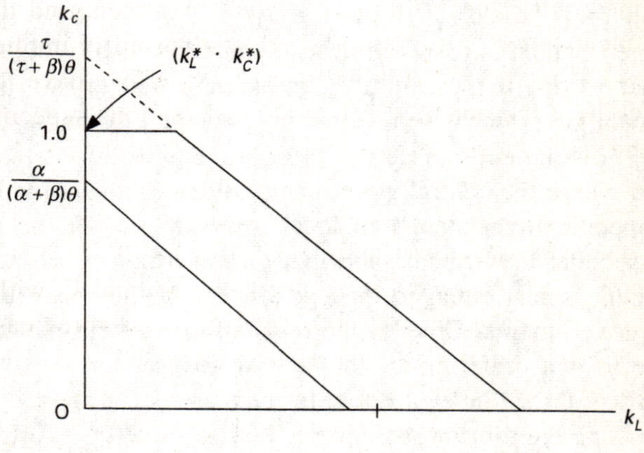

Figure 4.3 Equilibrium solution in case [ii]

specific investment, and local governments just fill in the gap of $\{\alpha/(\alpha + \beta) - \theta\}$ such that the equilibrium pattern of overall investment equals the local-preferred one. As a result, the total allocation of funds for the national–specific investment is strictly smaller than that preferred by the central government.

Case [ii] is shown in Figure 4.3. In this case, since $\alpha/[(\alpha + \beta)\theta] < 1 < \tau/[(\tau + \beta)\theta]$, $k_C = \tau/[(\tau + \beta)\theta] > 1$ is still not feasible. At equilibrium,

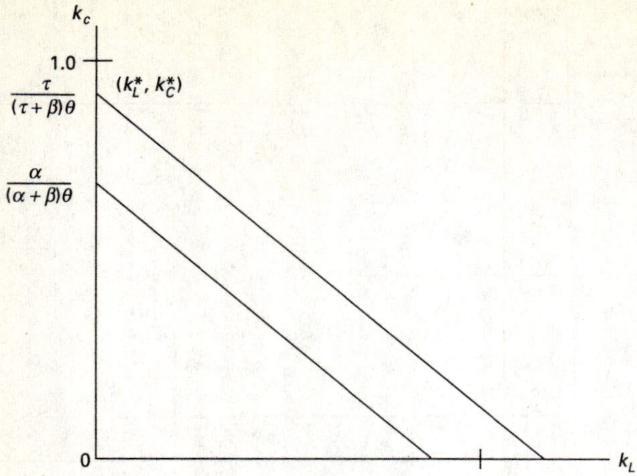

Figure 4.4 Equilibrium solution in case [iii]

$k_C^* = 1$, $k_L^* = 0$ (since $k_L = \{\alpha/(\alpha + \beta) - \theta\}/(1 - \theta) < 0$ implies disinvestment which is assumed away), and $\alpha/(\alpha + \beta) < k^* < \tau/(\tau + \beta)$. In other words, if the central government's budget ratio is greater than the local government's preferred investment ratio but smaller than the central government's preferred ratio, the equilibrium situation will be reached where the central government allocates all its funds for the national–specific investment and local governments do the same for the local–specific investment such that the resulting overall allocation of investment is just equal to the budget distribution between central and local governments. Clearly, the resulted investment pattern is less favourable to that preferred by the central government.

Case [iii] is shown in Figure 4.4. In this case, $k_C = \tau/((\tau + \beta)\theta) \leqslant 1$ is feasible. The equilibrium solution is that $k_C^* = \tau/((\tau + \beta)\theta)$, $k_L = 0$ and $k^* = \tau/(\tau + \beta)$. That is, if the central government controls sufficient funds for its preferred national–specific investment, the equilibrium allocation of investment will be equal to its preferred investment ratio; local governments do not allocate funds for the national–specific investment, but this does not affect the optimal solution.

In summary, we have shown that the equilibrium allocation of overall investment crucially depends on the budget distribution between central and local governments. The results are summarised by Figure 4.5. Our main conclusion is that the central government can directly achieve the optimal allocative pattern of resources $K_1/K_2 = \tau/\beta$ if and

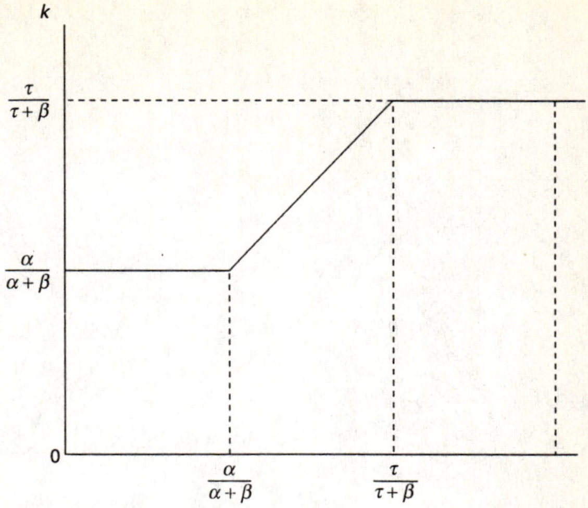

Figure 4.5 The relationship between the overall investment pattern and the budget distribution

only if its controlled budget is sufficiently large. Of course, we are aware that, in reality, this conclusion is valid only under certain circumstances. Under the centralised allocation of resources, inefficiency can arise from incentive failure and asymmetrical information. For the analytical purpose of this chapter, this complex situation is not dealt with.

4.3.2 Credit expansion for allocative adjustment

Under the decentralisation reforms, local governments gained a greater control over resources, and the distribution condition for the optimal allocation $\theta \geq \tau/(\tau + \beta)$ no longer held. In other words, the economy has entered the cases [i] and [ii] discussed in the preceding subsection. The problem faced by the policy-makers is simple: in order to achieve the socially optimal allocation of resources, more funds are necessary for the national–specific investment. Given the constraint on fiscal policy, the policy-makers resort to monetary policy, namely expansion of bank loans for fixed-assets investment to increase investment in the national–specific projects. In so doing, although real value of investment cannot be increased, the pattern of investment can be changed towards the centrally preferred one (i.e. $\alpha/\beta \rightarrow \tau/\beta$). The positive

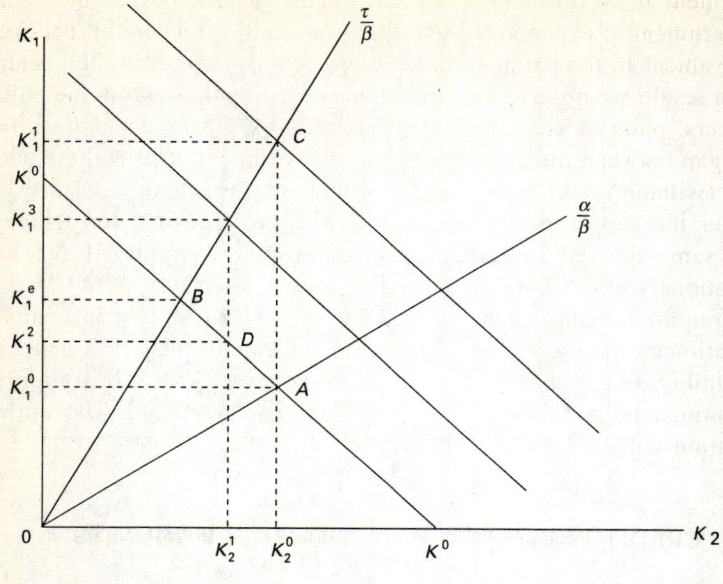

Figure 4.6 Credit expansion as a reaction to misallocation of resources

effect of such a policy is an increase in social welfare from improvement of allocative efficiency; the negative one is inflation (necessary for diluting real value of nominal investment fund).

This policy reaction is illustrated in Figure 4.6. Ray (τ/β) represents the investment pattern preferred by the policy-makers and ray (α/β) is the investment pattern preferred by local governments. Curve K^0K^0 represents the overall budget constraint in real terms and any increase in K_1 has to be accompanied by a reduction in K_2 by the same amount. Suppose the pattern of investment without monetary expansion is in point A because insufficient funds are controlled by the central government. From the central government's point of view, this pattern is not socially optimal. However, by expanding bank loans equal to $(K_1^1 - K_1^0)$ for fixed assets investment in favour of K_1, the policy-makers can change the pattern of investment from A to C so as to achieve a social optimum. The cost of this monetary expansion is inflation, equal to $BC/OB = (K_1^1 - K_1^e)$.

Knowing that it is the central government's interest to increase investment in K_1 to obtain an optimal allocation, local governments will rationally expect the credit expansion and therefore try to reduce investment in K_1 further (up to zero). This in turn pushes the central government to expand credit further (up to a level where all necessary investment in the national–specific projects is financed by the centre). As a result, we observe an expansionary credit policy. From the policy-makers' point of view, the extent of credit expansion depends on both the gap between the optimal pattern of investment (τ/β) and the actual one (without credit expansion), and the costs of infiation. Clearly, the larger the gap is, the more credit expansion is needed for achieving the same desired investment allocation. For example, if the non-inflationary allocation is D (which is a case when $\theta = K_1^2/K_2^1 > \alpha/\beta$), the required credit expansion is $(K_1^3 - K_1^2) < (K_1^1 - K_1^0)$. In reality, if inflationary pressure materialises (to an extent) and this generates 'disutility' (e.g. political pressure) to the policy-makers, τ/β is no longer a optimal target for the central government to pursue. The optimal solution will be between τ/β and α/β.

4.4 CREDIT EXPANSION AS A WORKABLE SOLUTION

In reaction to the investment behaviour of, and thus resource misallocation by, the localities during the reforms, the central government resorted excessively to banks for increasing investment in technical updating and in bottleneck sectors. Obviously, too much of the policy burden was placed on the banking system. The question then is: why did the central government not take alternative policy measures to achieve the desired allocation of resources and thus avoid excessive expansion of bank credit?

The answer is twofold. First, the central government did introduce other policy measures but they were not effective. Second, the policy-makers' choice was restricted by the type of economic reform they advocated. Third, the expansion of bank loans was workable also because of a rising household saving ratio. These three factors are dealt with in turn in the following three subsections.

4.4.1 Ineffectiveness of other policies

Both administrative and economic methods were employed by policy-makers to alter the investment pattern of local governments. The administrative measures included stipulations or provisions (*Tongzhi* and *Guiding*) issued by the central government. Considering industrial policy, the Central Committee of the Chinese Communist Party in 1978 made clear in its '*Decision to Speed Up Industrial Development*' that energy, raw material and transportation were the priority sectors. This policy has not been changed. In March 1981, the State Planning Commission prescribed '12 bans', including the banning of duplicated investment projects and of new projects that competed for raw materials with existing enterprises.[16] In December 1982, the State Council itself issued a document listing specific manufactured products whose investment must be controlled. They included cotton textile products, woollen textile products, automobiles, bearings, motors, TV sets, electric fans, washing machines, sewing machines, bicycles, mechanic watches, tobacco, wine, plastics, rubber products, etc. The central government has repeated this policy almost every year since then but the expansion of production of these products just seems unstoppable.

For example, the State Planning Commission, the State Construction Commission and the Ministry of Finance jointly issued a document forbidding investment for expansion of cotton-spinning capacity of the textile industry in March 1981, and has since then reaffirmed the same policy many times. What happened, however, was precisely the opposite, i.e. the rapid expansion of the cotton-spinning capacity. In 1988 alone, the total number of cotton spindles increased by 21 per cent from 26.0 million to 31.6 million. The increment between 1984 and 1988 was 5.5 million, equivalent to 54 per cent of that between 1949 and 1984 (Jiang X., 1991). During 1986–90, the planned increase of cotton spindles was 3.7 million but the actual increase was 15.0 million. As a result, the entire production capacity became excessive (excess spindles amounted to 10.0 million).[17]

The effectiveness of these administrative measures depended on whether it was in the best interests of the lower levels of government to implement such policies in their own regions (to be discussed in the next chapter). It was apparent that those who obeyed the administrative order would lose out to those who disobeyed; thus, it was safer to disobey. This is reflected in an open secret among Chinese officials: 'Those who follow directives get the worst of the system.' In our game, this meant that an obedient locality would suffer a decrease in its share of national industrial output. Violaters have to be punished in order to make the rule enforceable. But the limited administrative capacity (including monitoring and enforcement capacity) of the central government meant that the administrative measures have to be enforced by the provincial levels of the government. By the same token, provincial governments have to rely on sub-provincial governments. It seemed that no local governments were willing to enforce policies which re-

Table 4.13 Tax and profit as percentage of fixed assets (original book value)

	Tax & Profit			*Profit*			*Tax*		
	1980	*1985*	*1989*	*1980*	*1985*	*1989*	*1980*	*1985*	*1989*
Whole industry	25.6	23.9	18.2	16.9	13.4	8.0	8.7	10.5	10.2
Light industry	60.9	40.8	29.1	34.3	19.7	11.1	26.6	21.1	18.0
Heavy industry	17.9	18.7	14.1	13.1	11.5	6.8	4.8	7.2	7.3
Mining	14.2	7.6	2.0	11.1	3.4	–0.8	3.1	4.2	2.8
Raw material	21.6	21.2	17.8	15.1	11.6	8.2	6.5	9.6	9.6
Manufacturing	16.0	22.7	17.6	12.0	16.3	10.4	4.0	6.4	7.2
Rail transportation	7.2[a]	12.2	6.2	4.3[a]	8.1	4.8	2.9[a]	4.1	1.4
Highway transportation	15.5[a]	11.7	6.9	13.1[a]	9.3	4.1	2.4	2.4	2.8

Note: [a] 1982. Rail and highway transportation enterprises are the state-owned ones.

Source: SSB (1984a: 291–2; 1991a: 505, 511, 516; 1990c: 106–7, 124–5, 142–3).

stricted industrial expansion in their own regions. Given that the policy was violated by too many localities, the central government became virtually powerless in policing. It simply could not punish them all. Politics also played a rôle in this respect. Leaders of the central government need the support of leaders of lower-level governments, particularly in the circumstances of decentralisation reform. At the same time, the central government suffered from an information asymmetry problem and was unable to distinguish the performance of their local subordinates in the implementation of policies. In a dynamic setting, a policy which cannot be implemented will certainly lose its credibility. And this was precisely the case in China. The threat from the centre has generally been 'empty'.

Besides administrative means, economic means were also used to encourage investment in the centrally determined priority sectors. Differing from administrative means, economic means – mainly tax policy and interest rate policy – were designed to induce the investment in line with the centre's policy. On the fiscal side, differential sales tax rates were designed to encourage investment in bottleneck sectors (e.g. transportation and energy) and discourage investment in other sectors. They were so designed partly because of price control which was stricter over products of the bottleneck sectors. By imposing higher turnover tax rates on non-bottleneck sectors, it was hoped that price distortion could be reduced and thus investment misallocation minimised.

Because the return on investment of local governments in China

Table 4.14 Lending rates of fixed-assets investment (annual %)[a]

	Jan. 87–Sep. 88	*Feb. 88–Sep. 89*	*Sep. 89–Mar. 90*
Normal	8.64	9.90	12.78
Coal mining including energy saving projects	5.76	7.92	9.00
Energy, transportation and mining (iron and nonferrous metal)	5.76	7.92	10.26

Note: [a] For the term of 1–3 years.

Source: *Almanac of China's Finance and Banking* (1989: 157–65; 1990: 173–83); the PBC.

included not only profit but also taxes (to be discussed in next chapter), the differential-tax-rate policy actually exacerbated the sectoral imbalance of investment. For instance, the difference in profitability between the transport sector and industry was 2.7–4.1 percentage points in 1985, whereas the actual return to local governments (i.e. the sum of tax and profit remittances) ratios differed by 10.0–11.5 percentage points. The profitability difference between light industry and the mining industry was 16.3 percentage points, while difference in the returns between these two sectors was 33.2 percentage points. A comparison between other sectors reveals the same story (Table 4.13). It is not a coincidence that the bottleneck sectors were associated with much lower profits and tax return, especially in relation to investment.

On the monetary side, interest-rate policy (differential rates) was also used to encourage investment in the priority sectors (see Table 4.14). From the borrower's point of view, the interest rates for the priority sectors were about 20–33 per cent lower than the normal one. But this discounted interest rate had little impact on the overall investment return where the difference between transportation and industry and between manufacturing industry and other industrial sectors remained wide. As shown in Table 4.13, the financial return (sum of tax and profit) of investment in transport was much lower than that in industry; and the return in light industry was much higher than that in heavy industry. Within heavy industry, the return in mining industry was lower than in the manufacturing industry. From the lender's point of view, this policy actually discouraged lending to the priority sector because it meant that local bank branches making loans to the priority sectors would make less profits.

4.4.2 Constraints on policy options

To achieve the desired investment pattern without resorting to excessive aggregate expansion of bank credit, central policy-makers must either force local governments to abide by centrally determined investment patterns, reduce other categories of bank loans or ensure that alternative channels of financial intermediation are opened more widely. None of these options appeared acceptable to the policy-makers.

To influence the investment pattern of local governments, the central government could, for example, directly require that a minimum proportion of funds has to be used to finance investment in priority sectors or activity. They did not adopt this option partly because doing so would signal a political reversal in the direction of economic reform. The political constraints were very important. The power base of the reformist central leaders was largely the support of the local Party and government officials.

Since the differential sales tax rate policy was partly responsible for the unbalanced local investment pattern and was designed to offset price distortions, one may ask why not liberate prices altogether to eliminate distortions. There were two main factors precluding this policy option from being adopted. The first was that it was inconsistent with the gradualistic approach to reform advocated. The second one was that it would have caused a sudden redistribution of revenues between the centre and localities as well as among localities and among enterprises. This would not only create political tensions but also destroy the contract systems – both intra-governmental fiscal and enterprise management contract systems). In a word, radical price liberalisation would mean resetting the game and this was too risky to the policy-makers.

Cutting bank working capital loans was also not a feasible policy option. A significant part of bank loans for working capital investment (such as for government purchases of agricultural products) was irreducible and non-discretionary. Moreover, repayment of bank fixed-assets investment loans largely depended on the availability of working capital. Most fixed-assets investment projects were jointly financed by bank loans and non-bank loans (i.e. budgetary appropriation, domestic bank loans, foreign funds – most of their repayment was under guarantee by the Chinese government – and the internal funds, so called 'self-raised funds').[18] Finally, because a local government's access to capital markets was restricted by the policy-makers, cutting loans for working capital investment would drive local governments into a corner whereby the available production capacity would be wasted. Such an outcome was unacceptable to the policy-makers.

Bank loans for fixed-assets investment had to be expanded also because too much weight was placed on banks in financial intermediation (see Chapter 3). The underdevelopment of capital markets led to excessive financial intermediation through state banks. This factor also restricted expansion of firm size and thus internal mobilisation of financial resources within a firm. The underdevelopment of capital markets was partly due to a fear that a greater reliance on government bond issue would increase budgetary deficits. Another fear was that it would erode state ownership if households were allowed to buy up property rights. In addition, there was the concern that promotion of financing through capital markets might not necessarily improve resource allocation and at the same time might make investment control even more difficult.

Development of capital markets might make local governments more able to access savings and thus invest more in projects in their interests while neglecting investment in infrastructure. It has to be stressed that, with respect to allocation of resources, this concern may be partly justifiable. If local governments still dominate investment decision-making and the essence of the economic system remains unchanged, it would be difficult to expect the investment pattern to be altered much by allowing the issue of more bonds and shares. Development of capital markets through which investment is guided by profit maximisation would ultimately require a fundamental reform of state ownership. This was very difficult and risky and therefore not prepared for by the policy-makers. In addition, in China, capital markets had to be developed from scratch. Problems such as outdated accounting practices, imperfect information, lack of moral standards, lack of regulations and supervision, and absence of legal protection were all prevailing. There was certainly a greater risk for the government to embark on a course of rapid capital market development. This risk becomes greater still if the enormous number of medium- and small-sized enterprises and individuals are allowed to be involved. To policy-makers who were very unfamiliar with capital markets, their conservative attitude was not unreasonable.

It is worth noting that the behaviour of different levels of local governments was not identical. Table 4.15 reveals different priorities in in-

Table 4.15 Industrial investment priority of the governments at different levels (percentage of investment, 1986)

	1st	*2nd*
National	Coal(16.3)	Metallurgy(14.3)
Provincial	Electricity(22.5)	Coal(19.1)
City,	Electricity(27.0)	Light industry(21.0)
County & below	Light industry(>50.0)[a]	
	3rd	*4th*
National	Electricity(12.1)	Chemistry(4.9)
Provincial	Chemistry(12.7)	Light industry(10.0)
City,	Building material(10.7)	Textile(10.0)
County & below		

Note: [a] Author's estimation. During the period of 1981–5, total investment in the large and medium SOEs in light industry was ¥16.49 billion but total investment in the small SOEs and the COEs amounted to ¥52.20 billion. This accounted for 76 percent of the total investment in light industry during this period excluding village enterprises and individual investment.

Source: Xu, X. (1988); *Data of 1985 Industrial Census in China*, vol. 13. no. 1 (light industry), p. 200.

dustrial investment of the government at different levels in China.

In terms of sectoral allocation of investment, the lower the level of local governments the higher the investment priority given to industries with higher tax and profit returns (e.g. light industry). The reason is that the higher the level of government, the larger the territory upon which the social cost–benefit calculation of a project had to be based. Thus, the higher the level of government, the more consideration was given to the sectoral balance of the investment. In other words, *the higher the level of government, the larger the scope in which externalities are internalised.* Additionally, investment in the bottleneck sectors of transportation, mining and raw materials is on a large scale and of long duration. The return is uncertain since the future revenue generated by investment in these sectors accruing to the investors is subject to changes in the terms of central–local fiscal revenue-sharing scheme. Apart from sectoral consideration, time also entered investment decision-making. Construction projects in the bottleneck sectors were usually large ones which demanded, among other things, massive mobilisation of financial resources. These take a long time to complete and to become productive (more than 5 years according to

Table 4.16 Duration of completed capital construction projects (1986–7)

Number and investment scale		*Average duration*
Total number of capital construction projects	85 627	1 year 10 months
Number of large- and medium-scale capital construction investment projects	221	5 years 2 months
Of which, with scale (¥):		
5 – 10 million	1	1 year 10 months
10 – 50 million	71	3 years 7 months
50 – 100 million	51	4 years 2 months
100 – 500 million	77	6 years 7 months
0.5 – 1 billion	13	9 years 11 months
Over 1 billion	8	10 years

Source: SSB (1989d: 159; 104).

Table 4.16). The larger the project, the longer the time it would take to complete. Given the uncertainty accompanying the reforms, it was not in the best interest of lower levels of government to invest heavily for the benefit of the future.

The different investment behaviour of local governments is important to policy design (to be discussed in Chapter 8). Unfortunately, the reforms were one-sided in emphasising only the need to devolve greater decision-making power to the lower level governments and enterprises without accompanying measures to ensure greater national accountability. Taken to an extreme, there was a general view that the lower the level of government to gain autonomy, the better.

In summary, structural adjustment of investment patterns without resorting to the expansion of aggregate investment financed through bank loans was very difficult indeed. Expanding bank credit was effectively the easier way to satisfy more fully the demand for funds from both the central and local governments. Expansion of bank loans seemed feasible also because of the rising propensity of households to save in the form of bank deposits. In general, this has helped so far in alleviating inflationary pressure in the consumer goods market.[19]

4.4.3 Household long-term saving behaviour

Figure 4.7 shows that the household net saving ratio increased sharply in the period 1978–90.[20] It reached over 21 per cent in 1990 compared

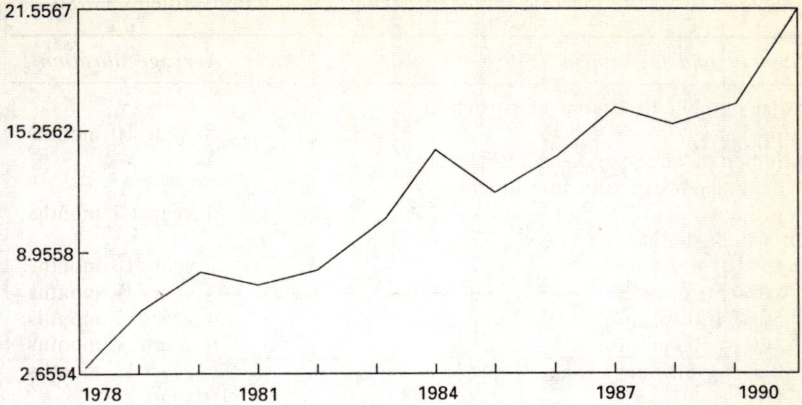

Figure 4.7 Household net saving ratio (%, 1978–90)

Table 4.17 Household savings ratio[a] (1987–90) (%)

	1987	*1988*	*1989*	*1990*
Hungary	–1.3	1.5	–0.3	4.7
Bulgaria	4.2	6.1	2.9	n.a.
Czechoslovakia	3.8	3.0	2.5	n.a.
East Germany	6.1	6.0	4.8	3.0[b]
USSR[c]	5.3	6.0	7.4	6.6
Romania	n.a.	n.a.	3.7	8.3
Poland	7.9	7.8	9.9	n.a.
China	11.8	8.2	13.3	16.9
China (broad)[d]	16.7	16.0	17.0	21.6

Note: [a] Ratio of increment in saving deposits to money income of the population. [b] Savings as percentage of disposable income. [c] Data for 1989 and 1990 for the USSR are lower than those reported by other sources. [d] Savings include increment in all financial assets (i.e. bank deposits, cash in hand and bonds and shares).

Source: Economic Commission for Europe (1991: 54); for China: Appendix 4.

with less than 3 per cent in 1978. Although the rise in saving propensity was not stable, the upward trend was very strong.

Household saving ratio is significantly higher in China than in reforming economies in CEE (Table 4.17).

Although the level of savings grew commensurately with the growth

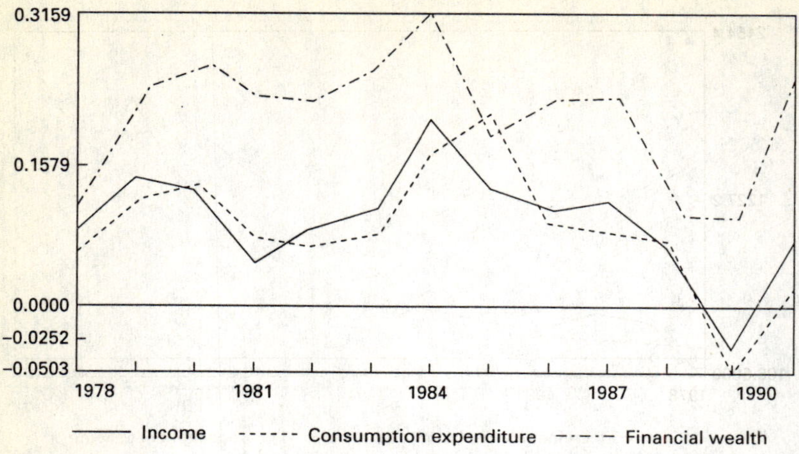

Figure 4.8 Growth of household disposable income, consumption expenditure and financial wealth (all in real terms; 1978–90)

in incomes, there has also been a striking and discernible increase in savings propensity among Chinese households. As Figure 4.8 shows, first, growth of consumption expenditure was slower and thus saving grew faster than income. When income growth slowed, consumption expenditure slowed as well; when income growth rose, consumption expenditure also rose but at a slower rate. Second, growth of household financial wealth never came below 9 per cent in the period 1978–90, even when income growth was negative.

This can be seen more clearly in Figure 4.9. An increase in household net savings seemed less dependent on changes in household income. Household consumption expenditure and physical investment were directly affected by changes in household income growth. Yet household net savings continued to increase in 1989 when the rise in household nominal income substantially slowed and real income actually decreased. This seems to suggest that Chinese household consumption/savings behaviour was asymmetrically procyclical. When income growth was high, savings grew at a higher rate, thus reducing pressure on the consumer goods market; when growth of income decreased, consumption expenditure but not financial wealth decreased accordingly. In other words, their financial wealth was not used to offset fluctuation of income flows when the income growth was in a downturn. As a result of such strong saving tendency, household financial

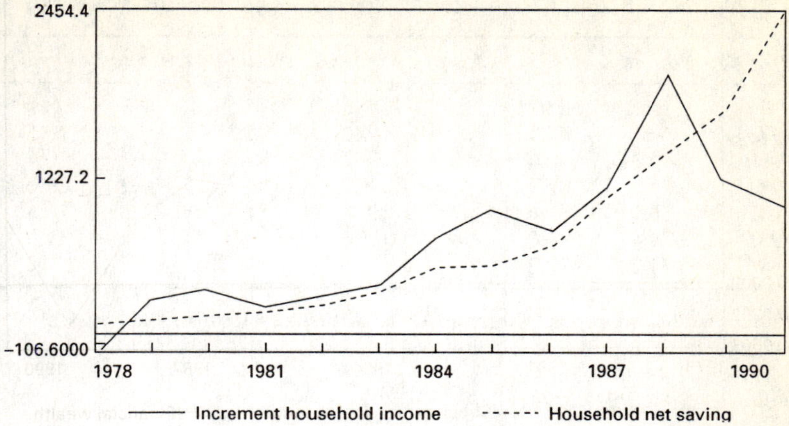

Figure 4.9 Household income and net saving (1978–90)

wealth/income ratio escalated. Between 1978 and 1990, it increased by 66 percentage points from 23.7 to 90.1 per cent.

Traditionally, an increase in monetary holding by households in a centrally planned economy is viewed as monetary overhang, reflecting shortages in consumer goods markets. However, as pointed out in Chapter 1, this is, by and large, not the case in China in the period under study. In particular, households' savings continued to grow even when inventories of consumer goods escalated (see Chapter 7). In fact, the impressive savings performance in China since the early 1980s is not abnormal if it is compared with the experiences in other East Asia economies (for a reference, see the World Bank (1993) *East Asian Miracle – Economic Growth and Public Policy*).

Theoretically, savings are important in the neoclassical development of the consumption function in terms of wealth effects (Haberler, 1941; Pigou, 1941, 1943, 1947; Patinkin, 1965). It postulates that net wealth of the private sector or the 'real balances' may break the constraint of current income on current consumption emphasised by the Keynesian approach. This implies that the purpose of savings is to smooth consumption. Based on intertemporal optimisation, the permanent income hypothesis (PIH) (Friedman, M., 1957) and the life-cycle hypothesis (LCH) (Modigliani and Brumberg, 1954) further establish the link between wealth and consumption. Forward-looking, they hypothesise that rational consumers tend to maximise utility through intertemporal allocation of consumption subject to the budget constraint of the

Table 4.18 Ratio of fixed-term to total household deposits (1978–90)

Year	*National*	*Urban*	*Rural*	*Year*	*National*	*Urban*	*Rural*
1978	n.a.	83.2	n.a.	1985	75.5	79.5	68.0
1979	n.a.	82.1	n.a.	1986	77.3	80.8	70.5
1980	76.3	80.9	65.2	1987	81.6	79.7	70.4
1981	75.7	81.7	63.1	1988	74.5	76.9	69.0
1982	76.9	81.6	67.6	1989	81.3	83.1	76.5
1983	76.4	81.0	68.3	1990	83.2	84.7	79.0
1984	74.2	79.2	65.2				

Note: Fixed-term deposits refer to those with fixed term of half year or longer.

Source: SSB (1991a: 275).

permanent income (PIH) or the lifetime income (LCH) (i.e. the present value of one's total income or total expected wealth). Chinese household saving behaviour is difficult to explain in such a theoretical framework.

Borrowing restrictions or liquidity constraints are the main arguments against the PIH and the LCH. Consumers have only limited access to capital markets through which the consumption pattern can be optimised. This is reflected in an apparently large marginal propensity to consume out of a transitory income in the empirical studies (for a survey, see Blinder and Deaton, 1985; Blundell, 1988). In the light of this argument, Chinese household saving performance may reflect borrowing restrictions or liquidity constraints. The detailed investigation and analyses are not in the scope of this study. However, the evidence indicates that the saving purposes themselves could be more important in explaining saving behaviour.

Chinese households tended to save for long-term purposes. This is reflected in their saving behaviour in terms of timing. They generally kept a high and relatively stable proportion of their total deposits in the forms of term deposits. Around 80 per cent of their deposits were fixed-term deposits with a duration of half-year or longer (see Table 4.18). According to the PBC, over two thirds of total household deposits are fixed for the term of one year or longer. Although even the fixed-term deposits are guaranteed to be withdrawable at any time, the long-term saving purpose is apparent.

More importantly, Chinese households were concerned not merely with their own consumption utility but also with that of their families, especially of their children. In the latter case, utility has a wider social

Table 4.19 Purposes of savings (1989, 1990)

	March 1989	*April 1990*	*Change*
Location of the sample	10 cities	20 cities	
Sample size	4786	8731	
Purposes of deposit (%)			
Children's education	21.2	22.8	+1.7
Purchasing durable consumer goods	20.9	13.0	−7.9
Marriage	12.4	11.1	−1.3
Housing	12.1	10.2	−1.9
Prudence	12.4	14.4	+2.0
Pension	11.7	13.2	+1.5
Business circulating funds	5.3	4.4	−0.9
Earning interest	4.0	11.1	+7.1
Reasons of withdrawal (%)			
Children's education	22.3	25.2	+2.9
Purchasing durable consumer goods	31.2	20.9	−10.3
Marriage	12.0	10.1	−1.9
Housing	11.0	10.9	−0.1
Purchasing bonds or shares	11.3	16.6	+5.3
Business	7.2	9.0	+1.8
Lending to others	5.0	7.3	+2.3

Source: *Financial Statistics and Analysis*, no. 31, 1989; no. 29, 1990.

content which may affect savers' social status. A survey of 10 000 households conducted in 1987 reports that the long-term saving purposes of households were family-oriented: over 72 per cent of them placed their emphasis on financing children's education, supporting the aged, meeting the costs of marriage and funeral expenses, and preparing for unforeseen circumstances and old age; 22 per cent of households emphasised the purchase of durable consumer goods, and only 0.5 of them were concerned with earning interest (China Economic Reform Institute, 1987). This is broadly consistent with two recent surveys on households' purposes of savings (in the forms of bank deposits) (Table 4.19). Among the withdrawal reasons listed, there was no mention of consumption expenditure except that of buying durable consumer goods. The predominant reasons were the same as those described above.

Since households have long-term saving purposes which are family-oriented, these long-term objectives cannot be fixed in terms of money value. First, they will change, and almost certainly increase, with an improvement in living standards and an expectation of rising expenditure demands in the future. Second, these objectives are influenced by

Table 4.20 Urban–rural difference in saving priority (1989)

	Urban	*Rural*
Children's education	1	2
Purchasing durable consumer goods	2	3
Marriage	3	4
Housing	4	1

Source: *Financial Statistics and Analysis*, no.32, 1989.

their neighbours. Households would therefore tend to save more subject mainly to growth rates of their own income and the desired wealth/income ratio of the society as a whole. As has already been observed in the late 1980s, before a desired wealth/income ratio has been achieved, Chinese households' desire to accumulate wealth could be so strong that their savings could still expand even when their income decreased.

It is interesting to note that the priorities of saving purposes of urban and rural households are different. As Table 4.20 shows, for urban households the most important saving motive is children's education, whereas for rural households it is house building/purchasing. This difference reflects the fact that in urban areas, housing is generally provided by a 'working unit' such as a factory, a school, a hospital, etc., but rural households have to look after themselves in housing. It can be expected that the importance of saving for housing in the urban area will increase as housing reform progresses.

In the long-term, the experiences in Japan and Taiwan may shed useful light on understanding households' saving behaviour in mainland China. In both Japan and Taiwan, households responded to the low initial wealth and high income growth by increasing savings at a higher rate. As a result, the households saving rates increased continuously. The high saving rates then gradually stabilised to a lower level as wealth/income ratios raised to a much more acceptable level and growth of income slowed. In Japan, the household saving rate increased from 12 per cent to 23 per cent during the high growth period until the early 1970s. It then dropped from 23.2 per cent in 1974 to only 14.1 per cent in 1990.[21] In Taiwan, the household saving rate increased from 3.6 per cent in 1955 to 28.5 per cent in 1986. It then declined to around 20 per cent recently.[22]

The strongly increased saving propensity of the households does not mean that it (or its growth) is stable. It fluctuates significantly (see Figure 4.7) in the short-term. A large change in the deposit rate might marginally affect savings.[23] For instance, in 1989 and 1990 when real deposit rates rose significantly because of lower inflation rates, the importance of earning interest increased (from 0.5 per cent to 4.0 per cent and from 4.0 per cent to 11.1 per cent respectively). The sensitivity of savings to change in interest rates seems to be the purchasing of durable consumer goods. In 1990, the relative weight put on earning interest increased by 7 percentage points, almost exactly offsetting the reduction in the weight attached to purchasing durable consumer goods.

Household saving/consumption behaviour is very important in understanding China's economic performance. The point made in this subsection is that the rising household savings in bank deposits, given the underdeveloped capital markets, helped to make expansion of bank credit a workable solution for the policy-makers when they had to increase investment for their priority activities – bearing in mind that the rise in household saving ratio is not stable in the short term.

Thus far, based on a centre–locality game in investment, bank credit expansion is explained as the central government's reaction to local governments' investment pattern. The latter is taken as given. The next chapter explains further why local governments behaved in the way they did in investment.

5 Local Governments' Ownership and Incentive Compatibility

The preceding chapter argued that the excessive expansion of bank credit and the violation of credit ceilings occurred because central policy-makers were compelled to increase bank loans as a means of rectifying the irrational investment patterns of local governments, and in particular, to ensure adequate investment in technical updating and in the bottleneck infrastructure sectors. This leads to the question as to why local governments tended to neglect investment in the priority sectors in favour of manufacturing and other activities. By focusing on the institutional and systemic characteristics of the Chinese economy and reform, this chapter will argue that although decentralisation based on the (effective) property rights of local governments[1] alleviated incentive failure,[2] it exacerbated problems of incentive incompatibility between the central and local governments in resource allocation. The chapter first describes the uniqueness of the Chinese economic system – local government ownership. It then applies theories on incentive compatibility to analyse the investment behaviour of local governments. Finally, it examines fiscal factors, which are related to local governments' ownership, in the incentive structure.

5.1 UNIQUENESS OF THE CHINESE ECONOMIC SYSTEM

The identification of systemic factors in investment behaviour in China requires a careful specification of institutional characteristics, particularly the role of local governments in economic activities. It is difficult to categorise the Chinese political economy system as either a unitary state or a decentralised federal state in a conventional way. Using social and political criteria, China is clearly a unitary state defined in terms of the constitutional sovereignty of the central government or parliament over local governments or local assemblies (Wilson, 1984). In economic terms, the nature of the Chinese system becomes equivocal. According to Hughes (1987), a unitary state is one in which expectations of uniform national standards of service and taxation are dominant, whereas a decentralised federal state is one in which a high degree of local autonomy determines the nature and level of local government activities even when this is at the expense of national economic and social objectives. On one hand, given that uniform national standards of taxation,[3] government services and even of wage payment were dominant, China was a unitary economy. On the other hand, since the autonomy of local governments could be exercised against the interest of the centre (e.g. against the new economic development strategy), China was closer to a decentralised federal state. Noting that provinces possess a high measure of autonomy and have sizeable financial means at their disposal, Plasschaert (1989) argues that one could speak of a *de facto* federation in China.

The difficulty of categorisation arises from the fact that, unlike local governments in both unitary and federal states which mainly provide local public goods and services (such as education, roads, refuse disposal, environment health, local planning, leisure and sport facilities, public housing, personal social services, etc.), China's local governments provide not only these but also possess property rights over the majority of enterprises. Concerning the latter function, Chinese local governments are 'entrepreneurs', but these 'entrepreneurs' are simultaneously the local authorities and agents of the central government.

China's economy in pre-1978 was conventionally categorised as a centrally planned economy (CPE), but its peculiarities have long been recognised by many outside analysts. For instance, Donnithorne (1967, 1972) describes China's economy as cellular, composed of a myriad of small discrete units. Lyons (1987) showed that, associated with Chinese planning organisations and procedures, a tendency towards fragmentation diverted China's economic development from that which was expected on the basis of theoretical considerations and the experiences of other large economies. Wong (1985, 1987) emphasises the importance of the role of the local sector in China's economy.

Study on the uniqueness of the Chinese economic system was recently significantly advanced. From a different perspective, Lin (1990: 293–98) argues that the essence of the Chinese system was not in its departure from Soviet-type planning, but in the basically unaltered Soviet system at local levels. Decentralisation in China resulted in a system of *polycentric Soviet-type planning*.[4] Applying the standard property-rights analysis and in comparison with the other CPEs, Granick (1990) concludes that property rights of local governments exist in China in both the pre- and post-1978 periods. In his words, 'The system of multiple principles, with property rights belonging to the local government, is a fundamental characteristic of contemporary Chinese society but not of the Soviet or East European centrally planned economies.' (p. 273) Although his study is based on a data sample which is heavily skewed toward the large- and medium-sized enterprises, he highlights five important elements of Chinese state-owned enterprises (SOEs): loose and easily overfulfilled production plans that offer only limited guidance to enterprises; the availability of allocated items outside the state materials allocation system; the existence of multiple prices for the same product and customer in a single region; multiple-level supervision of enterprises; and the nature of control over the appointment of managers and Communist Party secretaries within enterprises.

Public ownership in China takes two general forms: the SOEs and the collectively-owned enterprises (COEs). In Chinese convention, SOEs are divided into subgroups with different administrative ranks – such as ministerial or provincial, prefectural, county – and subordinated to the various local levels of government accordingly. Theoretically, since property rights of all the SOEs belong to the central government, representing all the people of China, the lower level of local governments, considered as hierarchical levels, should be agents of the centre. In reality, however, the lower levels of government in China are much more than agents: they are principals as well. As for COEs, their property rights belong in theory to those employed in the enterprises. But the owners are actually and effectively the levels of local governments to which they are subordinated. Essentially, the similarities between SOEs and COEs outweigh their differences: they are all government property. The main differences between them are that (a) SOEs are usually subordinated to levels of government at and above county level, while COEs are subordinated to levels at and below the county, and (b) COEs are usually not subject to central planning and operate more within the market. Table 5.1 shows the ownership structure of industrial enterprises in China in 1987.

As shown in Table 5.1, over 80 per cent of industrial output in 1987 was produced by the enterprises which were subordinated to the government at one level or another. The number of industrial enterprises subordinate to the central government was very small indeed: 0.27 per cent even excluding privately owned enterprises. These enterprises accounted for only 15 per cent of total industrial output, compared with 68 per cent for enterprises subordinate to lower tiers of government. This is in sharp contrast to the former Soviet Union. Even bearing in mind that the local government was merely an agent of the

Table 5.1 Subordination structure of industrial enterprises (1987)

	Number (000s)	(%)	*Gross value of output* (¥ bn)	(%)
Total	7 473 877	(100.0)	1381.3	(100.0)
Of which subordinated to:				
• The central government	5 222	(0.07)	209.7	(15.2)
• Provincial, prefectural and city (higher than the county level) governments	44 580	(0.6)	502.0	(36.3)
• County governments	94 618	(1.3)	168.8	(12.2)
– the SOEs	47 796	(0.6)	113.3	(8.2)
– the COEs	46 822	(0.6)	55.5	(4.0)
• City subdistrict governments	39 127	(0.5)	25.5	(1.8)
• Township governments	237 912	(3.2)	128.4	(9.3)
• Village authorities	708 000	(9.4)	116.5	(8.4)
• Other types:				
– Cooperatives	719 200	(9.6)	33.1	(2.4)
– Privately-owned[a]	5 553 330	(74.3)	50.2	(3.6)
– Domestic joint ventures	2 878	(0.04)	18.1	(1.3)
– SOEs-COEs	1 864	•	14.0	(1.0)
– SOEs-private	415	•	3.4	(0.2)
– COEs-private	599	•	1.0	(0.1)
– International joint ventures	771	•	8.6	(0.6)
– Unclassified	68 239	(0.9)	174.6	(8.7)

Note: [a] Most of them were self-employed. As residuals. Sum of percentage might not equal 100 because of rounding.

Source: State Economic Commission; SSB (1989b: 3–4, 388–9).

central government, most of the net value of fixed assets of industrial enterprises (at least 68 per cent) were employed by enterprises supervised by the government at the level of the USSR, and only 12 per cent was employed by the enterprises supervised at the lower level. The other 19 per cent belonged to enterprises jointly supervised by separate republics and USSR governments (Uno, 1991).

The subordination relationship between an enterprise and a tier of government does not automatically imply that the local government has property rights over the enterprise. Apart from the reasons given by Granick (1990), there is another point overlooked by him but which is vital to the argument of property rights of local governments. Enterprises (SOEs or COEs) submit their profits not to the treasury of the central government but to the treasury of the tier of government to which they are subordinated. This was the case even during the period of the first Five-Year Plan (1952–7).[5] Despite frequent changes in the fiscal system in China, this feature remains unchanged.[6] This fact is

Table 5.2 Budget revenue and expenditures of local governments 1952–90 (¥ bn)

	Budget revenue (1)	*Budget expenditure (2)*	*Ratio (3) = (2)/(1)*
1952–57	74.0	34.8	0.47
1958–62	163.6	118.7	0.73
1963–65	87.9	48.6	0.55
1966–70	173.9	98.1	0.56
1971–75	334.3	179.4	0.54
1976–80	418.6	265.7	0.63
1981–85	474.3	355.7	0.75
1986–90	817.6	844.6	1.03

Source: SSB (1991a: 221).

actually consistent with standard property-rights theory which regards profits as the residual of revenue belonging to the owners. What complicates Chinese intra-governmental financial relationship is that a local government's revenue from enterprises under its control are mixed up with those accruing from fiscal redistributions. Because of fiscal redistribution, the size of the return on investment by a locality that can be retained by that locality depends ultimately on its overall fiscal position (this point is covered shortly.)

The distinction between local government revenue from its own enterprises and its revenues from fiscal redistribution is vital in understanding the dual economic function of Chinese local governments (i.e. as the providers of both 'private' and local 'public' goods).[7] Since local governments own the majority of enterprises, they *directly* control a large proportion of the government revenues. Table 5.2 shows that local governments collected more revenues than their expenditure during 1952–90, except for the period 1986–90 when their expenditures expanded more quickly than their revenues.

Table 5.2 shows that Chinese local government as a whole is generally a net financial contributor to the central government. This is in sharp contrast to most other countries, where local 'self-generated' revenues are significantly less than total local revenues, with grants from the central government making up the difference. Among twenty-five countries in the 1970s studied by the World Bank (1988b: 434), local governments' 'own' revenues accounted for 9.9 per cent of total local revenues in Indonesia (the lowest) and for 89.7 per cent in Peru (the highest). Generally, they were between 60 and 80 per cent. In nineteen OECD countries, central grants accounted for about 25–56 per cent of total revenues of local governments (Hughes and Smith, 1991). It is worth mentioning that the Chinese situation is not surprising. Historically, this is analogous to the tradition where a subordinated local state paid tribute to the emperor.

The fact that local governments were net revenue contributors to the central government in China is frequently misinterpreted as the heavy reliance upon local governments as agents of the central government in tax revenue collection; in other words, local governments collected most of the government revenues on behalf of the central government. For example, the World Bank observes that:

> almost all tax revenues in the system accrue to the central government, which then shares them with provincial-level governments. China differs from many other countries, however, in that the central government collects very few of its own taxes. Rather, reliance is placed on local government, typically county-level government, for the collection of all revenues other than customs duties and selected excises (The World Bank, 1988b: 429).

It needs to be emphasised that the property rights of local governments in China are not always clear-cut. The complexity and thus the ambiguity of the system stem from three sources. First, property rights in principle and in practice were very different. On one hand, as mentioned above, SOEs belonged to all the people of China; on the other hand, the property rights of both types of enterprise were distributed amongst different levels of government. This 'mismatching' enabled the higher-level government to change to some degree the subordination of the SOEs. This is called 'transferring an enterprise among different levels of government' (*Qiye Shangshou He Xiafang*). Nevertheless, the majority of enterprises and of production were always under local government control (as will be shown in Table 5.3 which indicates that proportion of industrial output by the centrally-controlled enterprises never exceed fifty per cent).

Another unique feature is that various elements of public property rights in China are unbundled and separately associated with different government departments or units. Property rights consist of:

(a) the right to determine how the assets of enterprises are used, i.e. what to produce and how, etc.;
(b) the right to receive the profits from the enterprises;

(c) the right to sell, trade, or transfer the assets to another party, or simply to liquidate the enterprises (the World Bank, 1988b: 93).

In China, no single government organ is empowered to exercise the full property rights of a public enterprise. Moreover, there is a professional supervisory function of a given government departments (e.g. pricing) at the different hierarchical levels (e.g. provincial and prefecture).

Finally, the government at one level was simultaneously (i) the agent of the higher one in the hierarchy, and (ii) the principal of enterprises (i.e. exercising property rights) under its control. As a result, macroeconomic policy and microeconomic management were to an extent blurred and became difficult to distinguish. This situation resembles a special game where the larger game sets the rules of the smaller one. Although the lower-level players do not act simply on behalf of the higher-level players, the latter have the power to modify institutional settings and rules to fit the smaller games (to an extent, including the subordination of their enterprises). In this sense, neither the centre-in-command, nor the cellular image of the system is accurate. This is described as 'a fragmented structure of authority' by Lieberthal and Oksenberg (1988: 22).[8] Figure 5.1 illustrates the Chinese economic management system, where dual lines indicate ownership and subordination; solid lines, management and coordination; and dotted lines, specialised professional guidance.

Historically, the system of '*Tongyi Jihua, Fenji Guanli*' (unified central planning, multi-level management) was formed during the first Five-Year Plan (1953–7) when China began to learn central planning from the Soviet Union. Russian advisers recommended to the Chinese leadership that all enterprises be placed directly under central management, but the Chinese leadership preferred less detailed planning and sharing economic management between central and local government.[9] Thus, in 1954 – the second year of the First Five-Year Plan – the total number of plans was reduced from 257 to 161 and plan targets (indicators) were reduced from 3381 to 2454. The central government was in charge of 112 plans together with 1804 plan quotas concerning mainly heavy industry and infrastructure construction, whereas the provincial governments were in charge of 49 plans together with 650 plan quotas concerning mainly agriculture, local industry, local transportation, education, etc. In 1957, the proportion of total industrial output produced by the industrial enterprises subordinated to the central government was only 39.7 per cent. In terms of allocation of the physical resources,

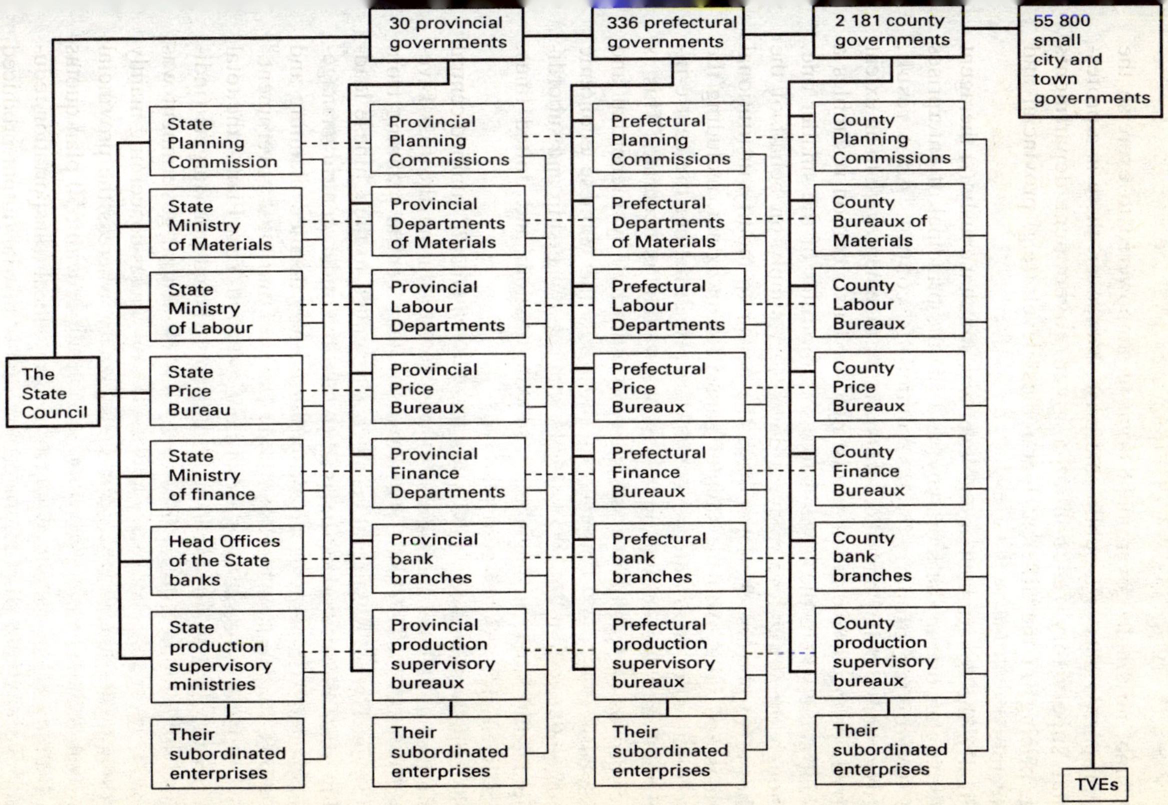

Figure 5.1 Multiple-level subordination and management of the government-owned enterprises (1989)

over 300 capital goods – or 60 per cent of total industrial output – were subject to central allocation through the State Planning Commission (Zhou, T. 1984: 70, 217–19). Compared with the former USSR – where the central planning agency, Gosplan, allocated the output of nearly 20 000 raw materials and central government ministries decided what happened to a further 50 000[10] – central planning in China was very limited, and the number of capital goods allocated by State Planning Commission and ministries never exceeded 869 before 1978.

The intellectual arguments against detailed Soviet-style central planning were twofold. First, China's economy was too large to be managed by a single power centre. It was impossible for the centre to coordinate economic activities efficiently. Second, central planning would suffer from incentive failure. According to Mao Zedong, 'two initiatives [the initiative of the central government and the initiative of local governments] are far better than one'.[11] In modern parlance, the problems of both information and incentive failure, as basic systemic problems associated with the economic system of the Soviet type were recognised. As a result, both the central government and the local levels of government were assigned the functions of entrepreneurs to grasp investment opportunities, mobilise resources, act as coordinating agents to explore opportunities and claim the residuals (i.e. profits). It was believed that sharing economic control between the central and local governments would enable China's economy to benefit from both centralised and decentralised government control.

The Chinese economic system has proved unstable in that there have been periodic cycles of centralisation–decentralisation cycles. Usually a distinction is made between administrative decentralisation and economic or market-oriented decentralisation. The former is defined as shifting the control over enterprises between central and local governments, while the latter is defined as decentralisation based on insulating enterprises from government intervention and on developing competitive market relations (e.g. Bernstein and Wu, cited in Wu, J. and Liu, J., 1991: 40–1). Decentralisation in China cannot be categorised fully by either definition. Although the locus of controlling power has been constantly swinging between central and local governments,[12] local governments are not only an agent of the centre but also a principal in their own right as well. Therefore, decentralisation in China has its own features reflecting the changes in the subordination of SOEs.[13] Table 5.3 shows the volatile changes in number and output of the industrial enterprises subordinated to the central government.

Table 5.3 Importance of the centrally-controlled industrial enterprises

	1957	*1958*	*1965*	*1972*	*1978*	*1987*
(1) Total number (000s)	169.5	263.0	157.7	219.6	348.4	1,920.8[a]
(2) Centrally subordinated ones	9 300	1 200	10 533	500	1 923	5 222
(3) Total output (¥ bn)	70.4	108.3	140.2	256.5	468.1	1 381.3
(4) Output of (2)	29.2	14.9	59.2	20.5	28.8	209.7
(5) =(2)/(1) (%)	5.49	0.46	6.68	0.22	0.55	0.27
(6) =(4)/(3) (%)	41.50	13.80	42.20	8.00	6.16	15.18

Note: (1): Excluding industrial enterprises at and below village levels due to unavailability of data for pre-1978.
[a] Total number excludes individual self-employed but includes industrial enterprises subordinated to villages as most of them emerged after 1978. (3) and (4): At current prices.

Source: SSB (1990c: 23–4, 34); Zhou, T. (1984: 70, 100, 137, 160); Lin (1990: 252, 254). Table 5.1.

As Table 5.3 indicates, there were two decentralisation drives prior to 1978. One was in the late 1950s and the other occurred in the early 1970s. The picture in 1987 is not as clear-cut because, unlike previously, the industrial boom after 1978 was mainly driven by local governments at and below county levels. Bearing in mind that the so-called SOEs are those that are subordinated to the county levels of government and above, the proportion of industrial output produced by the SOEs reflect the degree of decentralisation. This proportion declined from 77.6 per cent in 1978 to 59.7 and 54.6 per cent in 1987 and 1990 respectively (SSB, 1990c: 36; 1991a: 391). It is not in the scope of this study to examine the evolutionary processes in China's economic system in detail. What is important to the study is that, under such a system, neither policy rules in favour of central control nor those in favour of local control could generate lasting satisfaction.

As described in Chapter 2, the reforms in the 1980s emphasised that the most serious problem in the economic management system in China was the lack of the decision-making power of enterprises. Therefore, greater decision-making power was to be extended to enterprises as well as to local governments. The emphasis on enlarging enterprise autonomy, in addition to those of local governments, represented a major progress in Chinese reform policy. The reforms recognised in particular the need to separate government(s) at various levels from enterprises management, and to separate ownership from management, in order to give enterprises greater operational independence and make

Table 5.4 Approval limits for capital construction investment (¥ mn)

	State Planning Commission	*Provincial authorities*
Before 1984	Over 10	Below 10
Beginning 1985	Over 30	Below 30
March 1987	Over 50	Below 30
March 1987 (power, transportation and raw materials)	Over 50	Below 50

Source: State Planning Commission.

Table 5.5 Approval limits for fixed investment (Jan. 1985 – Mar. 1987) (¥ mn)

Level of government	*Capital construction*	*Technical updating*
Counties	1–5, a few 10	0.5–1
Reform-experiment-counties	5–10	0.5–2
Prefectures, cities, and provincial bureaux	5–10, some 30	3–5, some 10
Cities directly under provinces	10–30	10
Province-level cities	>30	>10

Source: Zhang S. *et al.* (1987a).

them responsible for own profits and losses. But the critical issue of property rights and how they were to be exercised was left unaddressed because of their ideological sensitivity. In practice, the so-called 'basic accounting units' (*Jiben Hesuan Danwei*)[14] under the traditional economic system were regarded as enterprises, and their autonomy was increased accordingly. Up to 1988, the State Council issued thirteen documents with ninety seven specific provisions to extend the autonomy of the enterprises. In general, autonomy of the enterprise director in production, trade, price setting, wages, recruitment, and use of retained bonus and welfare funds was increased considerably.[15]

Since the property rights of enterprises *had* to be exercised somehow, local governments actually gained most of the strategic decision-making powers of enterprises during the 'enterprise-centred' decentralisation reforms. They controlled essential business decisions such as investment,[16] appointment or dismissal of managers, profit distribution, mergers, takeovers, liquidation etc. As Byrd (1991) notes, during the reforms enterprises may have gained greater bargaining power but within an essentially unchanged and largely hierarchical supervisory system. Paradoxically, many traditional measures of decentralisation aimed at increasing the autonomy of local governments still dominated the process of reform. Tables 5.4 and 5.5 report the decentralised power of investment approval, and its hierarchical structure. The change in the investment approval power of the local authorities below provincial level is in line with that reflected in Table 5.4.

5.2 INCENTIVE INCOMPATIBILITY AND INVESTMENT BEHAVIOUR

5.2.1 Theories of incentive compatibility

Traditionally, government is studied by political science while economics studies human behaviour only in the market-place. Where the role of government is considered in economics, it is usually in the context of 'market failure' involving, for instance, the provision of public goods or income distribution. As a relatively new development, the theory of 'public choice' believes that the government can provide the solution to some problems but is the source of others. Defined as the economic study of non-market decision-making, public choice deals with the behaviour of man as both a political and an economic being. It makes the same behavioural assumptions for government, or more precisely for politicians and bureaucrats, as generally assumed in economics (rational, utilitarian individuals) and asks the same questions as traditional price theory (Do equilibria exist? Are they stable? Pareto efficient?). Furthermore, it depicts the preference revelation process as analogous to the market: voters engage in exchange, individuals reveal their demand schedules via voting, citizens exiting and entering clubs, etc. (Mueller, 1989: 3–4). The methodology that makes this analogy between the state and a person or between the state and a market is appealing; however, the analytical focus is generally placed on the state as a whole. The central–local government relationship with respect to administration is therefore studied as a case of the general principal–agent problem. Indeed, there have been inadequate attempts in Western economic theory to apply general decentralisation and control theory to the behaviour of local governments.

For the purpose of this study, another theory of interest is perhaps 'fiscal federalism'. Fiscal federalism originated from countries committed to political federalism such as the USA, Canada, Austria and Switzerland. In the literature, the classical federalist system is one in which local governments are concerned primarily with the efficient matching of local public expenditures to the preferences and needs of their population (Teibout, 1956). These recent studies are also restricted to issues of consumption of public goods supplied by local government, taxation and grants from central government (e.g. Oates, 1972; Topham, 1983; Hughes, 1987). In general, the benefits of fiscal decentralisation are that decisions of local governments may better reflect the preference of the local residents, and are therefore better positioned to gain information and control. The cost, however, is related to the inter-jurisdictional externalities or spillovers from certain local government actions. In terms of the macroeconomic stabilisation function of government, the consensus is that this should be assigned to the national government. Increasing international economic integration has even pushed the focus of macro policy on to an international level, for instance, the European Economic Community (Hughes and Smith, 1991). Overall, there is no *a priori* correct answer to the question of the optimal degree of decentralisation – it depends on the goods and services provided by local governments (Helm and Smith, 1987). It is worth noting that Breton (1985) formulates the term 'competitive federalism' and distinguishes 'horizontal' competition between governments on the same level of jurisdiction from 'vertical' competition between governments on different levels.

In a broad sense, the perceptions of public choice theories and the general discussion of the merits and demerits of fiscal decentralisation may shed useful lights on issues of central–local relations. However, because of the different nature of local governments in the West, the issue of profit-oriented investment by local governments has not arisen. Hence, there is little of direct relevance to China.

To establish an analytical framework, we turn to the incentive problem of an organisation. An economic organisation can broadly be viewed as a mechanism where economic decisions are determined as a function of information known by the self-interested individuals in the economy. There are two general problems in organisation- or mechanism-design:

(i) choosing the degree of decentralisation of decision making;
(ii) choosing the operating rules or instructions to motivate individual decision-makers to act in the interests of the organisation as a

whole, i.e. some form of incentive, either reward or punishment (Friedman, 1985: chapter 15; Marschak, 1989).

The necessity of decentralisation lies in the fact that perfect information is not available for decision-making. Since even imperfect information is costly to produce and to communicate, there are often important economies to be gained by breaking-up the problems into pieces and assigning particular subgroups to be responsible for each piece. Assuming that there is some division of knowledge, it is generally agreed that responsibility should be allocated to the person most appropriate. The decentralisation of decision-making, however, creates problems in organisational control when the participating individuals do not necessarily have identical interests. The issue of incentive is important. It is worth noting that in the debate between Lange-Lerner and Hayek over the possibility of socialism in the 1930s,[17] apart from the practical impossibility of perfect information, the incentive side of socialism was also challenged by Hayek (1935, 219–20).

The fundamental insight of mechanism theory is that incentive constraints should be considered equally with resource constraints and thus information constraints in the formulation of the economic problem. It is widely accepted that any institution, or rule designed to achieve the goals of an organisation, must be *incentive compatible* if it is to perform as desired. Incentive compatibility was introduced by Hurwicz (1972) to characterise those mechanisms for which participants in the process would not find it advantageous to violate the rules of the process. Incentive compatibility is also the basis of the modern theory of implementation. The basic idea is simple: the rule is implementable if, and only if, there is an incentive compatible mechanism, under which it is in the individuals' self-interest to follow the rule (Ledyard, 1989; Myerson, 1989).

With respect to both information and incentives, Radner (1989) summarises two sources of loss of efficiency concerning decentralised organisations:

(i) decentralisation of information, having the effect that individual actions will be based on information that is less complete than information jointly available to the organisation as a whole;
(ii) conflicts of interest and beliefs amongst decision-makers, leading to distortion of information and action.

For the purpose of this chapter, the focus is on the second source, particularly concerning the conflicts of interests or incompatible incentives among decision-makers. Since the period studied here is limited to 1978–90, the focus is on decentralisation and the problem of incentive incompatibility. The proposition is that given the property rights of the local governments, the drive towards decentralisation tends to generate misallocation of resources as a result of incompatible incentives between central and local governments as well as within local governments.

5.2.2 Local border-constrained investment

The basic problem in investment is how to allocate scarce resources amongst competing demands. Only when resources are allocated to their highest valued uses can economic output be maximised, in which case the allocation of resources is said to be 'Pareto efficient.' In the context of incentive theory, an efficient mechanism for resource allocation has to be incentive-compatible – namely, individual investors must have a common incentive to allocate resources to their highest valued uses – and to each of the investors, the measurement of value is the same.

In decentralised management of investment, the centre determines the rules under which local governments make their own investment decisions. The mechanism is as follows:

$$\text{Centre} \xrightarrow{V_c} \text{Local governments} \xrightarrow{V_p} \text{Investment Pattern}$$

where V_c is the set of decentralisation rules given by the centre, and V_p is the investment behaviour of the local government, given V_c.

Local governments in China are investors with unique characteristics. They are not only economic but also political and social entities. They are different from subnational governments or local authorities in market economies whose general functions are to provide public services and conduct redistributive activities such as education, social welfare, social housing, health care, etc. They are also different from individual investors in a market economy whose investment decisions are based basically on profit maximisation (i.e. maximisation of the present value of the profit stream generated by investment). Concerning the latter case, the difference in China is twofold. First, Chinese local governments are interested not only in profits, but also in other returns generated by investment such as taxes, employment and growth performance. Second, their concern is generally region-bounded, subject to the promotion mechanism and the design of success indicators. In other words, local governments have every incentive to enlarge their industrial base in order to generate more revenue and wealth, more employment in the regions under their jurisdiction,[18] and to profile their regions as high-growth performers.[19] The latter point merits attention because it is very important to local officials. Since leaders of local governments in China are appointed by higher levels of the government, the political career of local officials depends only on their immediate superiors. The higher-level government needs to monitor its subordinates but the monitoring is subject to the problem of asymmetric information. In order to ameliorate the monopoly of information possessed by lower government levels, the higher government levels seek independent 'yardstick' information (Schleifer, 1985). This is provided by comparing performance between local governments. The local governments maximise their utility (U):

$$\text{Max}_{\{Ps,\ Ts,\ Es\}}\ U = \alpha_1 P_s + \alpha_2 T_s + \alpha_3 E_s \tag{4.1}$$

S.T. V_c and availability of investment funds,

where P stands for profits, T for taxes and E for employment; α_i ($i > 0$; $\Sigma i = 1$; i = 1, 2, 3) are weights; the lower case letter s indicates the locality.

The point is that the utility of local governments is not profit maximisation of the project in question, but the maximisation of the sum of profits and taxes generated by, and the local employment related to, the project. The investment criterion is based on the same considerations. The lower the level of local governments, the narrower the local concern. The rationality of investment behaviour (V_p) is therefore *local utility-constrained* rather than profit-oriented. Since local governments' revenues come mainly from indirect taxes (which were the dominant source of local revenues, as will be discussed in section 5.3), and their social concerns are local border-bounded, they generally tended to invest within their own regions. That is: their investment is generally *local border-constrained*. A very simple comparison would suffice to demonstrate this point.

The contribution or return on investment in its own region to the utility of a local government (R_s) is the sum of P, T and E generated in its own region:

$$R_s = \alpha_1 P_s + \alpha_2 T_s + \alpha_3 E_s \tag{4.2}$$

while the return of investment in other regions (R_0) is merely profit because the T and E of other regions do not enter the utility function of the local government in question, or $\alpha_2 = \alpha_3 = 0$

$$R_0 = \alpha_4 P_0 \tag{4.3}$$

Since $R_s > R_0$, investment in one's own region is preferable compared with that in other regions, unless

$$\alpha_4 P_0 > \alpha_1 P_s + \alpha_2 T_s + \alpha_3 E_s \tag{4.4}$$

It is hardly surprising that the behaviour of local governments might be counter to national interest. Of course, China is an enormous country where provinces are usually larger, in terms of size and population, than a European country. However, decentralisation beyond the provincial level would jeopardise economic integration since the thirty provinces are subordinated by 336 prefectures, 2181 counties and 55 800 small cities and towns (1989 figures).

Aside from generating government tax revenues, investment generally affects employment and growth positively. Hence, there was a strong incentive for local governments to invest within their own regions. It is clear that the incentives of local governments in investment and those of the central government were incompatible. It may not be in the best interests of local governments to allocate resources according to centrally determined priorities because the latter were not territory-bounded. This confirms the view that inefficient allocation of resources is a property of the mechanism rather than an outcome (Holmstrom and Myerson, 1983).

5.3 FISCAL FACTORS IN INCENTIVE COMPATIBILITY

Where revenues are concerned, the utility difference between investing in one's own region and in other regions primarily depended on tax return. If all tax revenue belonged to the central government, or if tax revenue was of minor importance to local government's finance, then the geographical location of investment would be less important. However, the Chinese fiscal system was designed in such a way that:

(i) government revenue at every level was dominated by indirect taxes;
(ii) fiscal redistribution and investment return were not distinguished,

such that investment in regions with lower return was not penalised;
(iii) enterprise income tax rates were enormously in favour of small-scale investment (to ease the unemployment problem).

As a result, the fiscal system and policies encouraged rather than discouraged local border-constrained investment and local protectionism.

Government revenues from indirect taxes are important to government finance at every level. For instance, at the national level, the sum of construction tax, product tax, sales tax and VAT accounted for 54.7 per cent of total government budgetary revenues in 1988 (excluding income tax and debt revenue).[20] At the local level, the importance of industrial and commercial taxes was greater. Although column (4) in Table 5.6 is not an accurate calculation, it is sufficient to show the dominance of indirect taxes (industrial and commercial taxes) in revenues collected by provincial governments.

The heavy reliance of local government finance on indirect tax revenue means that where indirect taxes generated by investment were significant, the profitability of the investment became less important to local governments. In other words, local governments would tend to invest in projects with high tax rates despite their low profitability. This was evident in the discussion of the investment pattern of local governments in section 4.1. The absolute dominance of indirect taxes in the budgetary revenue of local governments strongly consolidated border-constrained investment behaviour.

Using the sum of profit and tax to evaluate the financial performance of an enterprise (either State- or collectively-owned) was a common practice in China. In industry, for example, there were six financial indicators relating to the sum of profit and tax (P + T): 1. P + T, 2. P + T as percentage of fixed assets, 3. P + T as percentage of total capital (funds) employed, 4. P + T as percentage of total gross output, 5. P + T per employee and 6. P + T remitted per employee.

However, there were only 2 indicators relating to profit alone: total profits and profit/sales rates.[21]

The second fiscal factor, fiscal redistribution, also encourages local border-constrained investment behaviour of local governments. In parallel with the attempt to increase enterprise autonomy, reforms in the 1980s extended greater financial autonomy to lower levels of local governments. Among the most important policies were the fiscal revenue-sharing schemes between neighbouring levels of the government, introduced in 1980. In order to provide the lower levels of government with stronger incentives to generate and collect more revenues,

Table 5.6 Importance of industrial and commercial tax revenue to the revenue of provincial governments (1987) (¥ bn)

Province	*Total revenues (1)*	*Loss subsidies (2)*	*ICT (3)*	*(4)=(3)/(1)*
Beijing	6.36	1.25	5.48	0.86
Tianjin	5.59	0.51	4.21	0.75
Hebei	5.76	0.54	4.79	0.83
Shanxi	3.36	0.34	2.88	0.86
Liaoning	10.80	1.48	9.10	0.84
Heilongjiang	5.38	1.39	5.53	1.03
Jiansu	10.72	0.95	9.12	0.85
Shanghai	16.51	0.59	11.31	0.69
Zhejiang	7.64	0.47	6.31	0.83
Anhui	3.88	0.47	3.38	0.87
Shangdong	7.28	0.72	6.23	0.86
Henan	6.32	0.35	5.35	0.85
Hubei	6.54	0.69	5.47	0.84
Hunan	5.44	0.39	4.52	0.83
Sichuan	7.59	0.89	6.40	0.84
Fujian	3.32	0.46	2.66	0.80
Guangdong	9.59	1.04	8.86	0.92
Jilin	3.76	0.70	3.03	0.81
Jiangxi	2.82	0.23	2.18	0.77
Shaangxi	3.36	0.34	2.88	0.86
Gansu	2.56	0.16	1.90	0.74
Inner Mongolia	1.94	0.46	1.77	0.91
Guangxi	3.05	0.35	2.45	0.80
Guizhou	2.15	0.25	1.94	0.90
Yunnan	3.75	0.50	3.52	0.94
Xizang	−0.004	0.10	0.043	−10.75
Qinghai	0.40	0.15	0.40	1.00
Ningxia	0.41	0.07	0.34	0.98
Xinjiang	1.16	0.34	1.16	1.00

Note: Total revenue is the revenue collected by the provincial governments (excluding loss subsidies to the SOEs). The amount allowed to be retained by each province varies (see Tables 5.11 and 5.12). ICT (industrial and commercial taxes) includes income tax levied on the non-SOEs and the self-employed businesses (¥10.50 bn). The sum of local figures does not come to the national figure because central government-owned enterprises are not included.

Source: General Planning Department of MOF (1989: 41, 54).

these fixed an amount or a proportion of revenues to be collected by subordinate levels and remitted to the higher level government for five years. Any amount collected above the fixed amount could be retained by the locality as an incentive. This kind of fiscal relationship between the central and local governments based on negotiation, resembles 'tax farming', which was the means by which medieval kings collected revenues in Europe.[22] The fiscal revenue-sharing scheme

Table 5.7 Revenue-sharing between the central and provincial governments set for 1985–90[23]

Province	*Retention ratio of the budget revenue collected (%)*	*Amount transfer to or from (−) the centre (¥ mn)*	*Extra-budget revenue as % of the budget revenue (1987)*
Beijing	48.2		93.8
Tianjin	39.5		68.5
Hebei	69.0		89.2
Shanxi	97.5		100.9
Liaoning	51.1		95.9
Heilongjiang	96.0		85.1
Jiangsu	39.0		78.0
Shanghai	26.0		58.6
Zhejiang	55.0		75.1
Anhui	80.1		79.5
Shandong	59.0		96.7
Henan	81.0		59.7
Hubei	66.5		67.9
Hunan	88.0		84.4
Sichuan	89.0		94.5
		(¥ mn)	
Fujian		235	79.5
Guangdong		772	70.1
Jilin		−397	111.7
Jiangxi		−239	94.0
Shaanxi		−270	100.9
Gansu		−246	83.2
	Fixed rate of annual increase in transfer *from the centre (10%) (Base year figure)*		
Inner Mongolia		−1783	128.9
Guangxi		−716	93.1
Guizhou		−743	68.4
Yunnan		−637	76.5
Xizang		−750	−3550.0[a]
Qinghai		−611	155.0
Ningxia		−494	117.1
Xinjiang		−1450	113.8

Note: [a] Budget revenue was −¥4 million and the extra-budget revenue was ¥142 mn.

Source: The MOF.

Table 5.8 Revenue-sharing between the central and local governments revised for 1988–90

Province or city	*Guaranteed revenue growth*[a] *(%)*	*Retention ratio of the budget revenue collected (%)*	*Amount transfer to or from (−) the centre (¥ mn)*
Beijing	4.0	50.00	
Hebei	4.5	70.00	
Liaoning	3.5	58.25	
Shenyang	4.0	30.29	
Harbin	5.0	45.00	
Jiangsu	5.0	41.00	
Zhejiang	6.5	61.47	
Ningbo	5.3	27.93	
Henan	5.0	80.00	
Chongqing	4.0	33.50	
Tianjin		46.50	
Shanxi		87.55	
Anhui		77.50	
Dalian		27.74 (27.26)	
Qingdao		16.00 (34.00)	
Wuhan		17.00 (25.00)	
Guangdong			1413 and 9% annual growth
Hunan			800 and 7% annual growth
Shanghai			10 500
Shandong			289
Heilongjiang			299
Jilin			−107
Jiangxi			−45
Shaanxi			−120
Gansu			n.a.
Inner Mongolia			−1842
Guangxi			−608
Guizhou			−742
Yunnan			−673
Xizang			−898
Qinghai			−656
Ningxia			−533
Xinjiang			−1529
Fujian			−50 (from 1989)
Hainan			−138
Hubei			−4.78% from Wuhan
Sichuan			−10.70% from Chongqing

Note: [a] The revenue growth is guaranteed in the sense that the regions have to make up the loss in case of a shortfall. Figures in brackets are the retention ratios of the increased revenue.

Source: The MOF.

between the lower levels of governments was designed in a similar spirit. This basic feature has remained unchanged since 1980 despite some minor modifications. Table 5.7 reports the revenue-sharing schemes between the central and local governments set in 1984 for the period 1985–90. Partly because of the newly gained fiscal independence of some cities from their provinces, the revenue-sharing schemes were revised in 1987 for 1988–90 (Table 5.8).

The schemes are self-explanatory. Looking at Table 5.7, seventeen provinces transfer part of the revenues they collected to the centre, while the other twelve received subsidies from the centre. In terms of the intra-governmental finance, this scheme was not extraordinary. Revenue-sharing is the mechanism used by central government to encourage local governments to collect revenue and to generate local governments' revenues consistent with their expenditure responsibilities. For the latter objective, there are usually two adjustment mechanisms employed:

(i) correcting 'vertical' imbalances, the misalignment of expenditure responsibility and tax capacity among levels of government;
(ii) reducing geographical or 'horizontal' imbalances between rich and poor regions to permit a more equal level of expenditure amongst them (The World Bank, 1988b: 430–38).

Under the Chinese economic system, however, since local governments controlled the bulk of investment these schemes would affect investment behaviour.

As we have seen, under the Chinese economic system local governments have a strong incentive to invest in their own regions because this generates not only profit in general but also tax revenue and employment for that region. Such incentives would be weaker if the revenues at the local governments' disposal were subject to arbitrary annual change by the higher level government, as was generally the case prior to 1980. By fixing the bilateral revenue transfers for five years, the fiscal revenue schemes strengthened the border-bounded investment behaviour at the lower levels of government.

Furthermore, by allowing the backward regions to hand a smaller (even negative) proportion of their revenue to the higher levels of government – equivalent to lower tax rates or subsidies on investment projects in these regions – the fiscal revenue schemes further protected and encouraged inefficient investment (with low profitability) in these regions.

Table 5.9 Actual return of investment to local government

		Region A	Region B
(I)	Investor region A	$(P_a + T_a)R_a + E_a$	P_bR_b
	Investor region B	P_aR_a	$(P_b + T_b)R_b + E_b$
(II)	Investor region A	$(P_a + T_a)R_a + E_a$	P_bR_a
	Investor region B	P_aR_b	$(P_b+T_b)R_b + E_b$

Note: Lower case letter 'a' indicates region A and 'b' region B. R is the revenue (P + T) retention ratio, $R_a<1$ and $R_b=1$. The difference between cases (I) and (II) is that in (I) profit tax is levied on enterprises by the local tax authority, whereas in (II) profit from investment is distributed amongst investors first, and profit tax is then levied by their own tax authorities independently. The policy was introduced in 1986. It is assumed that the same weights are attached to each component).

As far as inter-local flow of investment is concerned, the effects of the fiscal revenue-sharing schemes were a little more complex. To simplify the analysis, the central-provincial fiscal-sharing scheme is taken as an example and all seventeen remitting provinces are grouped as 'A' and the other twelve subsidised provinces as 'B'. The returns on investment in different regions are given in Table 5.9.

In Table 5.9, case (I), the condition for region A to invest in region B is

$$P_bR_b - (P_a + T_a)R_a - E_a > 0 \tag{4.5}$$

and the condition for region B to invest in region A is

$$P_aR_a - (P_b + T_b)R_b - E_b > 0 \tag{4.6}$$

Since $R_a < 1$ and $R_b = 1$, compared with the condition for investing in other regions

$$P_0 - (P + T + E)_s > 0 \tag{4.7}$$

the required profitability differential of the investment project needed for investment to flow from region A to region B decreases, but that for investment flow from region B into A increases, under the fiscal revenue-sharing scheme. Since it is generally true that profitability in A is higher than that in B, the fiscal revenue-sharing system discourages investment moving into the regions where it is most highly valued.

In case (II), the condition for region A to invest in region B is:

$$P_bR_a - (P_a + T_a)R_a - E_a > 0 \tag{4.8}$$

and the condition for region B to invest in region A is:

$$P_aR_b - (P_b + T_b)R_b - E_b > 0 \tag{4.9}$$

Compared with the condition [4.4], again the required profitability differential of the investment project increases for investment flow from region A into region B (i.e. inequality [4.8]), but remains the same for investment flow from region B into A (i.e. inequality [4.9] where R_b = 1) under the fiscal revenue-sharing scheme. Assuming $P_a > P_b$ in general, the scheme seems to encourage the movement of investment to the regions where it *is* most highly valued. However, since tax and employment considerations still favour local investment, the effect is marginal. Overall, the fiscal revenue-sharing schemes tends to encourage local border-bounded investment behaviour in local governments.

Local governments were further encouraged to invest on a small scale by the preferential income-tax treatments for small enterprises.[24] This policy was designed to promote small businesses so as to help to absorb the huge labour surplus in China's economy. Table 5.10 lists the eight ranges of tax rates applying to small-size SOEs and COEs in urban areas. The large difference in tax rates clearly favoured small businesses and thus small-scale investment.

According to an official of the Tax Bureau of Anhui province (Hu, L., 1988), large and medium-sized SOEs paid corporate income tax at the average rate of 55 per cent in 1987, whereas small-sized SOEs paid only 31 per cent. Compared with the COEs, SOEs paid a significantly higher rate (see Table 5.11).

The TVEs in the rural areas received even better treatment. Table 5.12 shows that income tax on township and village enterprises (TVEs) in Jiangsu province, where the TVEs were most prolific, was levied at very low rates (below 15 per cent). This enabled small enterprises, usually poorly equipped, to sell goods relatively cheaply.

It is worth mentioning that incentive incompatibility related to local government ownership and fiscal factors contributed to the persistence of the well-known phenomena such as soft budget constraints or non-bankruptcy of enterprises and soft credit during reform.[25] First, it is economically rational for local governments to subsidise the 'loss-making' enterprises, if the subsidies are smaller than tax revenues from them.

Table 5.10 Income-tax rates for small firms[a]

Profit (¥ 000s)	*Old rates* (%)	*Profit* (¥ 000s)	*New rates*
<0.3	7	<1.0	10
0.3–0.6	10	1.0–3.5	20
0.6–1.0	20	3.5–10.0	28
1.0–2.5	30	10.0–25.0	35
2.5–10.0	35	25.0–50.0	42
10.0–30.0	40	50.0–100.0	48
30.0–80.0	50	100.0–200.0	53
>80.0	55	>200.0	55

Note: [a] To be qualified as small SOEs, the industrial SOEs must simultaneously satisfy two conditions: (i) the historical value of fixed assets to be no more than ¥3 mn and the annual profits to be no more than ¥0.3 mn (¥4 mn and ¥0.4 mn respectively for those in Beijing, Tianjin and Shanghai). New rates applied to small SOEs after October 1, 1984 and to the COEs after January 1, 1985.

Source: MOF.

Table 5.11 Corporate income tax rates (%) in Anhui province (1987)

	Industry	*Commerce*	*Transportation*
SOEs	40.6	46.6	36.7
COEs	24.7	37.7	22.1

Source: Hu, L. (1988).

Table 5.12 Income tax on TVEs in Jiangsu province

	1980	*1983*	*1985*	*1986*	*1987*	*1988*
Profits (¥ mn)	2330	2982	4840	4254	4975	7582
Income tax (¥ mn)	242	366	595	597	706	944
Tax rate (%)	10.55	12.66	12.29	14.03	14.13	12.45

Source: *Reference Materials of Financial Studies*, no. 6, 1990, p. 5.

Second, under the fiscal contract system, fiscal transfers amongst local governments are recalculated every 3–5 years. So there are sufficient incentives to keep loss-making enterprises alive, even if the 'net' revenue (sum of tax revenues and subsidies) from them is negative.

Finally, the profits of the banking sector go to the central budget. It is beneficial for local governments to use bank credit to finance their enterprises' losses. These bad debts actually represent a financial loss to the central government and simultaneously a financial gain to local governments.

In summary, under the decentralised Chinese economic system based on local government ownership, local governments were able and motivated to invest primarily

(i) to increase production capacity in the existing manufacturing sector within their own regions (if the regions were 'resource-rich');
(ii) establish new manufacturing industries in their own regions to substitute for imports, from both abroad and other regions.

The central government's investment priority in technical updating and transformation of existing enterprises, and in transportation and communication, was neglected.

6 The Banking System and its Operation

This chapter examines the banking system and the related operations of credit control. It shows (i) that the banking system was designed as an integral part of the economic system and therefore had similar problem of incentive incompatibility, and (ii) that financial reform, whilst weakening central control, failed to change the fundamental design of the banking system. As a result of these characteristics, local governments gained a stronger influence over credit policy operations of local bank branches despite central government retention of control of the central bank and head offices of the specialised banks. The banking system effectively facilitated the interactive process of central and local investment. The chapter first examines the design of the banking system and the impact of financial reform. It then scrutinises in detail the banks' operations in credit allocation, including the regional allocation of credit, its screening and monitoring.

6.1 DESIGN OF THE BANKING SYSTEM PRE- AND POST-1978

Before 1978, the Chinese financial system was a monobank system, modelled after that of the former Soviet Union. The People's Bank of China (PBC) had a monopoly on currency issuance, transaction clearing, saving collection and lending for working capital investment. In 1950, it was authorised as the 'centre of cash, clearing and credit' to 'support the proportionate development of the national economy and to serve socialist construction.' (Yang, P., 1984: 425).

Except for the government-owned insurance company which ceased domestic business in 1958, virtually no other national and comprehensive banking institution existed between 1957 and 1978.[1] The Agricultural Bank of China (ABC) existed intermittently as a lender to the rural sector and as a supervisor of Rural Credit Cooperatives (RCCs). Foreign-exchange-related operations were handled by the Bank of China (BOC) which was a subsidiary of the PBC. In addition, the People's Construction Bank of China (PCBC) acted as a fiscal agent for budgetary transfer to enterprises in support of capital construction investment.

Banking in rural areas was handled by RCCs, which were the grass-roots units of the state bank.[2] Non-bank financial institutions and markets were non-existent, with the exception of limited international insurance services provided by the People's Insurance Company of China (PICC). Inter-firm finance was also absolutely prohibited.

The monobank system was directly controlled by the government. The PBC, or more exactly, its head office, was responsible for operational management of the whole banking sector including the implementation of monetary policy. Policy decisions however, were made by the State Council. The PBC was not treated as an enterprise but as a government department. Its financial outcome was an implicit part of the state budget. For example, in 1962, 20 per cent of the working capital quota provided by the bank was transferred into the self-funds of enterprises with no compensation to the bank (Yu, R., 1987: 85). Taking agricultural credit as another example, the total credit extended by the PBC and RCCs by the end of 1978 was ¥110 billion, of which ¥90.01 billion had been repaid. Of the ¥19.9 billion unrepaid loans, ¥5.2 billion that had been extended before 1961 was by 1981 exempted and about 70 per cent of the outstanding debt was overdue (CEM: 419). For each local branch, its profits and losses were internalised within the whole banking sector. Furthermore, there was no competition and no prudential regulations (such as capital adequacy, reserve requirement, liquidity, etc.).

The conventional view of the bank's role in China in pre-1978 was merely that of a passive or accommodating instrument of central planning. For instance, White and Bowles (1988: 28) claim that 'Under the old system, the banks were passive, administrative units with the major economic decisions being made by the planning ministries under the State Council.' The comment by Yang, P. (1984: 414) is more straightforward: 'Under the influence of the Soviet model, the bank became nothing but a bookkeeper, cashier and mint-master.' These views, though correct in the sense that the bank is an adjunct to central planning, are oversimplified.

Hsiao (1982) recognises that in performing financial surveillance functions, the bank's position fluctuated over time. It was stronger during periods of economic consolidation. In other periods, 'the bank became a captive of the state enterprises and turned into a limitless supplier of funds instead'. The fluctuating position of the PBC depended on development policy priorities and in particular on methods of financing increases in production in a given period. Liu, Hongru (1987: 9), the former deputy governor of the PBC, stated:

> There has been an abnormal practice that when the economy develops in an orderly manner, the role of the bank is weakened to that of accountant and cashier in order to secure supply of funds or somewhat as supervisor; only when the economy is in disorder and requires dramatic readjustment, does the bank demonstrate its position as monitor [regulator], playing an active part in economic adjustment.

The picture provided by Hsiao and Liu is closer to reality. But they assume, as do many others, that because the bank was entirely subservient to central government there was perfect and total control of local bank branches. The issue of incentives and behaviour of local bank branches was therefore overlooked.

The design of the banking system in China was integral to the design of the whole economic system which allowed local governments to control the local economies. In this design, banks were treated essentially as departments of government on a parallel relationship: the head office of a bank was aligned with the central government department; the provincial bank branch aligned with a provincial government department, and so on. The geographic scope of the financial intermediation function of banks was effectively restricted by the administrative border of government jurisdiction.

The role of local bank branches and the leadership of the local governments over these branches were emphasised from the beginning of economic planning in China. The first formal document of credit planning, 'Comprehensive Credit Planning Method of the People's Bank of China (draft)' (1952) stipulates that the bank county branches were the basic units (*Jiceng Danwei*) and the provincial branches, the intermediate units (*Huangjie Danwei*) (Yang Z. *et al.*, 1985: 36). It was stipulated in 1954 that 'The PBC is under the leadership of the central committee of the Communist Party and the local Party commissions' (CEM: 54). From 1958 until 1979, the local Party and government were in charge of appointment, dismissal, transfer, and promotion of bank personnel in places under their jurisdiction (Byrd, 1983: 12). In the practice of credit control, even during the first Five-Year Plan (1952–7) when economic management was most centralised, a separate credit quota was planned for all the local-government-run enterprises, and this was treated as a separate sector.[3] The provincial branches were allowed to use part of the credit quota reserve and the increased urban household savings above the planned quota (target) were allowed to be added to credit quotas for the local sector (for a brief review of credit management in the period 1952–78, see Appendix, A3).

The subordination of local bank branches to local governments was also reflected in the local monopoly of bank branches. These had the exclusive right to collect deposits within the localities and they only lent to firms within the localities. In this respect, the Chinese banking system was analogous to the previous American one under which monetary union was accompanied by *geographical restrictions* on interstate banking. In the USA, fragmented banking is associated with the American federal political system. Each state regulates its own state banks, and national banks are regulated under the National Bank Act of 1863. Until the 1980s, most states protected local bankers from out-of-state entry. Together with the prohibition of bank ownership of stocks (the well-known Glass–Steagall Act of 1933), this may be one reasons why banks play a less important role in industrial financing and management monitoring in the USA than in the majority of other developed economies. The US system is increasingly recognised as a mistake (Roe M., 1990; Masera and Portes, 1991).

The bank's position in China's bureaucratic hierarchy was quite weak. Unlike Gosbank, which was a ministry under the Council of Ministers in the former USSR, the PBC had an administrative rank lower than a ministry. Accordingly, the official rank of the director of a local bank branch was lower than the local government treasurer. Even so, the bank branches (even their head office) lost organisational independence from time to time. During 1958–62, all local bank branches were merged with the local treasuries; during 1968–77, the whole banking sector became part of the treasuries at various levels. (The PBC head office became a department under the Ministry of Finance of the central government, [Yu R., 1987: 2]). In this respect, China's banking system was more like that in the former Yugoslavia where six republics and two autonomous provinces had decisive control over the regional banks. The central control of the banking system in the former Yugoslavia was very weak. The central bank was not authorised or empowered to control other banks until the early 1970s. After that, monetary policy-making was still not centralised, for policy formation had to be based on the consensus of the eight People's Banks of the republics and autonomous provinces.[4]

In short, the banking system in China was under the dual control of the central and local governments. Although the degree of centralisation or decentralisation varied from time to time, this essential feature remained. Figure 6.1 demonstrates the institutional structure of the PBC in 1979.[5]

Within such a design, a local bank branch was the agent of both the

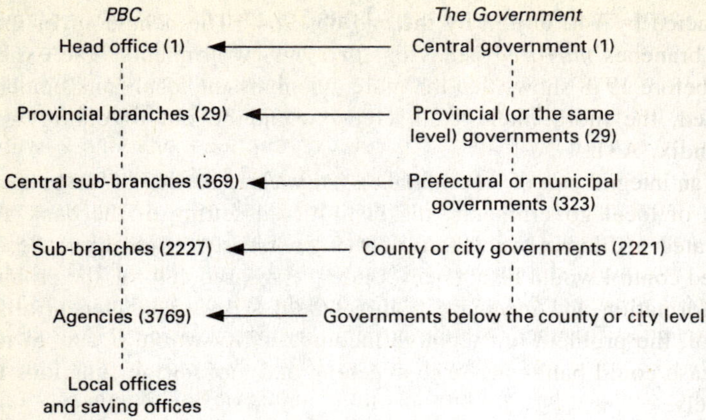

Figure 6.1 Institutional structure of the PBC (1979)

higher-level bank branch and the local government. The behaviour and interests of the PBC's head office and that of bank local branches were not identical, reflecting similar divergences between the central and local governments. The local branches were passive in terms of loyally supporting the local governments' objectives and plans, but whether or not this loyalty also extended to the head office of the PBC (thus the central government) largely depended on local governments which actually managed the local branches. When the degree of centralisation of economic management was relatively high, and thus local governments were cooperating closely with the central government, the local bank branches would function roughly in accordance with the directives of the head office of the bank; when decentralisation of economic management occurred, the local governments behaved to make local bank branches more 'creative'. This may conflict with the policies of the central government as well as of the head office of the bank. For instance, bank branches lent massively to meet the demand of local governments for local industrialisation during the Great Leap Forward (1958–60) when greater decision-making power was extended to local governments as well as local bank branches. Banks massively and blindly extended loans to meet the demand of local governments. Outstanding bank loans increased by nearly 2.4 times within three years, from ¥28.6 billion at the end of 1957 to ¥96.0 billion by the end of 1960. When government control was centralised after 1961, the bank branches behaved accordingly, and bank loans contracted by ¥40 billion by the end of 1964.[6] The behaviour of local bank branches *mirrored* behaviour of local governments. The experience before 1978 shows that the more autonomy the local bank branches enjoyed, the more likely bank credit would be out of control (see Appendix, A3).

As an integral part of an economic system characterised by the property rights of local governments, the institutional setting of the bank also generated a dilemma in which neither centralised control nor decentralised control would be efficient. Under centralised control, the problem of information and incentive failure would arise; under decentralised control, the problem of incentive incompatibility would occur. In neither case could banks perform screening and monitoring functions adequately.

Since the economic reform of 1978, greater emphasis was placed on the role of banks and monetary policy in mobilisation and allocation of financial resources. Correspondingly, the monetary sector has been considerably reformed. Banks multiplied, specialised and diversified. Between 1979 and 84, the Agricultural Bank of China (ABC), the Bank of China (BOC), the People's Construction Bank of China (PCBC), the People's Insurance Company of China (for domestic business; PICC), the Industrial and Commercial Bank of China (ICBC), and the Investment Bank of China (IBC) either became independent or were newly established. All these banks had specialised functions: ICBC was mainly engaged in urban banking business, with the purpose of promoting industrialisation and the expansion of commercial activities; ABC provided services to agriculture and the rural economy, and was also designed to guide and control RCCs. BOC specialised in foreign exchange related banking business; PCBC monitored state budget-financed investment, and was also engaged in general banking business. The China Investment Bank raised funds abroad and handled re-lending or on-lending of project loans extended to China by the World Bank and other similar international financial institutions. It is worth noting that, after 1987, the specialisation became less restricted. All were allowed to move towards comprehensive banking.

In order to exercise more effective control over multiple banking activities, the PBC was changed into the central bank in 1983 and most of its commercial functions were taken over by the newly established Industrial and Commercial Bank of China. As a result, a two-tier financial system took shape. After 1984, the course of pluralisation of financial institutions continued. A number of comprehensive banks, including the Industrial Bank of China, China International Trust &

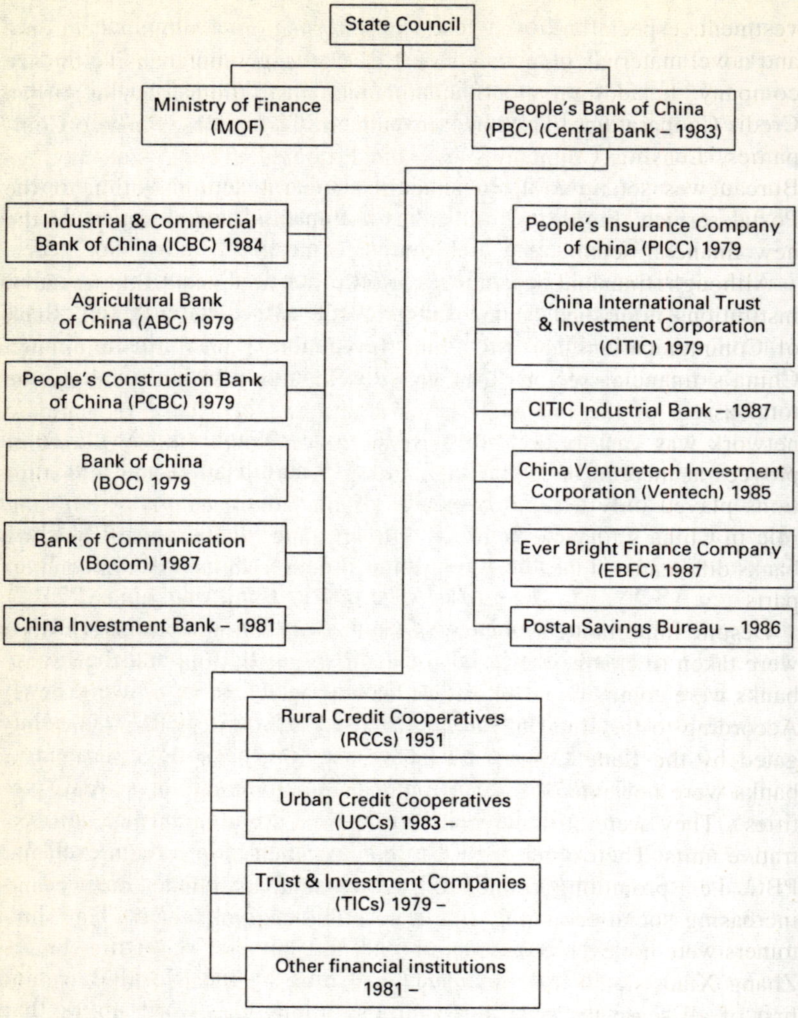

Figure 6.2 China's financial sector

Investment Company (CITIC), China Venturetech Investment Corporation (Ventech), the Bank of Communication (Bocom) and Ever Bright Finance Company (EBFC), came into existence. CITIC was the country's first and largest comprehensive trust and investment company, engaging in production, finance, trade and services. The Industrial Bank of CITIC was a subsidiary of the CITIC. Ventech dealt with risk investment, especially in the fields of information, biology, electronic and novel materials industries. The EBFC was a comprehensive finance company. In addition, non-bank financial institutions such as Urban Credit Cooperatives, Trust and Investment Companies, Finance Companies, Leasing Companies etc. mushroomed. The Postal Savings Bureau was set up in 1986 under the general administration of the Postal service. Figure 6.2 illustrates the institutional structure of the new financial sector.

Although financial institutions multiplied and non-bank financial institutions flourished, state banks (ICBC, ABC, BOC, PCBC, Bank of Communications and the China Investment Bank) still dominated China's financial sector. This group held about 85 per cent of the total assets of the financial sector at the end of 1989.[7] Its national network was vast, with 121 994 branches and over 1.42 million employees at the end of 1990 (SSB, 1991a: 641). Other financial institutions played only a supplementary, although increasingly significant, role in China's financial activity. The absolute dominance of the state banks differentiated the Chinese banking system from its Western counterparts.

Despite important changes in financial organisation, no decisive steps were taken to change the nature of financial institutions. First, no state banks were commercialised and the objectives set for them were vague. According to the 'Interim Regulations on Bank Management' promulgated by the State Council on 7 January 1986, the specialised state banks were not enterprises but 'independent economic accounting entities'. They were still government departments, though not administrative units. Their objectives were defined as the same as those of the PBC, i.e. 'promoting economic development, stabilising money and increasing social-economic efficiency'. The criteria for selecting customers were not even economic. In 1989, the governor of ICBC, Madam Zhang Xiao, stated that the specialised banks, as state banks, should first of all serve the economic policy of the government.[8]

Second, the principle of 'one level of local government, one level of bank branch' still applied. Even the central bank was no exception. Table 6.1 reports the internal structure of the state banks.

It is worth emphasising that even the central bank was no exception in terms of such an institutional design. When the PBC was transformed into the central bank in 1983, the State Council made it clear that 'In principle, the branching of PBC should be based on economic (not administrative) regions.'[9] However, in the Interim Regulations on Bank Management promulgated by the State Council on 7 January 1986,

Table 6.1 Internal structure of the main state banks (1990)

	PBC	*ICBC*	*ABC*	*BOC*	*PCBC*	*Administrative division of the government*
No. of units:						
Head office	1	1	1	1	1	1 (national)
Provincial head office	30	29	29	30	30	30 (provincial)
Separately planned city branch[a]	14	14	14	11	14	14 (provincial)
Prefectural (Municipal) branch	316	304	305	110	521	336 (prefectural)
County branch	2 048	2 066	2 161	788	2 429	2 182 (county)
City urban office	16	1 159	474	543	2 050	
City urban sub-office or Town office	2	6 244	–	–	1 214	
Deposit office	–	20 392	20 943	–	24 318	
Business office	–	–	30 798	–	333	
Others	92	589	685	–	685	
Total	2 519	30 798	55 410	1 483	31 595	
No. of Employees:						
Head office	2 332	695	677	1 905	(84	
Provincial head office	9 710	7 932	6 303	16 932	10 364	
Separately planned city branch[a]	4 237	4 937	2 031	3 210	4 832	
Prefectural (Municipal) branch	37 791	34 789	23 225	17 047	73 424	
County branch	70 269	142 323	113 924	32 630	120 743	
City urban office	602	112 044	20 306	1 647	–	
City urban sub-office or Town office	7	81 033	–	–	–	
Deposit office	–	93 753	29 379	–	–	
Business office	–	–	250 851	–	–	
Others	33 013	14 001	21 327	–	6 354	
Total	157 961	491 507	468 023	73 371	216 601	

Note: PBC: People's Bank of China; ICBC: Industrial and Commercial Bank of China; ABC: Agricultural Bank of China; BOC: Bank of China; PCBC: People's Construction Bank of China. [a] The separately planned city is the city whose credit plan targets are directly set by the head office and not by the provincial head office.

Source: SSB (1991a: 3, 641).

this item was changed into a rather more ambiguous term; 'the PBC sets its branches according to the need of economic development'.[10] The reason, provided by the deputy governor at the time, Mr Liu Hongru, was that PBC's branching had to be on the basis of government administration because in China's circumstances administrative regions and economic regions were identical and there was a need to coordinate branches of the specialised banks the local level.[11] He stated that, in principle, the PBC needed to set a branch in each of the economically developed counties. In practice, and as shown in Table 6.1, there was a county branch in every county no matter what its economic conditions. Given the bank's function in supporting local economic development, there was no reason why one county could have a bank branch and another could not. Therefore, the management of local bank branches, including those of the PBC, was still subject to the dual control of central and local governments. The traditional dual function of the local PBC branches was maintained. This was that the local bank branch had to carry out the macroeconomic policy required by the higher-level bank office on the one hand, and actively promote the local economic development on the other. In this respect, there was virtually no difference between branches of the PBC and the specialised banks. In terms of personnel management, the appointment and dismissal of bank directors still needed approval of the local Communist Party committee between 1979 and 1989.[12] The influence of local leadership on local bank branches was very strong. When two city branches of the ICBC (Shenyang and Guangzhou) were selected by their head office to conduct an experiment on 'management targeting responsibility' in 1987, their internal management strategy had to be approved by the municipal governments. The experiment was evaluated by the joint working group of the Head Office, provincial headquarters and municipal governments (ICBC, 21 July 1987). Moreover, whether or not bank directors could participate in major developmental decision-making of the localities depended on the local leaders. Since the official rank of directors of local bank branches was traditionally lower than that of local officials who directly reported to the local leadership (e.g. of the planning commission, the local treasuries), many bank directors still had difficulty in accessing top decision-makers at the local level).

It was essential for the directors of local bank branches to do 'good' work to maintain a close relationship with local governments and Party leaders. The 'good' work included services to the local leaders (information, consultancy and loans) and making these leaders understand

Table 6.2 Priority objectives of bank branches

1	Maximizing deposits
2	Increasing profits
3	Promoting economic development through the bank's specialized operation
3	Enlarging scale and operation
4	Optimizing allocation of credit funds
5	Speed up fund circulation
6	Achieving macroeconomic policy objectives
7	Maintaining credit and reputation
8	Satisfying requests and demand of the higher branch
9	Improving enterprise management
10	Guaranteeing enterprise financing

Source: A sample survey conducting in nine cities in 1985–6 (Zhang, S. *et al*, 1987b).

the banks' difficulties. 'You have to speak a good mandarin as well as a good local dialect', one bank director said.[13] This will be discussed in the following section.

In general, the main change in the design of financial institutions post-1978 was that one monolithic bank became five (including the central bank), while their non-commercial and locality-dependent nature remained. On the positive side, multiple banks and local bank branch subordination to the local government helped to finance local development more efficiently in terms of coordination between borrowers and lenders. Remarkably, it also helped in mobilising savings.It is widely agreed among foreign observers that Chinese financial intermediaries have been remarkably successful in mobilising financial resources. Yet few people see the institutional reasons for this. From the point of view of institutional design, an important reason might be that the incentives of the centre and localities, including bank branches, are compatible in this respect. Table 6.2 shows that the three top priority objectives of the local bank branches were all related to expansion, with maximisation of deposits the first of these. Meanwhile, achieving macroeconomic policy objectives and satisfying other requests and demands of higher bank branches were placed in positions of lesser importance.

Since financial reform failed to change the fundamental design of Chinese financial institutions, allocation of financial resources suffered from the same problems as under the pre-reformed financial system. Furthermore, the centre's credit control ability was weakened because of the greater coordination required given the multiple number of local bank branches. The flourishing non-bank financial institutions exacerbated this problem because most of them belonged to either the specialised bank branches or local governments and as such were actually more locality-dependent than the state banks as a whole. There were 745 trust and investment companies in 1989, of which 454 were owned by the specialised banks, 526 were at or under the prefectural level (Hong, Y. and Xu, S., 1989: 173).

The unchanged essence of the design of financial institutions was reflected in the allocation of financial resources. In the following three sections, regional allocation of bank loans, screening and monitoring functions of the banks are examined in turn.

6.2 REGIONAL ALLOCATION OF CREDIT CEILINGS

In the theory of bank lending, market failure due to asymmetric information between borrowers and lenders can result in credit rationing (e.g. Stiglitz and Weiss, 1981). Credit rationing has always existed in China's economy. However, it is characterised by regional rationing imposed by the central government not because of difficulties in accurate screening caused by imperfect information, but as a means for controlling the expansionary tendencies of local bank branches (reflecting the behaviour of local governments).

Before 1978, credit allocation was determined within the state credit plan in the form of mandatory credit ceilings or credit quotas for each locality which were often disaggregated at sectoral levels (e.g. industrial, commercial, agricultural loans, etc.). These were imposed on bank branches by the higher authorities on an annual basis. The bank branches then allocated loans to enterprises according to their production plan and planned flow of physical resources.

Similar to the situation before 1978, regional allocation of bank loans in the post-1978 period was determined by the state credit plan. The higher-level bank office allocated credit quotas or ceilings to lower level offices. The bank loan quotas were not allocated to banks but to local governments through the local bank branches. When the governments of nine cities gained managerial autonomy (as enjoyed by provincial governments) in 1988,[14] the PBC allocated credit quotas to them directly. In practice, outstanding bank loans to a locality were accepted and only the increment required approval. The process of determining bank credit quota for a locality was the same as the formation of the national bank credit quota or ceiling. Given the base ratio of economic growth and bank credit growth, determination of the planned national credit ceiling was based on three factors: the planned economic growth rate, the accepted rate of price rise, and the expected change in money velocity. For instance, if the base ratio was 1 (i.e. 1 per cent of the economic growth rate was related to 1 per cent of the bank credit growth rate; the base could be the previous year or average of the previous three years), the planned economic growth was 8 per cent, the accepted price rise was 4 per cent and the velocity of money was expected to slow down by 2 per cent, then the credit quota would be formed according to the following formula:

Credit quota = (1 × 8% + 4% + 2%) outstanding bank credit at the base year

Annual bank credit quotas were usually formulated and allocated in the final quarter of the year. The procedure involved three stages. To take the PCBC as an example:[15]

(i) In September of each year, instructions concerning credit plans were distributed downwards. This process was initiated by the head office of the PCBC.
(ii) Bank branches were required to forecast year-end figures for deposits and loans, and to propose a credit plan for the locality based on the actual figures for outstanding deposits and loans. The proposed credit plans of each sub-provincial branches were reported upwards to the provincial branches. After checking and adjustment, the provincial branches reported the proposed provincial credit plan to the head office of the PCBC at the end of October.
(iii) The comprehensive credit plan was balanced and adjusted according to the state investment plan and credit plan. Then, the disaggregated credit plan targets or quotas (including credit ceilings, deposit quotas, the surplus or deficit of loanable funds etc.) were allocated to each provincial branch which, after balancing and adjustment, allocated the approved credit plan (quotas) to the sub-provincial branches. The final quota of a locality was subject to intensive negotiation in which local governments would be involved.

With respect to the allocation of bank loans, what need to be noted are changes in the credit management system. Between 1979 and 1984, a scheme known as 'unified plan, multi-level management, linking lending with deposit and control of the difference (i.e. the difference between total deposit and total lending of the local bank branches)'[16] was introduced. Due to difficulties in 'controlling the difference', control was strengthened by changing it into 'contracting the difference' in 1981.[17] Under this arrangement, if more deposits were collected, the local bank branches were allowed to lend more for working capital investment (but not for fixed assets investment) subject to the total credit quota. Accordingly, if the planned deposit collection target failed to be realised, the branch may have had to leave the lending quota underutilised. The underlying idea was to stimulate the incentives of bank branches in mobilising deposits and to increase their autonomy while maintaining aggregate control.

After the establishment of the central bank, the most important changes in credit control occurred in 1985 and 1987. In 1985, instead of the head office of the PBC giving the annual borrowing quotas to local bank branches, the PBC directly credited the annual incremental borrowing allowance to the account of each of the specialised banks (SBs) held in the PBC. The SBs used these funds, together with deposits they collected, to facilitate lending.[18] Their lending was thus subject to both the imposed credit ceilings and PBC's lending to them. The SBs then allocated the borrowing allowances together with the credit ceilings downwards to local bank branches. Moreover, inter-banking was encouraged. Thus, the PBC was able to control lending by the SBs either through tightening credit ceilings, or reducing its lending to SBs or by doing both. In summary, the change in credit control in 1985 was twofold:

(i) the financial relationship between the PBC and the SBs became commercialised, at least nominally;
(ii) the regional allocation of bank credit was mainly through the SBs.[19]

Another important change was in 1987 when the role of the PBC in credit allocation was enhanced. First, provincial PBC branches were empowered to decide on the extension of short-term loans to other bank branches.[20] Second, a PBC special lending scheme was introduced. This included the PBC loans to less-developed localities, PBC loans for local economic development, loans for purchasing hard currency and loans for the development of fourteen coastal cities and the Special Economic Zones (SEZs). These loans were allocated directly by the PBC head office and its branches. Third, the PBC branches in

Shanghai and Shenzhen were empowered to change the control and allocation of bank loans within the locality. Branches of the SBs received credit quotas directly from local PBC branches instead of from their head offices.[21]

Despite these 'reform' measures in credit allocation and control, the behaviour of bank branches did not change significantly. Since local bank branches remained subordinate to local governments, who were eager to expand local manufacturing capacity, direct controls through credit ceilings or quotas could not and were not removed to curb unauthorised credit expansion. A senior official of ICBC stated that in formulating the credit plan, ICBC managers began with assessing the financial needs of the locality. Use of funds was determined first, then the source of funds was considered. Usually, the shortage of funds was left to the higher level branch (Shao Qiuming, 18 December 1989).

Facing expansionary demands for funds from every branch, higher-level bank offices always had difficulties in determining how to allocate the borrowing allowance from the PBC to their branches. Here we see the problem of asymmetric information at work. The higher-level bank branches had less knowledge than their lower-level branches about the justifiable needs for credit in the local economy, about the potential in saving mobilisation and about other relevant information. This resulted in a well-known phenomenon in the allocation of bank credit (or ceilings): uniform rate of expansion or 'uniform cutting' in credit contraction among localities (*Yidao Qie*: 'slicing across the board with one knife'). This partly explains why it is difficult to fine-tune China's economy.

Since the design of institutions remained fundamentally unchanged, local bank behaviour mirrors local government behaviour. This can be seen by examining the banks' screening and monitoring functions. To these two functions the following two sections turn.

6.3 SCREENING

Screening is necessary because a bank cannot rely entirely on the rate of interest to select borrowers. The reason is simple. On one hand, those who offer (accept) higher rates may have a higher propensity to default (moral hazard) or take excessive risks in using funds. On the other hand, because of imperfect information the lending bank may not know the true characteristics of the borrower. So, in a market economy, bank screening of borrowers is important but difficult.

The screening function of the Chinese banks was even more difficult because of their institutional peculiarities. The bank's dual objectives of pursuing its own as well as the larger social interests were often conflicting. The conflict was usually resolved by giving priority to social benefits. A senior officer of the ICBC, Mr Ying Zhihai, reported that bank management involves two types of 'efficiencies': 'social efficiency' and 'bank efficiency'. When these conflict, every branch of ICBC must give priority to the improvement of social efficiency.[22] The 'Standard Procedure of Industrial Credit' of ICBC makes it very clear that the central criterion for extending credit is social efficiency (or benefit).[23] The problem was that 'social efficiency' was a very vague concept. Therefore, the needs of government became the dominant consideration. According to the 'Interim Regulations on Bank Management' promulgated by the State Council on 7 January 1986, the specialised state banks should lend to enterprises 'according to government policy and the government plan'. Let us first examine the banks' screening function in lending for fixed assets investment.

Bank loans for *fixed assets investment* were subject to both the bank fixed assets investment loan quota and the fixed assets investment quota. The latter was allocated by the State Planning Commission to every provincial planning commission, and the provincial planning commissions to prefectural planning commissions and so on. The ICBC stipulated that a credit plan for technical updating investment must be geared to the plan for technical updating and transformation of the governments at each level. The credit plan formation was initiated by provincial branches according to the borrowing plan of the economic commission and the enterprise supervisory bodies. The province-initiated plans were balanced and adjusted by the head office of the ICBC, together with the State Economic Commission and relevant ministries. Then, the national credit plan for technical updating and transformation was scaled downwards.[24]

Quotas for *capital construction loans* were actually allocated to ministries by the State Planning Commission, together with the PBC, to supplement the state budget appropriation. Bank *technical updating loans* were managed by the specialised banks. In coordination with the central ministries, head offices of the specialised banks directly allocate part of the technical updating loans, usually to a selected number of large SOEs. The remaining quotas were allocated to local branches of the specialised banks. The purpose and allocation of loans for economic development of backward regions and for local economic development were more specific. The specialised banks often act as

Table 6.3 Examples of the size classification of industrial projects (annual production capacity)

	Large	*Medium*	*Small*
Iron and steel complexes (000s tonnes steel)	≥1000	100–1000	<100
Synthetic ammonia (000s tonnes)	≥150	45–150	<45
Plastics (000s tonnes)	≥30	10–30	<10
Farm chemicals (000s tonnes)	≥30	3–30	<3
Power stations (000s kilowatts)	≥250	25–250	<25
Cars (000s)	≥50	5–50	<5
Cotton textiles (000s spindles)	≥100	50–100	<50

Source: Fixed Assets Investment Department of SSB (1987: 336–43).

agents of the PBC in managing these two types of loans. Therefore, bank autonomy in screening was very limited in China. This is also evident from the lending procedure of bank loans for fixed assets investment.

A project was usually initiated by an enterprise through its supervisory body or by the latter itself in a form of the 'recommended project'. Before an application for bank loans for fixed assets investment could be made to the bank, the recommended project had to be certified by the local government planning commissions (or the economic commissions if the project concerned technical updating and transformation). Two commissions of the government at each level were assigned the autonomy to approve the projects according to the government levels and the policy. In general, large- and medium-size projects needed to be certified by the State Planning Commission or the State Economic Commission; only very large projects required State Council approval;[25] small-size projects were certified by provincial level commissions or below. Table 6.3 provides a few examples about the size classification of the investment projects.

If a project was difficult to classify by size (production capacity), then approval depended on the scale of investment involved. Generally, the smaller the investment scale of a project, the lower the level of governmental approval required (see Chapter 5, Tables 5.4 and 5.5).

After a recommended project had been certified, a feasibility study group was organised. The group usually included the initiators, the planning commission or the economic commission and other government departments which might be involved (e.g. the government treasury would participate if the bank loans entailed subsidised interest payments). At this stage, the bank might or might not be invited to participate (although the head offices normally required their branches to take part in the project feasibility study). The conclusions of feasibility study could be influenced by many factors. The most significant was the opinion of the local leadership. If the feasibility study reached a positive conclusion, the project was included in the annual fixed assets investment plan of the planning commission. Only those projects which were on the list of the planning commission were entitled to apply for bank loans for fixed assets investment.

The success of a project in getting bank loans for fixed assets investment depended on five conditions:[26]

(i) The project had been included in the government investment plan.
(ii) The investor could provide 10–30 per cent of total funds, with the funds deposited with the PCBC in advance (6 months).
(iii) The project could be completed according to the plan schedule.
(iv) The technology employed was advanced and feasible, supply of the required raw materials was assured and the completed project could be put into operation.
(v) The product was competitive in the domestic or international markets, and the loan could be repaid on time.

Bank fixed assets investment loans required collateral which could be either fixed assets that belonged to the borrower or a third party who had the ability to repay the loans for the borrower. In case of repayment default, the banks were entitled to dispose of the collateral and/or call upon the guarantees.[27]

There are two immediate problems associated with such investment control practices. First, although the investment decision was made substantially by government planning commissions and other supervisory departments, they assumed no accountability for the economic consequences of the investment. The function of banks in project screening was restricted. The local bank branches had at most only limited choices from the investment list prepared by local governments. Table 6.4 shows that quite a high proportion of bank technical updating loans were earmarked by the local governments.

The main reason given by local bank managers for problematic loans in 1985–6 was that the projects (or the clients) 'had a considerable impact on the local economy and on local budget revenue', or 'the local governments demanded the loans' (Zhang, S. *et al.*, 1987b).

Second, the larger the project, the higher the level of governmental authorisation required. In order to circumvent such controls and

Table 6.4 Technical updating loans earmarked by local governments (ICBC local branches) (%)

Year	*Proportion*	*The highest*	*The lowest*
1985	50.3	65.9	26.7
1986	73.3	94.0	41.3

Note: City branches of the ICBC.

Source: Xu, X. (1988).

Table 6.5 Average scale of new capital construction projects in Sichuan province (1984)

	Total	*Central*	*Provincial*	*Prefectural and County*	*Town and village*
Number	3861.0	325.0	339.0	3197.0	n.a.
Investment (¥ M.)	3397.7	1657.5	301.5	1438.7	n.a.
Proportion (%)	100.0	48.8	8.9	42.3	n.a.
Average scale (¥ 1,000)	880.0	5100.0	889.0	450.0	35.0

Source: Zhang, S. et al (1987a).

bureaucracy, local governments had an incentive to design projects sub-economic in size and conceal their true costs, thus leaving it under-funded. Table 6.5 shows that the scale of distribution of capital construction projects amongst different levels of the governments in Sichuan province in 1984 followed the pattern of an inverted pyramid. The township and village projects, while accounting for nearly 83 per cent of the total number of projects, had an average scale of only 0.69 per cent of the central projects.

Moreover, not every condition required in the procedure was met in practice. Some, such as (iii), (iv) and (v), were quite vague. Others posed problems of enforcement, such as condition (ii) and the collateral clauses. For instance, in 1985 it was stipulated that the self-raised fund – the fund not come from the government or banks – for capital construction investment be deposited in the Construction Bank in advance. In the following year, this rule was specifically known as the 'deposit six months in advance' requirement (Financial Encyclopedia (II): 1386). However, according to the governor of the PCBC, only 60–70 per cent of the self-raised investment funds were deposited into the PCBC according to rule (ii) set by the State Council.[28] It was very rare for a bank actually to liquidate the borrowing firm or call upon guarantees. This was due partly to problems in other aspects of the economic system (such as the problem of transferability of the property rights, lack of regulation, lack of a social security net etc.).

The design of financial institutions and credit policies all worked towards the integration of interests of local governments and the local bank branches. It is also worth noting that local economic performance has conventionally been the criterion in evaluating the performance of the local bank branch manager, and this performance was also vital to the career and promotion prospects of local government officials. Moreover, since no local bank branch was allowed to mobilise savings from other localities, the quantity of deposits it could mobilise was closely linked to the quantity of funds the locality itself could obtain through appropriations from higher-level government and loans from the local bank. The support of local government was in turn essential to the local bank for the expansion of its business and for welfare provisions for its employees (e.g. construction of new bank offices, employees' housing, recruitment of new employees, education and employment of the staffs' children, etc.). There was therefore a close and symbiotic relationship between the local bank and the local government. Local bank branches were consequently highly motivated to lend to projects preferred by the local government. Available funds were centred on this locality concern.

As with bank lending for fixed assets investment, bank screening of applications for loans for working capital investment was also restricted. Consider the reform of December 1982 when banks were authorised by the State Council to manage the working capital of the SOEs. When the PBC was transformed into the central bank in the early 1980s, this function was taken over by the ICBC.[29] In December 1982, the State Council approved new provisions (jointly drafted by the State Economic Commission, the State Planning Commission, the Ministry of Finance and the PBC) on the management of circulating funds. The provision stipulated that banks must not provide loans for working capital investment if the intended project duplicates existing production where there exists excess capacity or if stocks are already above plan quotas.[30] The reforms, however, were internally inconsistent. On the one hand, they stipulated that government department must not force the banks to lend. On the other hand, allocation of bank loan quotas for working capital investment was still to be decided by banks in consultation with government treasuries and enterprise supervisory bodies.[31] The policy was based on the false assumption that the incentives of local governments at different levels were compatible with those of the centre, and that local governments would assist bank branches to exercise the required screening.

The reforms were disjointed even on the surface. In order to avoid making bank loans the sole source of finance for working capital and to reduce lending risk, the PBC stipulated that in principle the government department approving the capital construction investment had to be responsible for financing working capital. Specifically, banks could only provide working capital loans to a new project if 30 per cent of the 'normal' working capital needs were provided by the investors.[32] For enterprises already operating, a proportion of the production fund was also required to be used to finance working capital (10–30 per cent). In cases where fixed assets investment was financed through state budgetary appropriations, banks were allowed to finance all the working capital investment needed. As a result of both the bank's institutional nature and lending policy, the banks actually financed all the incremental working capital of all SOEs and most of the incremental working capital of COEs.

6.4 MONITORING

In the market economies, monitoring is important for several reasons. First, it can lessen the problem of asymmetric information and thus reduce risks of adverse selection and moral hazard. Second, it can help build cooperation between lenders and borrowers.

Bank monitoring is related closely with corporate control and is not quite the same under different financial systems. Conventionally, Western financial systems are often categorised either as market-based systems or bank-based systems (e.g. Bayliss and Butt Philip, 1980), or the 'outsider' and 'insider' systems (e.g. Corbett and Mayer, 1991). In the former, such as in the UK and the USA, security markets play a more important role in corporate finance. Banks hold little or no corporate equity and do not generally sit on boards. They are thus not closely involved in internal corporate business. Banks exert their control from outside through decisions to refinance loans or to place companies in financial distress, e.g. into bankruptcy.[33] The market mechanism which keeps corporate management alert is the threat of loss of control resulting from mergers and takeovers. In bank-based insider systems, prevalent in most other Western countries and typified by Japan and

Table 6.6 Properties of insider and outsider systems

Outsider systems	*Insider systems*
Dispersed ownership	Concentrated ownership
Separation of ownership and control	Association of ownership with control
Little incentive for outside investors to participate in corporate control	Control by interested parties (banks, related firms, and employees)
Hostile takeovers that are costly and antagonistic	Absence of hostile takeovers
Low commitment of outside investors to long-term strategies of firms	Intervention by outside investors limited to periods of clear financial failure
Takeovers may create monopoly	Insider systems may encourage collusion

Source: Corbett and Mayer (1991).

Table 6.7 The role of banks in corporate control in four economies

	UK	*China*	*Japan*	*Germany*
Do banks hold corporate equity?	No	No	Yes	Yes
Do banks sit on the boards of firms?	No	No	Yes	Yes
Can banks place distressed firms into bankruptcy?	Yes	No	Yes	Yes
Are there hostile takeovers	Yes	No	No	No

Note: Part of the table is from Corbett and Mayer (1991).

West Germany, banks play a more important role in corporate finance. They are thus involved more directly in corporate management and monitor their customers more actively. Banks often directly own equity in the non-financial corporate sector and have representatives on the boards of corporations. Bank ownership and representation allow banks to intervene in corporate management from the inside.[34] The properties of these two systems are shown Table 6.6.

Compared with their counterparts in the UK, Japan and Germany, Chinese banks had no control over corporate management either from within – such as was the case in Japan and Germany – nor from outside, such as in the UK (see Table 6.7). Although advantages and disadvantages of 'insider' and 'outsider' systems are arguable in terms of corporate control, the Chinese system has almost no control over their customers at all.

In pre-1978 China, banks only financed working capital of enterprises. The bank's monitoring function was to ensure that transactions of the enterprises corresponded to approved plans and to guidelines of the cash plan and credit plan in particular. (As in the former Soviet Union, monitoring was to keep 'temporarily free transactions balances' of enterprises to a minimum and to exercise the bank's micro surveillance function; Hodgman D.R., 1962: 117, 119.) Since bank branches were under the control of local governments, they reported and made recommendations to the level of government to which they were subordinated. Unlike in market economies, the banks exerted no direct control either from inside or from outside.

It may be postulated that the entire economic system was highly inconsistent. On the one hand, it was undesirable to have one centre, representing the whole people, as one homogeneous owner to run the entire economy. This had already been recognised by the Chinese leadership in the mid-1950s. Yet property rights of local governments effectively existed in the Chinese system! On the other hand, no property rights were equitised and no transactions involving property rights were allowed. As a consequence, corporate control was vested in government at every level and fragmented among different government management departments. Worse still, corporate finance and its financial returns were muddled with fiscal redistribution.

Under reform, all these fundamental features and defects of the economic system remained unchanged. Restricted by the unchanged fundamental design of the financial institutions, the bank monitoring function continued to be jeopardised in China.

As units authorised by the state with 'working capital management', bank branches were required to inspect enterprise activities and examine the implementation of working capital circulation plans on a quarterly and annual basis. Their reports had to be submitted to both higher-level bank branches and the local governments.[35] Since local governments actually controlled both the enterprises as well as the bank branches, bank monitoring was unlikely to be objective or effective. For instance, although bank monitoring focused on ensuring that enterprises raised their own circulating funds from internal sources,[36] enterprises rarely used their own funds to supplement their working capital needs and the leverage ratio of working capital continued to decline. Another important objective of bank monitoring was to prevent enterprises from using working capital for fiscal purposes, such as price and loss subsidies, etc. Ironically but not unexpectedly, according to the Deputy Prime Minister, Mr Zhu Rongji, the amount of such misused funds reached ¥104.1 billion at the end of 1991.[37] This was equivalent to about 6 per cent of total outstanding loans extended by the state banks.

The banks did have some power to punish enterprises if they were dissatisfied with their use of working capital loans. The measures included:[38]

(i) increasing lending rates (20 per cent higher interest rate was charged for above-quota working capital loans and overdue loans; 50 per cent higher for loans misuse);
(ii) enforcing immediate repayment of misused loans (capital plus interest);
(iii) early recall of misused loans;
(iv) stopping part or all of lending;
(v) withdrawal of all loans extended.

In practice, most of these measures were not enforceable and were not actually taken. Banks effectively had only one weapon, which was to increase lending rates, i.e. measure (i). Even in this respect the banks could not impose sanctions if problem loans were 'caused' by changes in government plan and policy.

As for bank loans for fixed assets investment, there were virtually no specific provisions for bank monitoring. Although banks financed an increasing proportion of fixed assets investment, their role in corporate control was still highly restricted. The guarantor's responsibility for repaying loans was stressed but such repayment was rarely enforced by the banks. Bank monitoring was also hampered by fiscal policies concerning loan payment and loss subsidies which actually encouraged borrowing for fixed asset investments. The repayment of loans was actually tied up with the fiscal revenue of the governments at every level. This resulted, on the one hand, in bank risk being largely reduced because loan repayment was actually backed by the governments' budgetary revenue.[39] On the other hand, banks became more dependent on the government because the proportion of the loan to be repaid was decided by the fiscal authorities. Table 6.8 indicates that bank loans for fixed assets investment were subsidised very heavily. Between 1981 and 1988, all subsidies exceeded the nominal interest payment even before inflation was taken into account. During 1981–4, the subsidies, as a proportion of the total lending, usually exceeded

Table 6.8 Subsidies to bank fixed investment loans to the SOEs (1979–88; ¥ bn)

	1981	1982	1983	1984	1985	1986	1987	1988
(1) Before-tax profit used to repay bank fixed investment loans	2.1	3.5	4.8	6.6	9.8	13.9	16.4	24.7
(2) Subsidies equivalence[a] [(1) 45%]	0.9	1.6	2.2	3.6	4.4	6.3	7.4	11.1
(3) Bank loans repaid by taxes	0.6	1.0	1.4	2.1	3.1	3.2	4.8	5.0
(4) = (2) + (3)	1.5	2.6	3.6	5.7	7.5	9.5	12.2	16.1
(5) Bank fixed assets investment loans[b]	13.3	23.8	30.7	45.2	70.5	100.6	128.7	155.9
(6) = (4)/(5) (%)	11.3	10.9	11.7	12.6	10.6	9.4	9.5	10.3
(7) Lending rate[c] (%)	4.0	4.4	4.4	4.4	7.0	8.6	8.6	9.1

Note: [a] Estimated average corporate income tax rate. For the large and medium-size SOEs, the rate was 55 per cent.[b] Year-end outstanding.[c] For fixed assets of the term 1–3 years. The figures are annual average. Where lending rates for technical updating investment and for capital construction investment differ, arithmetic average is calculated.

Source: General Planning Department of the MOF (1989: 145; 137). (5): *Almanac of China's Finance and Banking* (1990: 52–3). (7): the PBC (1)88: 46–7).

Table 6.9 Loss compensation of the SOEs (1978–85; ¥ bn)

Year	*Loss* (1)	*Loss subsidies* (2)	*As % of total* (3) = (2)/(1)	*Exemption or reduction of taxes* (4)	*As % of total* (5) = (4)/(1)	*(1) + (4) as % of the state budget revenue* (6)
1978	11.532	6.017	52.18	0.600	5.20	5.90
1979	11.677	6.733	57.66	2.834	24.27	8.97
1980	14.087	5.098	36.19	4.539	32.22	9.26
1981	12.638	6.421	50.81	4.931	39.02	11.17
1982	19.686	5.265	26.75	4.553	23.13	9.06
1983	23.992	10.300	42.93	5.528	23.04	13.07
1984	19.993	6.800	34.01	4.678	23.40	7.83
1985	25.893	12.100	46.73	7.434	28.17	10.61

Source: Zhang, B. (1988).

the lending rate by around 6–7 percentage points.

In fact, not only was interest payment subsidised but also any final

Table 6.10 Number of bankruptcy cases dealt with by courts

	1988	*1989*	*1990*	*1991*
Number of cases accepted and heard	5	98	32	117
Number of bankruptcy cases announced	n.a.	n.a.	n.a.	57

Source: *Abstract of Newspapers and Magazines* (*Baokan Wenzhai*), 24 March 1992.

loss incurred by enterprises (after interest payment subsidisation) was compensated by the state budget through loss subsidies and exemption or reduction of taxes (Table 6.9). Banks therefore did not need to worry too much about the repayment of their loans.

Table 6.10 shows that only 252 bankruptcy cases had been accepted and heard by courts by the end of 1991. It is not surprising that banks had virtually no bad debt provisions. Because profits of the banking sector go to the central budget, it is advantageous for local governments to use bank credit to finance their enterprise losses. These bad debts actually represent a financial loss to the centre and simultaneously a financial gain to the peripheries.

In summary, during the economic reform which commenced in China in 1978, financial reform was recognised by the policy-makers as a very important component. However, the focus of financial reform was placed on the limited pluralisation of financial institutions, including the establishment of a two-tier banking system, without changing the nature of the institutions. As before, the allocation of bank-loanable funds was controlled by both central and local governments. Heavy subsidies from the governments at all levels for enterprise borrowing were retained. Despite the establishment of the two-tier banking system and decentralisation of the banks' operation, all banks' profits and losses as well as liquidity risks were still effectively internalised.[40] It is reasonable to conclude that while fiscal reform attempted to change 'eating out of one big pot' into 'eating in separate kitchens', financial reform preserved the 'big pot' of the national banking network. Furthermore, under decentralisation, local governments' control over local bank branches was strengthened. Given the persisting defects of the financial system, the monetary authority was left with no alternative but to provide extra funds to the central government to finance its priority investment which local governments were unwilling to undertake. The nature of banking system therefore contributed to both the unbalanced investment pattern of local governments and to the central government's reliance on bank credit expansion for adjusting the overall investment pattern. Indeed, bank operations merely reflected and facilitated the interactions between central and local governments investment behaviour as depicted in earlier chapters of this study. This explains why the effectiveness of credit control ultimately depended on the State Council and its determination to impose central policies on local governments. Before the central bank was established, the State Council directly commanded provincial governments and ministries – not the PBC and its provincial branches – to tighten credit control.[41] After the PBC was transformed into the central bank, the State Council had to operate monetary policy through the PBC and the specialised banks. The reliance on the banking system to enforce central policy was, as we have tried to show in this chapter, hampered by systemic defects. Thus, when urgent measures were needed in the face of weak enforcement through the banking system, the State Council had to resort to direct orders to provincial governments and ministries to 'strengthen the banking and credit management' or in more straightforward terms, to take decisive measures to stop credit expansion. This was what happened in April 1985 and September 1988 when the central government decisively and effectively imposed austerity measures.[42]

7 Tight Money in 1988–9: A Case Study

This chapter looks at the processes, effects and limits of tight monetary control in 1988–9. Tight money in this period merits scrutiny because it was central to the stabilisation programme introduced to fight the sharp price rise and economic overheating. In fact, 1988 was the only year in which bank credit ceilings had been maintained since 1979,[1] and the extension of bank credit in the first nine months of 1989 was also below these ceilings.

The chapter begins with an overall picture of China's monetary policy and its effectiveness during the stabilisation programme in this period. It next analyses the transmission mechanism of tight money, and finally tight money's costs and limitations.

7.1 TIGHT MONEY AND ITS EFFECTIVENESS

Households' very strong saving propensity is a key factor in explaining successful mobilisation of financial resources and the general absence of unmanageable excessive demand in China under reform. Nevertheless, inflationary pressures were generated by the continual expansion of bank credit. The annual increase in the retail price level was 3.6 per cent between 1978 and 1985, but reached 7.3 per cent in 1987. In the short term, the increase in the household saving ratio is not stable. A close inverse relationship between changes in household saving ratio and changes in the inflation rate can be observed: a fall in the household saving ratio was accompanied by an increase in the inflation rate. Table 7.1 shows it to be −0.60 during the period 1979–90 compared with 0.30 in 1954–78. This negative correlation became stronger in 1984–90 than in 1979–83.

In 1988, growth of total household deposits in the first seven months was minus 7 per cent compared with 50 per cent and 42 per cent in the same period in 1986 and 1987 respectively. August 1988 witnessed an unprecedented net withdrawal of ¥2.61 billion (or 0.73 per cent) of total household bank deposits – the first such occurrence since 1970. This was accompanied by a surge in the retail price level from 9.5 per

Table 7.1 Correlation between changes in household saving ratio and retail price inflation (1954–90)

1954–78	*1979–90*	*1984–90*
0.30	–0.60	–0.76

Note: Household savings include bank deposits, cash and other financial assets holdings.

Source: Appendix A5 and own calculation.

cent in January 1988 to 25.4 per cent in September 1988 (compared with the same month the previous year). Most worrying of all, the acceleration of price increases led to run on banks and panic-buying occurred three times nationwide between April and August 1988. Over 120 bank branches crashed when angry depositors were unable to withdraw cash because the banks had run out of cash reserves.

Frightened by these unexpected events, policy-makers in September 1988 launched the stabilisation programme ('economic rectification and adjustment'). The ultimate aim was to stabilise the economy and make growth sustainable. The immediate objectives were:

(i) economic growth rate was to be lowered to an appropriate level (7–8 per cent);
(ii) inflation was to be reduced significantly in 1989, and reduced further still afterwards.

It was also hoped that efficiency could be improved significantly by adjusting the investment pattern, coupled with control over aggregate demand. Since excessive aggregate demand was believed to be the key factor causing economic overheating and thus accelerating inflation,[2] control was focused on both the scale of fixed assets investment and retail sales of consumer goods. The targets for 1989 intended fixed assets investment to be cut by 21 per cent and retail sales increased by 15.6 per cent (all in nominal terms).[3] Because of bank dominance in mobilisation of savings and in external corporate financing given changes in national income distribution and saving pattern under reform, the stabilisation programme was centred on monetary policy.[4] This was aimed at curbing the expansion of bank loans (especially loans for fixed asset investment) and to encourage the households to save more to reduce demand pressures.

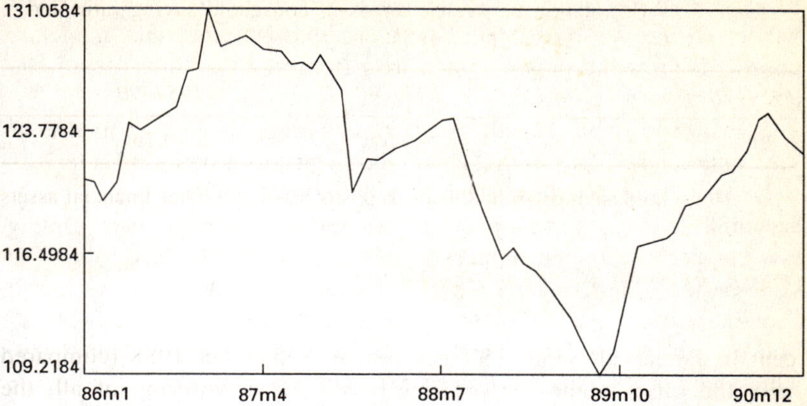

Figure 7.1 Bank loans index (1986–90, same month of previous year = 100)

Table 7.2 Percentage increase in the stock of bank loans (1985m9–90m8) (previous September = 100)

1986m8	*1987m8*	*1988m8*	*1989m8*	*1990m8*
122.7	122.6	120.9	108.6	120.8

Note: Include the loans extended by RCCs.

Source: The PBC.

The policy proved very effective. Expansion of domestic loans for fixed assets investment not only ceased, but the amount of loans actually decreased. The cut in loan extended (flow) in 1989 was ¥21.0 billion, equivalent to 22.7 per cent of that extended in 1988. That accounted for 58.6 per cent of the cut in total investment in fixed assets (or 93.8 per cent of the cut in state investment) in 1989 (SSB, 1991a: 143). In fact, the cut in bank loans for fixed assets investment in 1989 was greater than this. Taking into account other funds provided by state banks for fixed assets investment, such as PBC loans to the state budget, the cut amounted to ¥25.2 billion,[5] or 70.2 per cent of the total decrease in the fixed investment in 1989. In practical terms, fixed assets investment can only be feasible if a minimum amount of funds can be made available. Paralleling the cut in loans for fixed assets investment was a significant slowdown in the growth of total bank loans. Taking the stock of bank credit (including those of RCCs) as a whole, Figure 7.1 illustrates that it responded to the tight monetary policy. Its growth dropped immediately in September 1988 when monetary policy was tightened.

The slowdown in growth of bank (including RCCs) credit can be seen more clearly by taking September-August as a period (Table 7.2).

Table 7.2 suggests that in the period 1988m9–1989m8 (i.e. September 1988 – August 1989), about 12 percentage points of bank lending was cut because of the tightened monetary policy compared with the same period in other years. Since the stock of bank loans at the end of September 1988 was ¥1103.6 billion, this means that about ¥132 billion of bank loans (equivalent to 8.3 per cent of the GNP in 1989) which would normally have been extended was not lent.

Monetary policy both succeeded and failed in its ultimate objectives. It succeeded in that the inflation rate was brought down as desired. It failed in that growth of GDP dropped much more than targeted – by 7 percentage points from 10.9 per cent in 1988 to merely 3.9 per cent in 1989 and 5.0 per cent in 1990 against the target of 7.0-8.0 per cent. Furthermore, it created a series of other problems such as increased SOEs losses, greater misallocation of resources, growth of bad debts, etc. These will be discussed in section 7.3.

Since the responses of both investment in fixed assets and consumption expenditure were central to the successful outcome of the stabilisation programme, the question taken up in the next section is: what were the transmission mechanisms between the monetary policy and aggregate demand?

7.2 TRANSMISSION MECHANISMS

This section shows that cutting or suspension of investment projects combined with tight credit ceilings were decisive in demand management. The success in investment control led not only to a direct reduction in aggregate demand but also to an immediate reduction in the household consumption expenditure. Even when growth of investment, and thus income, recovered, growth of household consumption expenditure still lagged behind because of household savings behaviour (discussed in Chapter 4, Section 4.4.3). This further reinforced the initial demand control.

It is generally accepted that investment is related to the cost of capital (thus profitability of investment) on one hand and to the availability of funds for investment on the other (Eshag, 1971). Monetary policy could affect investment through the channels of either cost of capital or availability of funds. For instance, the cost of capital can be changed by altering the rate of interest. The availability of funds for investment can be affected by availability of credit which partly depends on reserve ratios, etc.

Availability of credit has been considered an important channel for the effects of monetary policy on economic activity (Hawtrey, 1919; Roosa, 1951; Gurley and Shaw, 1960; Friedman B., 1981). In neoclassical economics, capital markets are usually assumed to be perfect; thus, there is no difference between debt financing and equity financing (Modigliani–Miller proposition). Accounting for market imperfections, especially asymmetric information, an alternative approach stresses the existence of credit rationing (e.g. Hodgman, 1960; Jaffee and Russell, 1976; Stiglitz and Weiss, 1981). Credit rationing affects availability of funds for investment because, to a different degree, firms are equity constrained (Greenwald and Stiglitz, 1986a, 1986b). This is the case in China but for different reasons. As discussed in Chapter 3, capital markets are still underdeveloped in China. In other words, the substitutability between debt financing and equity financing is highly imperfect. More importantly, securities issues as a whole do not raise substantial funds. For example, they accounted for less than 5.5 per cent of physical investment in the UK over 1949–82 (Mayer, 1987).

In practice, monetary policy measures for investment control vary in different economies and in different time periods of the same economy. Other things being equal, the effectiveness of monetary policy depends on:

(i) the importance of external financing of investment;
(ii) the importance of credit in external financing; and
(iii) the possibility and costs of alternative external financing, e.g. equity financing.

Since bank credit became a very important external source of fixed assets investment in China in the 1980s, monetary policy could play an important role in affecting investment.

Although the cost of investment was not irrelevant in the interactive process of investment between the centre and the localities in China, its importance was almost entirely eliminated by fiscal factors. First, property rights of local governments meant that tax revenues were equivalent to return on investment in the form of profits. As a result, many loss-making investments (if the net sum of profit and taxes was positive) actually contributed positively to local revenues. Next, intergovernmental fiscal arrangements allowed subsidies to loss-making enterprises to be excluded from the revenue of local governments. This therefore internalised the profit-and-loss account of the entire state sector. Furthermore, since investment returns and fiscal redistribution were mixed up, low-return investment was effectively protected. Finally, fiscal policies were designed to reduce the cost of investment to such an extent that not only full interest, but also a considerable part of the principal, of bank fixed assets investment loans were actually repaid out of the state budget as a whole. Given all these features, it is not surprising that the key financial factor determining the level of investment in China during the period under study was the control over availability of credit.

In principle, the imposition of bank credit ceilings should have been sufficient to stop unwanted credit expansion if the ceilings were credible and comprehensive. However, as has been argued, bank credit ceilings were exceeded because policy makers had to allow them to be exceeded in order to protect priority investments. For credit ceilings to be feasible, either local governments have to alter their investment pattern for a given investment scale or their investment scale must be reduced, given the pattern. It was the latter that policy-makers decided to achieve in 1988. As already mentioned, the target set for 1989 was to cut nominal investment by 21 per cent. This target was applicable to every locality. Investment control was administratively exercised, mainly through cancelling new investment projects and suspending existing ones. Credit control by reducing the availability of funds was employed as the chief economic means to reinforce such a 'crackdown' campaign. Credit control in 1988–9 covered not only fixed assets investment loans *per se*, but also working capital loans. The latter is relevant for fixed assets investment control because it is often used illegally for fixed assets investment.[6] Working capital was also necessary for putting completed investment projects into operation (considering that all increment in working capital of the SOEs since 1979 was provided by domestic loans). The experience of credit control in 1988–9 reflected the policy-makers' determination to control investment.

To reduce the availability of funds to local governments, a great effort was made to enforce bank credit ceilings. First, in order to signal that breaking credit ceilings was no longer allowed, the State Council took over monetary management from the Head Office of the PBC. Unlike the usual practice,[7] it directly issued the 'Decree on Further Control over Money [Supply] and Stabilising Finance' on 27 September 1988. The decree reaffirmed that extension of bank credit had to be within ceilings. A crucial factor was that provincial governments, together with provincial PBC branches, were made accountable for maintaining provincial credit ceilings. Second, in October 1988 the central government launched a nationwide financial inspection to back up credit control. The inspection was led by the newly established 'State Council's Inspection Office'. 'Leading groups' headed by provincial governors in each province were also set up. Between October 1988 and January 1989, 21 814 inspection teams, comprising 97 010 staff,[8] were organised to do the job. Financial institutions were first asked to carry out self-inspection. Then 13 052 of these institutions (65 per cent of the total) were randomly chosen for outside inspections. It was reported that ¥35.3 billion over-due loans and 'risk debts' were repaid as a result.[9] Third, since lending of non-bank financial institutions was not subject to the credit ceilings (until 1989), lending of the Trust and Investment Companies (TICs) was frozen at the June (1988) level. At the same time, in September 1988 a ¥2 billion special deposit was required from the TICs. In the following October, a ¥5 billion special deposit was required from the PBC's branches in Guangdong province and the Shenzhen Special Economic Zone. In 1989, credit ceiling control became more timely and comprehensive. In addition to annual credit ceilings, the PBC began to impose quarterly credit control with monthly examination of bank credit extension. The coverage of credit ceilings was enlarged to include non-bank financial institutions and direct financing, e.g. issuance of enterprise bonds and shares. Fourth, in order to weaken the control of local governments over management of local bank branches, the central government took over power from the provincial governments by appointing and removing governors and vice governors of provincial branches of the PBC in 1989.[10] Appointments and removals of governors and vice-governors of local branches of the SBs required the consent of PBC branches at the same level and were submitted to the next higher level for approval.[11] At the same time, a low bank credit ceiling (increment) was set for 1989, at only ¥160 billion – only 3.2 per cent higher than the credit ceiling for 1988. Indirectly, the financing capability of both banks and non-bank financial institutions was reduced by raising the required reserve ratio from 12 to 13 per cent from 1 September 1988. The SBs' required deposits at the PBC were maintained at the level of 5–7 per cent of their total deposits. This strengthened the PBC's financial power in its lending operations (to be discussed shortly).

With respect to the cost of capital, the level of lending rates (constant

Table 7.3 Changes in bank lending rates (1985–90) (% per annum)

	Aug.85	*Sep.88*	*Jan.89*	*Mar.90*	*Aug.90*
Working capital	7.92	9.00	11.34	9.00	8.64
Fixed assets investment					
1–3 years (including 3 years)	8.64	9.90	12.78	10.08	10.08
3–5 years (including 5 years)	9.36	10.80	14.40	11.52	10.80
5–10 years (including 10 years)	10.08	13.32	19.26	11.88	11.16
Change in retail price level[a]	9.70	25.40	27.00	3.30	4.00

Note: [a] Percentage increase compared with the same month last year.

Source: The PBC.

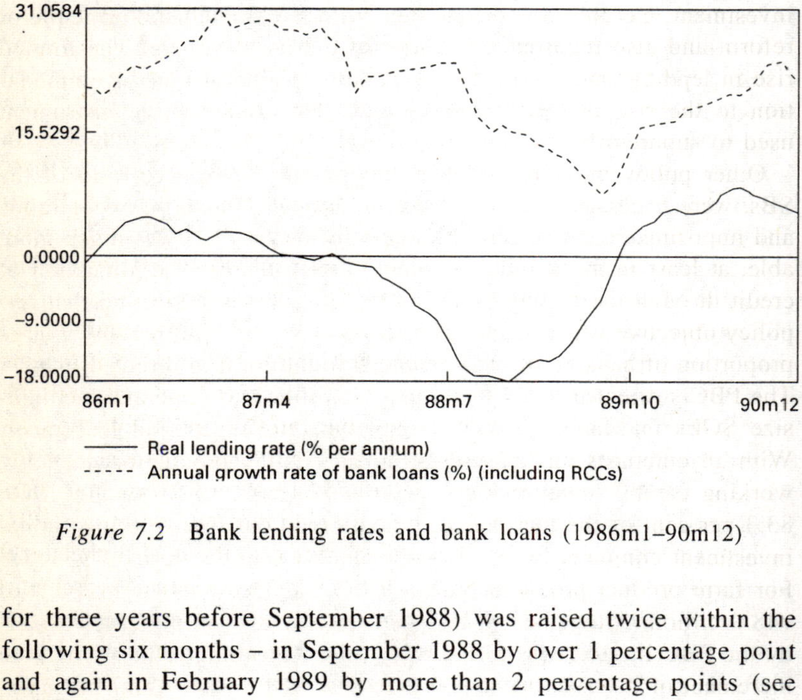

Figure 7.2 Bank lending rates and bank loans (1986m1–90m12)

for three years before September 1988) was raised twice within the following six months – in September 1988 by over 1 percentage point and again in February 1989 by more than 2 percentage points (see Table 7.3).

Although measures were taken both to reduce availability of funds and to increase the cost of capital, the effect of the latter on the demand for loans was insignificant because the increase was much smaller than the inflation rate, leaving a substantial decrease in real lending rates in 1989. If any relation between real lending rates[12] and growth of bank loans can be observed at all, the effect was a positive one, with a few months' time lag (see Figure 7.2). All available evidence suggest that the limited rise in lending rates had no negative effect on investment in China's economy. This is actually not abnormal. One of the more established facts in macroeconomics is that investment and the cost of funds are either non-correlated or only weakly correlated even in the developed market economies.

In theory, channelling credit control through higher lending rates meant that banks had financial resources as well as incentives to lend, but did not lend because there was inadequate demand for loans due to the high cost of borrowing (i.e. high lending rate). In China's case, this required real lending rates to be higher than the investment return, in terms of the sum of profit and taxes generated in proportion to total investment. Yet this was inconsistent with the gradualistic principle of reform and also required a redesign of the fiscal system. The limited rise in lending rates in 1988–9 is better explained as an accommodation to the rise in deposit rates rather than as an active instrument used to suppress borrowing.

Other policy measures, such as increasing the reserve ratio of the SBs, were necessary for allocative purposes. By raising reserve ratios and imposing excessive reserve requirement, the PBC was much more able, at least in its financing capability, to influence the allocation of credit through its lending policy to the SBs (bearing in mind that one policy objective was to adjust allocation of resources). In 1989, a large proportion of bank credit was extended in the form of directed loans.[13] The PBC's directed loans totalling ¥27.4 billion to large and medium-size SOEs in March, August, September, November and December. With an emphasis on full utilisation of existing production capacity, working capital loans received priority in credit extension. In 1989, 83.3 per cent of the increment in bank credit was for working capital investment compared with 71.8 per cent on average during 1984–8.[14] For farm product procurement, the PBC extended short-term loans of ¥48.0 billion. Altogether, at least 52 per cent of working capital loans by the PBC in 1989 was directed lending. According to the ICBC, the increment of its credit to 40 000 industrial SOEs was ¥45.57 billion in 1989, of which 68.8 per cent was extended to 6615 large and medium-sized industrial SOEs compared with 46.5 per cent in 1988.[15] Directed lending was necessary because local bank branches tended to protect enterprises subordinate to local governments and thus left centrally controlled enterprises underfunded.

Table 7.4 Fixed investment of the government sector

	1988	*1989*	*1990*
Total projects	166 000	126 500[a]	123 000
(of which new projects)	78 000	37 000	55 800[b]
The projects cancelled or or suspended	14 400[c]	18 000	n.a.

Note and Source: [a] It was reported that the number of projects was 3536 less than in 1989. [b] Number of the completed projects comes from SSB (1990a: 160, 204). Other figure: *People's Daily (Overseas Edition)* 2 March 1989; 22 February 1990, and 23 February 1991. [c] Cancelled or suspended in the final quarter of the year.

Tightening credit as a means of investment control was effective. A large number of existing fixed-asset investment projects were suspended or cancelled and the number of new projects were sharply reduced (see Table 7.4). Although nominal growth of fixed asset investment in 1989 decreased by 8 per cent against a targeted cut of 21 per cent, fixed asset investment dropped by about 17.3 per cent in real terms in 1989.

The success in investment control in 1989 caused a sharp fall in the growth rate of aggregate output. Although household income grew faster than national income during reform, the former was closely related to the latter. A fall in national income directly affected household income (see Figure 7.3).

Since households had a long-term saving purpose, the decrease in income directly caused a decrease in consumption expenditure and the increase in savings was maintained although at a slower rate. In 1989, nominal household money income increased by ¥111.8 billion, of which ¥80.8 billion was expended on consumer goods and services. In real terms, household money income decreased by 3.5 per cent and real household consumption expenditure fell by 5.0 per cent. Remarkably, growth of household savings increased in 1989. In nominal terms, it grew by 21.5 per cent compared with 21.3 per cent in 1988 (in real terms, 3.0 per cent and 3.5 per cent respectively). The household saving ratio also increased slightly from 16.0 in 1988 to 17.1 in 1989, despite negative growth of real income. In 1990, growth household income resumed and reached 9.1 per cent in real terms. Households increased their savings dramatically while their consumption expenditure rose by only 2.7 per cent (their saving ratio rose to 21.6 per cent).

The response of household consumption expenditure was a very important factor behind the successful demand management which re-

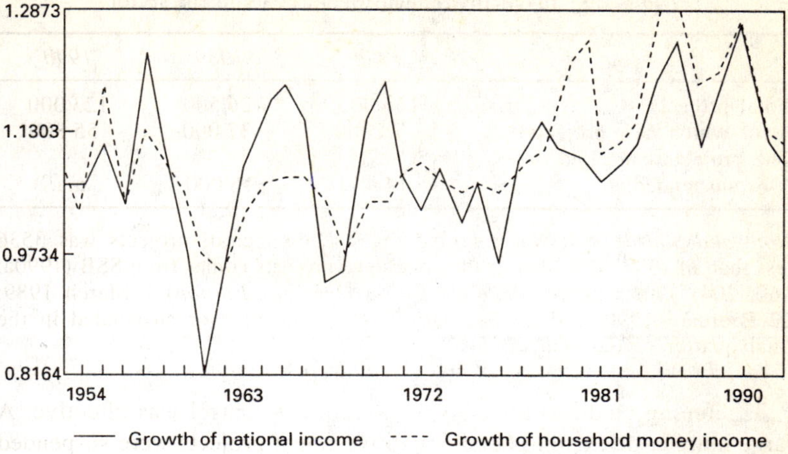

Figure 7.3 Growth of national income and household income (1954–90)

Table 7.5 Deposit rate for households (1985–90) (% per annum)

	Aug.85–Aug.88	*Sep.88–Jan.89*	*Feb.89–Mar.90*	*Apr.90–Aug.90*	*Aug.90–Dec.90*
6 months	6.12	6.48	9.00	7.74	6.48
1 year	7.20	8.64	11.34	10.08	8.64
3 years	8.28	9.72	13.14	11.88	10.08
5 years	9.36	10.80	14.94	13.68	11.52
8 years	10.44	12.42	17.64	16.20	13.68
Change in retail price level	10.15	26.24	14.65	1.52	1.43

Source: The PBC.

lied largely upon tight credit control. Since deposit rate policy was more actively used in the period 1988–90 than previously, it merits some discussion. As described in section 4.4.3 of Chapter 4, Chinese households save mainly for long-term purposes. A small change in deposit rates therefore has only marginal effects on household savings. However, a large rise in real deposit rates would significantly affect the household saving ratio. Provided that interest earnings are not withdrawn from the saving account, the same amount increases simultaneously in both household bank deposits and household income, *ceteris paribus*, which leads to a significant increase in the household saving ratio. Table 7.5 reports changes in deposit rates during the period (1985–90).

Table 7.6 Indexation of deposit rates (% per annum)

	Basic rate	*Subsidy rate*	*Total*
4th quarter 1988	9.72	7.28	17.00
1st quarter 1989	13.14	12.71	25.85
2nd quarter 1989	13.14	12.59	25.73
3rd quarter 1989	13.14	13.64	26.78
4th quarter 1989	13.14	8.36	21.50
1st quarter 1990	13.14	0.78	13.92
2nd quarter 1990	11.88	0.93	12.81
3rd quarter 1990	10.98	0.00	10.98
4th quarter 1990	10.08	0.00	10.08

Note: For the term deposits of three years and longer.

Source: The PBC.

Moreover, inflation indexation (adding subsidy rates to the base deposit rates) was introduced in September 1988 to term deposits with a duration of three years or longer. The subsidy rates were calculated as the mark-up, i.e. the difference between interest rates and retail price indexes in various localities. Table 7.6 shows the basic rates and average subsidy rates.

To encourage savings, household deposit rates were raised twice in 1988–9 by between 2.88 and 7.2 percentage points (Table 7.5, the differences between the first and third column). In 1989, the extra payment due to an average increase of 2.7 percentage points in deposit rates amounted[16] to ¥12.1 billion.[17] The additional interest payment due to deposit rate indexation is estimated at ¥9 billion.[18] All together, ¥21.1 billion was added simultaneously to household bank deposits and money income in 1989. This was equivalent to about 2.3 per cent of household money income in that year. In 1990, in order to encourage spending, nominal deposit rates were cut by between 2.52 and 3.96 percentage points (see Table 7.5, the differences between the third and fifth column). But because of the sharp drop in the inflation rate, the real deposit rates increased substantially. For example, the one-year-fixed-term deposit rate effectively increased by about 10.5 percentage points – from about minus 3 per cent to about 7.5 per cent. The average increase in real deposit rates is estimated at 9 percentage points, equivalent to about 5.0 per cent of household money income in 1990. In other words, about half the increment in real household money income in 1990 was due to increases in deposit rates. Reflected in the household

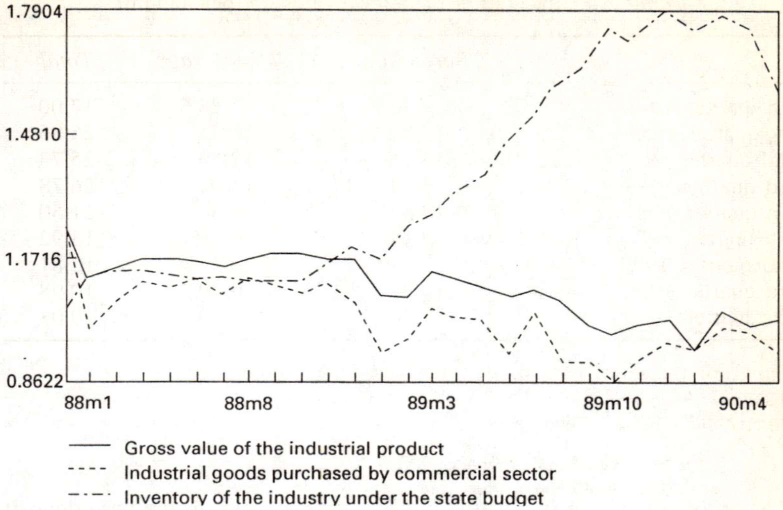

Figure 7.4 Changes in industrial output, industrial goods purchased by commercial sector and industrial inventory (1988m1–90m4) (Same month previous year = 1.00)

saving ratio, it increased from 17.1 per cent in 1989 to 21.6 per cent in 1990.

The decrease in real incomes together with a continued high household saving propensity caused growth of retail sales to fall below target. It grew by only 8.9 per cent in nominal terms against a targeted 15.6 per cent. In real terms, it was minus 8.9 per cent.[19] Actually, both fixed assets investment and retail sales in 1990 were still significantly lower than in 1988 in real terms by 7.5 per cent and 15.6 per cent respectively.

The reduction in demand and sales caused a massive pile-up of unsold stocks which in turn adversely affected production. The impact of the fall in demand on industrial output is clearly evident in Figure 7.4. The close relationship between industrial output and industrial goods purchased by the commercial sector is apparent.[20] Although growth of the gross value of industrial output is calculated at fixed prices, the negative relationship between rapid accumulation of industrial inventories (at current prices) and the slowdown in growth of industrial output is also visible in the figure.

The growth of the gross industrial product fell from 20.4 per cent in October 1988 to 0.9 per cent in September 1989 and minus 2.1 per

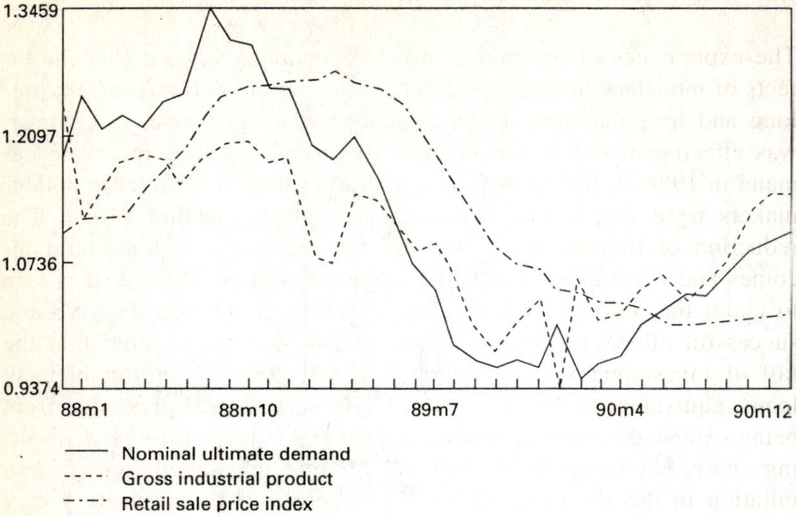

Figure 7.5 Changes in nominal ultimate demand, industrial output and price level of retail sales (1988m1–90m12) (Same month previous year = 1.00)

cent in the following month. The growth then gradually recovered as result of government stimulatory policies. In the meantime, the fall in aggregate demand led to the sharp deceleration of inflation. In 1989 the rise in the retail price level was 17.8 per cent against 18.5 per cent in 1988, but fell to just 2.1 per cent in 1990. On a monthly basis, the retail price level continued to rise from 25.4 per cent in September 1988 to 27.9 per cent in February 1989, but fell steadily to 7.4 per cent in December 1989 and to just 0.4 in August 1990. Using the sum of retail sales and the fixed assets investment of the state sector as an approximate index of ultimate domestic demand,[21] Figure 7.5 shows that both changes in industrial output (at constant prices) and the retail price level were closely related to trends in ultimate demand during 1988–90.

The accumulation of inventories was accelerating during the 'economic rectification'. The piling-up of inventory explains the fact that although both fixed assets investment and retail sales declined, the growth of the GNP was still 3.95 and 4.99 per cent in 1989 and 1990 – in real terms, – neither are very low by international standards.

7.3 COSTS AND LIMITS OF TIGHT MONEY

The experiences of developed market economies suggest that the effects of monetary tightening (through interest rate policy) are felt after long and irregular lags. Tight monetary policy in China, in contrast, was effective within a narrow span of time in curbing aggregate demand in 1988–9. By making credit ceilings effective,[22] Chinese policy-makers were able to cut investment dramatically within a year. The reduction of investments led in turn to reductions in household incomes and eventually in consumption expenditures. Overall, it is safe to claim that during 1988–9, tight monetary policy had decisive and successful effects on demand management, bearing in mind that the fall of investment was overwhelming – about ¥132 billion in bank loans, equivalent to 8.3 per cent of GNP in 1989, was prevented from being extended between September 1988 and August 1989. The resulting sharp fall in aggregate demand brought down both growth and inflation in the short run. However, the costs of the austerity policy were also dramatic.

First of all, as mentioned earlier, the growth of GNP fell from 11 per cent in 1988 to 4.0 and 5.2 per cent in 1989 and 1990 respectively, lower than targeted (7–8 per cent). Meanwhile, unemployment increased. By the end of 1989, the number of SOEs and urban COEs workers with their jobs suspended or semi-suspended reached 6.68 million or 6 per cent of the total. The registered number of self-employed in the urban area decreased by 3.61 million.[23] More than 10 million 'farmer-workers' returned to their villages.[24]

Second, enormous losses occurred. As discussed in Chapter 2, in China's industrial sector, resources are utilised inefficiently by large numbers of local manufacturing enterprises which are poorly equipped. High-speed growth is essential for such industries to be profitable. Successful control over demand slowed industrial growth from 20.8 per cent in 1988 to 8.5 and 7.6 per cent in 1989 and 1990. This resulted in a huge increase in the number of loss-making enterprises as well as in total losses. After-tax profit as a percentage of sales in industrial enterprises at and above the township level was 8.5 in 1988. Without any changes in tax rates, it dropped to 6.3 (by 26 per cent) in 1989 and to 3.3 (by 61 per cent) in 1990.[25] The declining trend of profitability was, of course, not new. The extent of the decline during 1989–90, however, was very remarkable. Nearly 70 per cent of profits of industrial SOEs in the state budget were wiped out between 1988–90; it was ¥77.9 billion in 1988, but ¥24.6 billion in 1990 (SSB, 1991a:

Table 7.7 Estimates of the total losses of the SOEs (¥ bn)

	1988	*1989*	*1990*
(1) The loss subsidies from the state budget	44.6	60.0	66.5
(2) The total reported losses [(1)/0.856)]	52.1	70.1	77.7
(3) The total true losses[a]	93.8	154.2	170.9

Note: [a] Estimated as 80% more than (2) for 1988, and 120% more for 1989–90. This is because the amount of losses which occurred in 1989 or 1990 was much larger than in 1988.

81). The proportion of industrial enterprises in the state budget which made losses increased from 12.2 to 31.3 per cent between 1988 and 1990. The reported losses of industrial SOEs in the state budget more than quadrupled during 1988–90 (SSB, 1991a: 81). Usually, losses made by the SOEs were covered by subsidies from the state budget. Recently, however, because of the fiscal difficulties, subsidies to SOEs could only cover a proportion of their actual losses. For instance, in 1988, SOEs losses amounted to ¥52.1 billion, but the subsidies were only ¥44.6 billion or 85.6 per cent of total losses.[26]

In fact, the official figure for loss-making SOEs is not realistic. A considerable proportion of actual losses went unreported by enterprises in recent years because they were inclined to report profits in order to take advantage of the profit-retention scheme and to protect bonus and welfare payments. According to a survey conducted by the MOF and its local departments in nine provinces and municipalities, 78.6 per cent of the industrial SOEs surveyed deliberately hid losses to varying degrees. The total amount of hidden losses during 1986–90 was 1.8 times that reported.[27] Another survey of 40 158 SOEs conducted by the ICBC (Industrial and Commercial Bank of China) found that 41.2 per cent of enterprises surveyed had similar problems. The amount was also larger than the figure of loss reported (*People's Daily*, 5 December 1991). Taking the above factors into account, Table 7.7 provides a rough estimate of real losses of SOEs in 1988–90.

The estimates for 1989–90 might be conservative. Nevertheless, they indicate the scale of reported and hidden SOE losses. COEs were no exception. For instance, losses made by village industrial enterprises also increased from ¥1.85 billion in 1988 to ¥4.74 billion in 1990 (total number of TVEs dropped by 378 000 (2.0 per cent) during 1989–90).

Third, the problem of inefficient resource allocation was not resolved. Most of the investment projects cut or suspended were for technical

Table 7.8 Asymmetrical change in fixed investment of the State sector (1986–90, ¥ bn)

	1986	*1987*	*1988*	*1989*	*1990*
Capital construction investment	10.2	16.7	23.1	2.3	15.2
(of which energy industry)	6.2	7.3	7.2	3.5	11.2
Technical updating investment	17.0	13.9	22.2	–19.2	4.1

Source: SSB (1991a: 143, 150).

updating and transformation. It is clear from Table 7.8 that technical updating investment in the state sector was affected much more than capital construction investment when total investment was cut.

The problem of irrational resource allocation was also reflected in deteriorating product quality. As noted in Chapter 2, in the last quarter of 1989 only 73.7 per cent of output came up to standard – a much lower percentage than before.[28] In 1991, this ratio further declined to 59.46 per cent. This is extraordinary, inasmuch as one would expect improvement of product quality when inventory grows and market demand slackens. One explanation is that product quality deteriorated because the better producers were more badly hit than other producers because of the tight credit control and the local protectionism of trade.

Fourth, the fragility of banks increased. Taking the economy as a whole, outstanding bank loans expanded by 7.9 times between 1978 and 1990. As a proportion of GNP, they increased from 53 to 95 per cent.[29] This means that if average interest rate was 10 per cent in 1990, total interest charge would account for 9.5 per cent of the GNP. An economy with such a debt burden is surely highly vulnerable to business cycles and trade conditions. When the economy is booming, everything is fine; but when it enters a downturn, problems of illiquidity and insolvency would mount. From this point of view, tight money would hit not only the economy in general but also the banks themselves. Sales profitability of the industrial SOEs under the state budget declined from 8.7 per cent in 1988 to 2.6 per cent in 1990.[30] According to survey data of 769 industrial SOEs by the Economic Institute of Chinese Academy of Social Sciences, interest payment as a percentage of value added increased from 5.84 in 1988 to 9.24 in 1989 (Tang, 1992). At the same time, the problem of non-performing loans worsened. The reported and hidden SOEs losses were financed only partly by subsidies from the state budget (less than 40 per cent according to Table 7.7). The remaining part was virtually financed by bank credit.

Very few enterprises (at the level above township) went out of business because of losses. In September 1989, deferred loans reached ¥110 billion,[31] equivalent to 11 per cent of total outstanding loans.[32] More seriously, tight credit control not only exposed the inefficient firms, but it also hit higher-performance firms because they were forced to pay back bank loans. According to a survey conducted in nine provinces, only 30 per cent of repaid industrial working capital loans was justifiable (Niu, R. *et al.*, 1990). Furthermore, a debt chain known as the 'tri-angle debt' (i.e. inter-firm trade credit) in China developed, directly threatening normal transactions between enterprises. It was so serious that, in 1992, an 'Office for Triangular Debt Clearing' was formed, headed by a deputy prime minister. Eventually, over 30 billion additional bank loans were extended to break the debt chain.[33]

In summary, tight money was powerful because it reduced availability of funds for investment through credit control by making credit ceilings credible. Credibility of these ceilings depended upon the determination of the centre and the obedience of local governments. Success in investment control reduced the growth of household income. Since Chinese households save for long-term purposes, the reduction in income directly affects their consumption expenditure. In comparison, the effect of increases in deposit rates on household savings was marginal. On the surface, the higher deposit rates seemed to help increase household savings. This was because higher deposit rates led to more interest being paid on a unit of household bank deposits and this interest payment was simply added on to bank deposits rather than being expended. In the very short term, although austere monetary policy was effective in bringing inflation down through aggregate demand management:

(i) it was excessive;
(ii) it was unable to achieve stable and sustainable economic growth.

The costs of tight money were high. More importantly, the systemic problems of China's economy remained unresolved. Expansionary monetary policy was resumed after September 1989, and it was quite possible that another stop–go cycle would be repeated.

It is worth noting that the limitations of monetary control does not mean that proper degrees of monetary control should not be implemented during the restructuring of the economic system. For instance, if the policy was internally more coherent, i.e. if the links between investment, income and household consumption expenditure were better understood, the excesses of investment clampdown might be less severe.

8 Summary and Policy Issues

8.1 SUMMARY

The package of policy and systemic reforms introduced by the Chinese leadership in 1978 comprised two major components. One was a shift in development policy away from the previous pattern of extensive growth based on the priority development of the producer goods sector. The new development strategy was aimed at achieving more balanced, proportionate and sustainable development based on intensive growth and increased economic efficiency. To enhance efficiency, the new strategy entailed the sectoral reallocation of resources away from the input-intensive producer goods sector towards the less-input-intensive consumer goods sector. Both the open-door policy and the emphasis on consumer goods production were essential to enhancing efficiency: the former through greater participation in the international division of labour and the import of advanced technology; the latter improved living standards and thereby raised workers' incentives.

The other component was a more fundamental and long-term solution to increasing economic efficiency as a prerequisite to balanced and sustainable development: market-oriented systemic reforms which could enhance allocative efficiency as well as the operational or internal efficiency of firms (enterprises). Indeed, these two components – the shift in development policy priorities and market-oriented systemic reforms – were indivisible. In particular, systemic reforms were aimed at creating new institutional arrangements conducive to the implementation of the new development strategy.

Reforms in China have proved remarkably successful. China's real GDP grew by an annual average of about 9 per cent during the 1980s. Strong growth of aggregate output was accompanied by very significant increases in living standards. But China's economic performance since reforms began has also been characterised by a number of shortcomings. It is not clear whether economic efficiency, say as measured by total factor productivity, has increased substantially. Growth has been fuelled largely by excessive investment, especially in the manufacturing sectors. This type of growth has led to periodic overheating with the accompanying problems of inflationary pressures, sectoral disproportions and macroeconomic imbalances and instability. Weaknesses in the infrastructure sectors, in transport and telecommunications, which were an inherited legacy of the pre-1978 economy, have been exacerbated both by rapid economic growth in general and by an unbalanced pattern of investment characterised by under-investment in basic industries and infrastructure. The sectoral pattern of investment and of capacity expansion, together with serious bottlenecks in infrastructure, suggest that there is considerable misallocation of resources. This type of growth has been made possible by a remarkably accommodative monetary stance by the central policy-makers, with seemingly uncontrollable and imprudent growth of monetary and credit aggregates. Excessive monetary expansion inevitably resulted in macroeconomic imbalances and instability, forcing the central government to restore economic order through traditional and harsh administrative methods of macroeconomic and monetary control – the use of which run counter to the stated policy aim of market-oriented reform. This has led to periodic stop–go cycles in Chinese policy making and performance. The costs of each austerity programme, as has been shown in Chapter 7 of this study, are very high indeed. In view of the insufficient progress in increasing economic efficiency, the growing sectoral imbalances and the inherent macroeconomic instability, it is reasonable to conclude that the type of economic growth witnessed during the 1980s is unlikely to be sustainable in the long term unless a substantial capital inflow continues to take place. For growth to be sustainable, the underlying policy and systemic defects have to addressed. One of the most serious problems concerns the financial system – a system which continually exhibits excessive and destabilising monetary and credit expansion.

This study has presented six basic arguments to explain continuous monetary expansion in China during reform.

1. As argued in Chapter 3, monetary expansion was driven by the expansion of bank loans, especially banks' finance for fixed assets investment. The central bank played an important role in supporting such credit expansion through its massive lending to the specialised banks (SBs).
2. Excessive bank credit expansion (at least in terms of exceeding planned targets) can be explained in a game-theoretic framework: as a product of an investment game between central and local governments. Chapter 4 argues that in this game, investments for technical updating and transformation of existing enterprises – as well as for infrastructure – were inadequately financed by local governments. To adjust and

rectify this unbalanced investment pattern in order to promote and maintain economic growth, central policy-makers were compelled to provide more funds for these investments by, in a sense, violating their own prudent credit policy. The growth of state budgetary revenues was limited by decentralisation, and changes in the relative importance of the government, enterprise and household sectors brought about by reforms meant that the central government was no longer the main saver. Households had become the most important source of savings. Unable to resolve problems of resource allocation directly, the policy-makers therefore resorted to banks for more funds. In other words, bank loans had to be expanded to meet the needs. Chapter 4 also explained why other measures for rectifying the unbalanced pattern of local governments, and for adhering to stated credit targets, were either technically or politically not feasible. The use of the banking system to solve the problems of underfinancing of priority investment was the easy option for central policy-makers.

3. Such a game situation arises from incompatible incentives between the central and local governments. The problem of incompatible incentives is argued in Chapter 5 to be embedded in the Chinese economic system characterised by local government property rights. Although decentralisation reform without a fundamental change in the system design alleviated the problem of incentive failure, it exacerbated the problem of incentive incompatibility in resource allocation. Decentralisation and reforms succeeded in strengthening the incentives for local governments to promote rapid economic development and maintain high investment levels, but these incentives at the same time led to a divergence from the direction of investment preferred by the centre. Because of its peculiar systemic features, a local government in China acted simultaneously as investment decision-maker, tax collector and local employment manager. It was concerned not only with increasing profit, but also with tax revenue and employment generation in the locality under its jurisdiction. Its investment decision-making was therefore (i) local-border constrained, and (ii) biased towards establishing industries with higher tax rates, such as processing industries, which could broaden its tax base. Such investment behaviour was magnified by the fiscal system which combined fiscal redistribution and investment return. Low return of investment was effectively subsidised by higher levels of government through fiscal redistribution. The very heavy reliance of government revenues upon indirect taxation further encouraged

such investment patterns because to local governments, tax revenues were equivalent to after-tax profits of an investment project. Given the dual function of local governments as tax collector and residual claimer of investment profits, the tax policy actually encouraged investment in processing industries. This was the case despite fiscal measures designed to discourage such investment. Local governments were further encouraged to invest in smaller-scale projects because of preferential income-tax treatments for small enterprises. This further militated against investments in infrastructure which were usually very large in scale.

4. Chapter 6 examined in greater detail the structure and processes of the banking system which made expansion of bank credit a workable solution for the central policy-makers seeking to ensure adequate investments in priority areas. Bank credit was shown to be effectively the best way of satisfying demand for funds from both central and local governments, given (i) the expansion of household savings associated with changes in national income distribution favouring the household sector; (ii) the rising households' saving ratio, and (iii) the excessive financial intermediation between households and the enterprise sectors, through the state bank system, given an underdeveloped financial market and lack of both portfolio choice for savers and alternative channels for financial intermediation.
5. Chapter 6 also argued that the institutional characteristics of the Chinese banking system meant that local bank branches had a vested interest in pursuing the interests of the local governments rather than in defending or enforcing policies of their headquarters. This facilitated central-locality interactions in investment and hence excessive credit expansion. From an institutional perspective, the banking system in China was dually controlled by central and local governments. Local bank branches were agents of local governments rather than higher bank branches. The subordination of local bank branches to local governments was further magnified by (i) local monopoly of deposit collection, (ii) disjointed objectives of supporting local economic development while carrying out macroeconomic policies, and (iii) explicit deposit insurance and non-failure of local bank branches (the problem of moral hazard). Within this systemic setting, decentralisation reform simultaneously stimulated mobilisation of savings and exacerbated segmentation of loans allocation, both favoured by the local governments. At the same time, this gave both central and local governments easy access to bank loans.
6. In the short term, bank credit can be very effectively controlled by

cutting investment through administrative means. However, as argued in Chapter 7, austere credit control was easily exaggerated under the Chinese system and entailed very high economic and social costs. A general tight policy would not work because it was against the interests of an individual local government and the centre would have had great problems in monitoring it. It thus lacked creditability. In order to show absolute determination, the policy-makers had to overdo it. In such a situation, austere monetary policy would cause recession in the short term. In addition, inadequate understanding of household saving behaviour also contributed to an excessive reduction in demand. In responding to a decrease in income, households cut their consumption expenditures rather than use part of their financial wealth to smooth their consumption flow. Furthermore, since allocative problems cannot be resolved and the bad debt problems of enterprises worsen during a very tight monetary regime as a result of both falling demand and increasing interest rates, tight money could actually destabilise the economy in the longer term.

8.2 POLICY IMPLICATIONS

Against China's overall economic performance in the past fourteen years, the above findings do not suggest that the monetary expansion was a disaster. It effectively financed the priority investment of the central government. However, in this process the problem of excessive liquidity of financial assets of the economy emerged. Chinese policy-makers have hitherto been fortunate in generally avoiding unmanageable excess demand for consumer goods because of the rise in household voluntary savings. But this rise is not always secure and the longer-term savings behaviour of Chinese households remain inadequately understood. When the economy overheats through expansion of investment fuelled by excessive bank loans, a sharp rise in inflation may occur together with a drop in the household saving ratio. Should this happen, the government would face immense difficulties in macroeconomic stabilisation given the inadequacy of existing macro control instruments. At a deeper level, what is more worrying is not monetary expansion *per se* but the continued extensive development in the real economy.

The findings of this study suggest a number of implications for policy.

First, the study has sought to demonstrate that the three key problems in the Chinese economy (as described in Chapter 2) – weak macroeconomic control, slow improvement of efficiency, and fragility of banks – are interrelated. This suggests that excessive monetary expansion cannot be resolved by tighter monetary control alone. Given the systemic and institutional peculiarities of the Chinese economic system, monetary control is not 'exogenous' but 'endogenous'. Macroeconomic control was weak because extra funds had to be raised to compensate for an unbalanced investment pattern by local governments, which reflect allocative inefficiencies. An accommodating monetary stance in turn further discouraged improvement of allocative efficiency and fulfilled the demand for credit from inefficient enterprises, leading to growth of non-performing loans and erosion of the capital base of the banking system. Fragility of banks also developed because too much of the banks' profits was extracted by the central government for its priority investment, and at the same time non-performing loans mounted in relation to the slow improvement of allocative efficiency. So, improvement of aggregate monetary control has to be based on micro-level improvement in the allocation of resources. In order to improve allocative efficiency of resources, the problems associated with the economic system, and the present defective architecture of Chinese financial institutions and fiscal policies have to be resolved. In this respect, financial and non-financial spheres are interlocked, and macroeconomic and microeconomic issues in both systemic and policy spheres cannot be separated.[1]

Second, in the process of monetary expansion, the essential factor is incentive incompatibility between central and local governments, as well as within local governments in resource allocation under decentralisation. In this sense, monetary expansion can be attributed to partial economic reform – economic reform without reform of local government ownership. It is in this particular type of asynchronised reform process, that one can see the origin of monetary expansion. More precisely, this expansion was produced by the Chinese economic system based on local governments' ownership under conditions of decentralisation *pari passu* with restricted alternative channels of financial intermediation.

Ownership reform, whether in the form of joint-stock companies, public limited companies or other forms where property rights are clearly defined, together with greater market competition, would help not only in improving the internal efficiency of a firm (as is often claimed), but also allocative efficiency. More importantly, these changes would address the root cause of monetary expansion and the related liquidity risk and fragility of the banking system. On the surface and in the short term, industrial profitability would be improved immediately after part of debt capital has been converted into equity capital – interest payment becomes profit. Through changing money into risk-bearing equity, industry's gearing ratio would be lowered and the capital base of the banking system could be strengthened. In addition, a proper ownership reform would help in resolving the well-known problem of the centralisation–decentralisation dilemma: the policy favouring centralised investment control generated incentive failure on the lower level and inability of administration on the upper level; the policy in favour of decentralised control exacerbated the problem of incentive incompatibility. Such a dilemma has its roots in local government ownership. Since governments at all levels were dominant players in markets, the primary game in China's economy was not between government and autonomous individual firms, but between central and local governments. More precisely, the game was played between higher- and lower-level government with policy rules being set by the former.

Third, monetary expansion could be reduced by encouraging alternative channels of financial intermediation, e.g. issuing more government bonds. The government's reliance on bank loans rather than government debt to finance necessary expenditure is often discussed under the heading of 'quasi-fiscal' activities.[2] By creating this quasi-budget deficit, the government actually worsens the problem. First, its true magnitude is not explicit and thus it is difficult to receive a warning signal about the scale of this. Next, in terms of liquidity management, bank deposits are much more difficult to deal with than government bonds. Finally, the increasing quasi-budget deficit created obstacles for market-oriented banking reforms, such as commercialisation of the state banks.

Fourth, given an economic system characterised by the property rights of local governments, neither centralised control nor decentralised control would be desirable. Under relatively centralised control, the problem of information and incentive failure would arise; under relatively decentralised control, the problem of incentive incompatibility would occur. In neither case could the banks screen and monitor properly. In this respect, the extreme view that the more the control over resources is decentralised, or the lower the level of government to gain autonomy the better, is one-sided.

Fifth, increasing interest rate needs caution. This is not because the lending rate has little effect on the demand for loans and the deposit rate has only an insignificant effect on saving. It is because it would worsen firms' profitability and therefore the government's current account as well as the banks' bad debt problem. Such effects of a rise in interest rate will become stronger, bearing in mind that the rise of the gearing ratio of the industries has been continuing.

Sixth, apart from systemic factors, the households' consumption or saving behaviour can also contribute to an excessive response of demand to an austere policy. Households' consumption expenditure is very sensitive to income and thus investment. A reduction in their income would consequently reduce their consumption expenditure. By contrast, their savings are much less affected by their income reduction because they save for long-term purposes. This saving behaviour is a very beneficial factor for resource mobilisation. In this area, interest rate plays only a marginal role. However, the rising household saving ratio is not stable.

8.3 RELEVANCE OF THE WESTERN APPROACH TO FINANCIAL REFORM

It has been argued that behind the problems of monetary control in China are fundamental problems associated with defective system and institutional design. Before entering into discussion of policy issues based on the findings, it is worth reviewing very briefly the extent to which Western theory and experience can offer guidelines to financial reform in China.

Earlier literature on the development process stresses the importance of investment and capital accumulation (e.g. the Harrod–Domar growth model). Drawing upon the experience of the Great Depression in 1929–33, Keynes (1936: 351) argued that in a market economy there is a natural tendency (liquidity preference) to push the real interest rate too high to provide adequate inducement to invest. Unless this tendency is curbed, using every instrument society has at its disposal, the economy cannot settle on a full-employment equilibrium. After the Second World War, the common development strategy adopted by the developing economies was industrialisation. The government either acted directly to establish state-owned industry through budgetary funding, or it intervened in the financial sector to provide cheap funds for the priority industrial sectors. To encourage investment, a low-interest-rate policy was generally adopted.

Since the mid-1970s, the main intellectual bases for financial sector analysis and policy advice have been associated with McKinnon (1973) and Shaw (1973). The central idea of the McKinnon–Shaw analysis is that real rate of growth is gravely retarded by artificially low financial prices (including rates of interest and exchange rates), which cause financial restriction and repression (Shaw, 1973: 3–4). On one hand, low interest rates reduce the flow of loanable funds through the organised banking system; on the other hand, they encourage inefficient use of financial resources. The policy recommendation is therefore financial liberalisation, i.e. abolishing interest ceilings and directed credit programmes, deregulation, promoting market-oriented financial competition and so on. However, like the earlier prescription of financial control, financial liberalisation may be one-sided. It focuses on the negative aspect of government financial control, and neglects more fundamental factors in economic development.

Partly because of the influence of changing intellectual perspectives about the role of the financial sector, many developing countries shifted their policy in favour of financial liberalisation in the late 1970s and the 1980s. Some Latin-American countries experienced a series of bank panics and collapses during the introduction of a radical financial liberalisation process, whereas in Asia the story was more encouraging because its attitude towards financial liberalisation was less radical. A recent World Bank Development Report (the World Bank, 1989) provides a synthesis of current wisdom about the relationship between financial systems and development. It concludes that: 'In the past, governments' efforts to promote economic development by controlling interest rates, directing credit to priority sectors, and securing inexpensive funding for their own activities have undermined financial development.' The World Bank clearly recommends financial liberalisation. However, drawing on the experiences of financial liberalisation in Argentina, Chile, Uruguay and several Asian economies since the mid-1970s, the World Bank warns that liberating financial institutions from interest-rate or credit controls cannot by itself ensure that the financial system will develop as intended. It could result in destabilising capital outflows, high interest rates, bank failure and corporate distress, as it did in the Southern Cone countries. It suggests that financial liberalisation needs to be undertaken alongside macroeconomic reforms, to be accompanied by restructuring insolvent banks and firms and by adequate regulation and supervision. Overall, the conditions for the development of a more robust and balanced financial structure listed are:

- restoring macroeconomic stability, building better legal, accounting and regulatory systems;

- specifying rules for disclosing information more fully;
- levying taxes that do not fall excessively on finance (The World Bank, 1989, pp. 1–5).

The World Bank's recommendations are more sophisticated and balanced than that of McKinnon-Shaw. There are, however, problems. First, their suggestions are too general to be applied in practice. Moreover, it takes time to build financial foundations including legal, accounting, regulatory systems and information disclosure – and how to exercise better monetary control during the unavoidable transition period is virtually unknown. McKinnon (1989) admitted that knowledge as to how best to achieve financial liberalisation remains seriously incomplete. Second, the possible negative (often damaging) effects of tight money and high interest rates on the supply side have not received adequate attention. Bearing in mind that many firms in financially distressed economies are not competitive and are very vulnerable to external financial shock, the costs of the macroeconomic stability policy might be too high to bear, at least politically. Third, little discussion is devoted to the design of financial institutions for industrial financing and corporate control at the micro level. Where restructuring financial institutions is discussed, attention is generally given to the development of a more broadly based financial system, privatisation and autonomy of government-owned banks and so on. In other words, design of financial institutions for promoting growth is a subject that has yet to emerge in the development literature (Collier and Mayer, 1989).

More recently, McKinnon (1991) emphasises that there is an optimal order of economic liberalisation, which may vary for different economies depending on their initial conditions. In his view, from 1985 to 1991 the Soviets had the wrong order of liberalisation – before proper fiscal and monetary control over the Soviet economy was secured, they decontrolled prices, floated the exchange rate, privatised SOEs, and decentralised decision-making (McKinnon, 1991: 120). He further argues that fiscal control and government budget balance should precede financial liberalisation. Otherwise the government has to rely on inflation tax or undue reserve taxes on depositors to generate revenues (ibid., pp. 4, 8). To secure government revenues, he particularly recommends introducing VAT to profits, interest, rents, wages and salaries for reforming socialist economies (McKinnon, 1991: 134–5). He also suggests a major recapitalisation of both banks and enterprises before privatisation and decentralisation can safely take place (McKinnon, 1991: 7). In a broad sense, McKinnon's recommendation comes a step closer to the real problem facing the policy-makers. Nevertheless, it still has a considerable distance to go before being of immediate practical applicability to the Chinese reality.

8.4 SOME ISSUES FOR FURTHER POLICY RESEARCH

Since the problem underlying monetary expansion during reform is institutional in nature, improvement of monetary control has to be based on improvement of the system, particularly ownership and related financial system design. This does not, however, mean that a 'big bang' approach should be applied. Summarising lessons about the transformation processes in the CEE, Portes (1991) makes the criticism that too much was expected too quickly. The extreme 'big bang' approach (adopted in Poland and Czechoslovakia, for instance) is based on the idea that it is necessary to do everything simultaneously because everything depends on everything else. Although this is the ideal approach, it is administratively and institutionally non-implementable. Instead of the expected 'J-curve', the transformation prospects more closely follow an 'L-curve'. Focusing on feasibility, this section discusses only a few issues for further policy research in relation to this thesis.

The detailed policy recommendations for financial reform are beyond the scope of this study. However, based on the findings and their implications, some policy issues and areas need to be highlighted for further research.

(i) How to conduct ownership reform

Ownership reform, especially privatisation of SOEs, is almost a standard policy recommendation to the reforming economies.[3] In China's case, we do see the necessity for changing the property rights of the government (both central and local). The real issue is, what is the least costly way to do this? It might be more appropriate first to restructure corporate governance, the reasons being that:

(i) ownership reforms are better conducted by a single institution which exercises property rights fully;
(ii) ownership reform takes a long time during which the problem of ineffective corporate control would have to be dealt with;[4]
(iii) restructuring corporate governance itself (e.g. imposing a bottom-line discipline) is desirable for ownership reforms.

To reform government's property rights, segmented property rights have to be united into one single institution and *this* institution has to be corporatised or commercialised. First, all property rights of the government-owned enterprises should be delegated to the 'enterprise supervisory bodies'. These bodies may be divided (or merged) if too many (or too few) enterprises fall under their supervision. They should be empowered with full autonomy, compatible with a large corporation in a market economy, including that of investment (purchase or sale of physical or financial assets), the management of their subordinate firms, and production and pricing. At the same time, this has to be imposed with bottom-line discipline, i.e. financially, they have to stand on their own feet, making a good return on investment or failing to do so on the basis of their own success in competition. Among the necessary policy changes, capital accounts have to be set for each newly-formed corporate body (initially capitalised at the historical value) and their performance must be publicised. More importantly, capital account transactions must be encouraged and facilitated; barriers should be removed for free exchange of property rights legal entitlements. At present, there is limitation on inter-locality portfolio and direct investment flow.[5] Theoretically, agents with diverse endowments or preferences require exchange to obtain marginal benefits. If agents have differing marginal rates of substitution then trade exists benefiting both. The Coase Theorem states that, with regard to efficiency, the initial allocation of legal entitlements does not matter, so long as they can be freely exchanged.

The fact that corporatisation or commercialisation often refers to transformation of SOEs into managerially and financially autonomous entities merits emphasis (e.g. Kahn and Peck, 1991; Wood, A. 1991). According to the World Bank,[6] internal management of an enterprise in a market economy can be divided into three layers. At the bottom layer is cost control. The middle layer is centred on profits. Management at this layer sets output, price and inputs. At the top layer lies the investment decision-making. There is a big difference between an enterprise and a basic accounting unit. There could be hundreds of basic accounting units within an enterprise, but there is only one legal person, represented by the investment decision-making body. If an enterprise extends its investment decision-making power into its subordinated accounting units, the action amounts to suicide. Since an existing Chinese SOE, as a basic accounting unit, is comparable only with the lower layers of a corporate body in a fully-fledged market economy, the attempt to transform it into an independent enterprise is misleading. That is why corporatisation of enterprise supervisory bodies, rather than corporatisation of enterprises themselves, may be a better policy choice. The former is particularly desirable when a very low industrial concentration is taken into account. The corporatisation of enterprise supervisory bodies implies the creation of the M-form organisation.[7] The 'central office' of this organisation (acting as a 'surrogate' capital market), can provide a superior mechanism for allocating investment resources to different subsidiaries and therefore help restructure industry. Furthermore, such an organisation would have plenty of room for manoeuvre by reorganising itself through capital account transactions.

One of the difficulties in industrial restructuring is how to motivate local governments to promote industrial restructuring so as to integrate the local economy into domestic and international markets. At least three policy changes must occur. One is that industrial protection through fiscal redistribution must be discontinued over a *medium term*, say, five years. This requires decontrolling prices further, stopping the policy that allows 'paying bank loans before taxes or with taxes', equalising tax rates and setting criteria for fiscal redistribution which are not related to the investment return of local industry. The second is that the tax-collection system has to be centralised and policy against local trade protection must be legislated and enforced. This requires a strong central government. The third necessary change is that local governments have to be separated from the newly-formed corporate body, i.e. local governments' property rights have to greatly change. The next subsection deals with this issue.

(ii) How to reduce liquidity risk of the financial system

In relation to the first issue, a privatisation programme needs to stick to the money–equity swap: part of monetary balances should be exchanged for ownership entitlement of the newly-formed and commercialised corporate bodies including banks.[8] Money–equity swap as well as new issues may also reduce an already existing liquidity risk and frangibility of banks. It is better for the government to issue bonds than to rely on bank loans to finance new investment in infrastructure.[9] The money–equity swap should be applied to the state banks. So far, changing sole government ownership of the state banks is not a consideration. It is more urgent to rebuild a sound capital base for these banks because the present capital base is in effect negative.[10] In restructuring the banks' ownership, government borrowing from banks (both explicit and implicit) should be replaced by government bonds, and the government issues bank shares to the household sector and uses part of the proceeds to redeem government bonds. How large a proportion of bank equity should be sold is a practical issue. Most developed market economies have mixed ownership in the bank sector. For instance, in Austria, Germany, France, and Italy, the government owns about half the banking sector assets (Gardener and Molyneux, 1991: 35).

The above measures would require a broad capital market to facilitate the issue and transaction of bonds and shares, including contracts enforcement. Furthermore, given the present locality-constrained lending behaviour of banks, orderly development of capital markets could improve allocation of resources. If a well-established enterprise issues bonds and shares, it could break its financing constraint. Limited bank loans, therefore, would not restrict its development and expansion. In fact, the shift from bank financing to bond financing of a firm is a natural one in the evolution of a market economy. To explain such a shift, Diamond (1989) argues that the early development stage of a firm relies more on bank loans because of asymmetric information, while in the later stage – when it has built up its reputation – it turns to the bond market for finance.

The need to develop capital markets is in contrast to the World Bank's assertion that China does not necessarily require a broad capital market to sustain its development in the near future. The World Bank recommends a gradual transformation of banks into financial conglomerates as the demands for services arise (*China International Seminar on Financial Sector Reforms in Hainan, China*, The World Bank, 1991).

What should be noted is that a large-scale security issue would generate inflation if this issue was not taken into account in credit control. Since enterprise and localities' great enthusiasm, when issuing shares, is spurred by the gain in mobilisation of funds for their investment expansion, shares issuance will not reduce demand for bank credit. Money supply will increase if bank lending is not adjusted in accordance with the share and bond issuance. This calls for policy coordination between bank lending and issuance of securities. At present, the quota-setting of bank credit increment in China does not seem to take security issuance into account. This point is worth emphasising, bearing in mind that since 1978 bank credit control in China has almost always been weak.

It must also be warned that promotion of alternative channels of financial intermediation (e.g. through capital markets) might not necessarily improve resource allocation, and at the same time might make investment control even more difficult. Where both central and local governments still make investment decisions, their competition for resources through capital markets might not result in an improvement in resource allocation. At the same time, development of capital markets would make local governments more easily able to access savings and thus invest more in the projects in their interests. It has to be stressed that, with respect to allocation of resources, development of capital markets through which investment is guided by profit maximisation would ultimately require the fundamental reform of state ownership.

In addition, in China, capital markets have to be developed from scratch. Problems such as outdated accounting practices, imperfect information, lack of moral standards, lack of regulations and supervision, and absence of law protection are all-prevailing. There is certainly a great risk for the government in embarking on a myopic capital markets campaign. In other words, the adoption of laws, accounting and auditing systems, regulations and supervision from the developed market economies must not be delayed.

(iii) How to restructure financial institutions for a better corporate control

The money–equity swap would lead to either the 'outsider' financial system or the 'insider' financial system (see Chapter 6, section 6.4). One of the major advantages of the insider system is that it alleviates free-rider problems caused by diffused ownership or creditship. In other words, since problems of asymmetric information and lack of incentives to monitor are less prevalent in the insider system, the latter allows more effective corporate control.[11] When there are many owners or creditors, corporate monitoring and control are difficult because an individual owner or creditor bears the full costs but shares the benefits (Balow and Jhoven, 1978; Gertner and Scharfstein, 1989).

With an insider financial system being the objective model, the money–equity swap should not create dispersion of ownership, although the households' money holdings are nevertheless dispersed. To reconcile the contradiction, it might be more appropriate to create non-bank financial intermediaries, such as unit trust or mutual funds, venture capital companies and other investment funds, to exercise corporate control. These institutions themselves issue shares to pool dispersed funds.[12] It is also necessary to create a number of funds (such as pension funds, local development fund, etc.) to which a proportion of shares is distributed free. The pension funds would look after pensioners of both old and newly transformed enterprises. Under the present system, pensions are paid out by each firm revenue. Also, an insurance business needs to be promoted. More importantly, banks need to be allowed to possess the firm equity (as practised in Japan and Germany). Sheard (1985) revealed that for 72 per cent of Japanese firms the largest lender was one of the firm's top five shareholders. Since banks in China already lend heavily in fixed assets investment, a proportion of their outstanding loans may be changed into equities to enable them to exercise effective monitoring.[13] Accordingly, the banks' monitoring functions need to be greatly strengthened.

The extent to which a bank possesses a firm's ownership, and a firm possesses a bank's ownership (i.e. the extent of ownership interlocking), needs to be carefully regulated. Shifting ownership of banks from the government to large industrial groups would increase concentration. The formulation of an organisation similar to *Keiretsu* in Japan would be desirable if it helped to break local monopoly and promoted competition. However, formulated bank–industrial groups might undermine sound banking if there is no adequate prudential regulation framework. For instance, industrial groups in Chile in the late 1970s acquired the privatising banks and used them to make excessive loans to group firms (The World Bank, 1989: 127).

To enable and facilitate the money–equity swap and expansion of the financial sector, government cadres need to be transferred massively into this sector, in accordance with the restructuring of government functions. Such a transfer is very important, not only for the sake of the financial sector *per se* (which has the broadened functions of screening and monitoring), but also so as to reduce the obstacles of reforms. If the gradualist strategy is to succeed, then the interest of 'cadres' must not be ignored and should be compatible with the transition to a market economy.

(iv) How to maintain monetary control during the ownership reform

It has been made clear that fundamental problems, i.e. ineffectual monetary control (and thus monetary expansion) cannot be found in monetary control *per se*. Given the fundamental design of the system, there is only very restricted room for manoeuvre if monetary authorities are to achieve their objectives (i.e. to facilitate growth while maintaining financial stability). However, this by no means undermines the importance of monetary control. In the short term, monetary policy has proved a powerful weapon for stabilising price levels. The proper monetary control is particularly important where ownership reform takes place. One of the difficulties of monetary policy design during a major structuring transformation, as pointed out by Kaser and Allsopp (1992), is that monetary rule or targets are hard to formulate, since it is highly likely that the demand for money will vary considerably during transition and structural change.

Since bank credit has to be controlled to stop continuing monetary expansion, bank credit ceilings need to be used continuously as main monetary policy instruments during economic transition, at least in the first few years. For this instrument to be effective, the credibility of ceilings is crucial. At this point, the PBC has to be authorised to use whatever means are necessary to punish the violation. As far as the general level of interest rate is concerned, this needs to be maintained at a level at which inefficient firms are under more pressure to be rationalised but where the investment associated with industrial restructuring as a whole is not too dear.

To improve monetary control, it is also necessary that the independence of the PBC in the control operation is increased. Budgetary borrowing from the PBC (both explicitly and implicitly) has to be converted into treasury bonds. As regards branching of the central bank, it might be necessary to set up seven PBC regional branches in seven economic regions (i.e. the lower-reaches valley of the Yangzi River, the Pearl River delta, the region round the Bohai Sea, Northwest, Northeast, Southwest, and Mid-China). Provincial but not the lower level branches of the PBC can be retained. The PBC's business of direct lending could be transformed into an independent financial institution. It is also conceivable that the ICBC could be divided into a few smaller banks.

8.5 THE SECOND-BEST SOLUTION

Policies must be feasible if they are to be implemented. In practice, the key issue has to be, who is to be relied upon to implement them. Bearing in mind that in a vast country like China accomplishing economic transition takes a considerably long time, the government at all levels will inevitably continue to play a key role in the economy. The difficulty is that, on one hand, China is too big to be governed effectively by a single power centre and, on the other hand, because Chinese society has traditionally been atomised, a weak central power usually means a rise of 'aristocratic economy', blocking integration of the domestic markets. This leads to consideration of a very important aspect of policy design: what should the role of provincial government be in economic management?

According to Granick (1990: 23), the situation can be viewed as a large, repeated Nash equilibrium game where the national government plays with the provincial ones; within which the provincial governments play with the next-lower-level regional governments and so on. The larger game sets the rules of the smaller game. Although the higher-level players have the power to modify the rules to fit the smaller games, they cannot go too far, otherwise the larger game would break down. Considering both the desirability of, and constraints on implementing policy, the second-best solution for improving financial management during the gradualistic transition would be to internalise the externality problems at a provincial level. In order to implement the recommended policies better, the central government needs to mobilise its administrative capacity to concentrate on monitoring provincial government. Meanwhile, provincial governments need to be granted more autonomy in determining the way in which policies are implemented and how their provincial economies are managed. There is a great potential economic gain in increasing the degree of economic integration within a province, even if the economic integration at inter-provincial levels is slow. In other words, within a province, the externality problem is internalised from a provincial government's point of view.

The focus of monetary control and financial reforms has to be placed on industrial competition and restructuring. Successful industrial restructuring and rationalisation would significantly relieve the pressure upon some bottleneck sectors in China's economy, such as energy and raw materials. The existence of these bottlenecks constituted the policymakers' primary concern in resorting to bank loans for fixed assets investment. The shortage of supply was largely superficial because of inefficient use of the products of these sectors. The important point is that competition does not have to be 'classical'. For instance, competition in so-called government-guided market economies (e.g. Japan, South Korea) may be termed as oligopolistic, even nationally monopolistic. In each dynamic industry in Japan, there have always been several large firms, though not many, sometimes exceeding ten.[14] The competition is essentially oligopolistic, dominated by the group known as *Keiretsu* (firms centred on affiliated banks and financial institutions). The six largest *Keiretsu* are Mitsubishi, Mitsui, Sumitomo, Fuyo,

Dai-ichi•Kangyo, and Sanwa. Almost half the largest 200 firms in Japan are members of one of these groups. These six groups account for roughly 40–55 per cent of sales in natural resources, primary metal, industrial machinery, chemical and cement industries. Because of vertical integration, group firms are three times as likely to trade with group members as with non-members. These trading relationships are reinforced by cross-shareholdings in the group (Gerlach, 1987). In South Korea, the competition is not even oligopolistic because the economy is virtually monopolistic domestically. Around 60 per cent of total production is attributed to the three largest conglomerates (Song, 1991). As the term 'Korea Inc.' implies, Korea could be compared to a large multinational firm whose domain of business operation is the world market (Yung, 1991).

It has to be admitted that uncertainties about the economic system's future landscape in China increases alongside the advance of economic reforms and 'open-door' policy. Monetary policy and financial institutions are not entirely designable. Domestic as well as international politics, social and cultural factors all play a very important part in their evolutionary process. In this respect, there is not much that economists can do about it.

Appendices 1–5

A.1 DATA ISSUES OF INDUSTRIAL CAPITAL STOCK

Data for industrial fixed capital stock published by the State Statistical Bureau (SSB) is not appropriate for analyses. There are two main problems involved. First, price changes are not taken into account. Second, residential housing is included in the capital stock. The annual data for net capital stock consists of the sum of the previous year's figure plus newly commissioned fixed assets (excluding work in progress) in current prices, subtracting the value depreciated and scrapped. Unless prices of investment goods remain stable, such data series cannot correctly reflect the real trend in capital accumulation. As is well-known, prices of capital goods have not been stable in China, therefore data reconstruction is required.

Chen K. et al, (1988a) have made valuable efforts in estimating real fixed capital stock for Chinese state-owned industry which is independently accounted for and covers 1952–85. They break down annual figures of newly-added fixed assets into four categories: non-residential construction, residential housing, equipment and others. They then construct price indexes to deflate each category and combine the deflated components (excluding residential housing) to form a new series of capital stock at a constant price. However, the revised data series by Chen et al (1988a) still has problems:

(i) The proportions of components of fixed investment in the entire state sector are applied to state industry. Therefore, the difference between industries and non-industrial sectors is ignored.

(ii) For 1952–77, outlay shares for the basic construction component of investment expenditure is taken to represent the overall total.

(iii) Instead of using time-series data for the annual value of overall construction output (in current and constant prices) to obtain an implicit deflator for the construction price deflator, they collected data for the years 1957, 1965, 1978 and 1985, indicating cost per square metre of factory structures, to measure construction costs directly. Such a method is not convincing.

The most commonly used materials in construction are steel, timber and cement but, due to shortage of timber, cement is increasingly substituted. Nevertheless, the consumption of steel, timber and cement as a whole is still a good indicator of the real scale of investment. This, using a reasonable price deflator, should be roughly consistent with consumption of the above three main construction materials. Table A1.1 suggests that, when comparing the last three rows, row (4) seems more reasonable than row (5) in showing the real construction scale. It is for this reason that (1), rather than (2), is used to deflate construction investment valued at current prices.

To overcome the shortcomings listed above, fixed net industrial capital

Table A1.1 Price deflator and investment scale

		1957	*1965*	*1978*	*1985*
1	Construction *P* deflator	1.00	1.01	1.15	1.54
2	Cost per square metre	1.00	1.37	1.50	2.93
3	Construction investment of capital constructions	100	124	341	824
4	Real investment =(3)/(1)	100	123	296	535
5	Real investment =(3)/(2)	100	91	227	281
6	Steels used in key constructions	100	160	408	894
7	Timber used in key constructions	100	92	118	136
8	Cement used in key constructions	100	203	541	1090

Note: Construction *P* deflator is a quotient (total product of construction at current prices divided by total product of construction at constant prices). (3)–(8): All figures are indexes.

Source: (1): SSB (1990a: 49–50); (2): Chen, K. *et al.* (1988a: 249); (3): SSB (1987b: 68); (6)–(8): SSB (1987b: 61–63).

stock of state industry (independently accounted) is constructed as follows:

Step 1 Annual fixed investment of the state sector is decomposed into three categories in per centage points – capital construction, renovation and others (SSB, 1989a: 354; 1990a: 157).

Step 2 Each of the three categories is broken down into four components in per centage points: investment in construction, residential housing, equipment and others. By deducting residential housing investment from construction investment, results in non-residential construction investment (for capital construction: SSB, 1987b: 67–8; 1990a: 164; for renovation: SSB, 1987b: 220; 1989d: 178; 1990a: 190; for other investment: SSB 1987b: 330; 1989d: 256; 1990a: 213).

Step 3 Industrial fixed investment is also broken down into construction, and renovation among others (as percentage). Because data are not available for the period 1952–80, corresponding ratios have been estimated according to the differences between industry and the state sector in the 1980s. On average, the industry spent 11.34 per centage points less on capital construction (or 11.34 per centage points more on technical renovation) than the state sector during 1981–7) (for the State sector as a whole: SSB, 1989a: 354; 1990a: 157; for industry: SSB, 1989c: 25).

Step 4 The newly commissioned fixed capital of the state industry (independently accounted) is broken down into capital construction, and renovation among others, using the outlay ratios of fixed industrial investment of the state sector obtained in step 3.[1]

Step 5 Each of the three types of fixed assets in step 4 is further decomposed into construction, residential housing, equipment and others using the ratios obtained in step 2.

Step 6 Rearranging the components of fixed assets in forms of

Table A1.2 Net capital stock of the independently accounted state industry (original and revised) (1952–89; ¥ 100 mn)

	1952	*1953*	*1954*	*1955*	*1956*	*1957*	*1958*	*1959*	*1960*	*1961*
(a)	148.8	175.7	219.5	249.5	282.5	334.6	435.6	571.9	721.8	800.8
(b)	100.8	118.9	152.3	193.9	237.7	335.9	461.9	590.1	636.8	660.7
	1962	*1963*	*1964*	*1965*	*1966*	*1967*	*1968*	*1969*	*1970*	*1971*
(a)	855.4	889.6	951.7	1040.0	1120.0	1176.0	1229.0	1294.0	1462.0	1610.0
(b)	661.6	687.5	743.8	788.9	808.6	820.4	845.9	992.9	992.9	1105.2
	1972	*1973*	*1974*	*1975*	*1976*	*1977*	*1978*	*1979*	*1980*	*1981*
(a)	1806.9	2033.6	2196.4	2428.3	2621.8	2882.2	3193.4	3466.7	3730.1	4032.3
(b)	1261.4	1444.1	1541.7	1709.2	1819.6	1987.1	2191.8	2307.0	2392.8	2480.0
	1982	*1983*	*1984*	*1985*	*1986*	*1987*	*1988*	*1989*		
(a)	4375.0	4767.8	5170.0	5956.2	6744.8	7677.9	8795.2	10160.8		
(b)	2580.1	2708.1	2815.9	3176.2	3482.3	3820.3	4154.1	4530.8		

Note: (a): Fixed capital stock (originally valued); (b) Net fixed capital stock.

Source: (a): SSB (1990c: 66). Depreciation rate: General Planning Department of MOF (1989: 124); SSB (1991a: 28).

construction, residential housing, non-residential construction, equipment and others obtained in step 5.

Step 7 Deflating the value of non-residential construction using a deflator of the construction industry's gross output; deflating the equipment value using a heavy industrial output deflator; and other assets can be deflated by the retail price index (data for heavy industry price deflator: SSB, 1990a: 56–7; for construction industry: SSB, 1990a: 49–50; for retail price deflator: SSB, 1990a: 250).

Step 8 The above can be added together to arrive at a newly commissioned industrial fixed capital in real terms.

Step 9 The net capital stock estimates are derived as follows for 1952–89:

$$RKN_t = RKN_{t-1} + DRKO_t - (RKO_{t-1} + DRKO_t/2) \cdot DPR_t$$

where *RKN* denotes real net capital stock; *DRKO* added real gross capital stock; *RKO* real gross capital stock; *DPR* depreciation rate and *t* time.

Table A1.2 lists the original and revised data series for net capital stock of state industry which is independently accounted.

It is worth noting that data for fixed capital stock is available only with industries *at and above* township levels (excluding village enterprises and individually-owned ones which accounted for 21.9 per cent of total indus-

Table A2.1 Required supplementation of working capital (1983–8; ¥ bn)

	1978	*1983*	*1984*	*1985*	*1986*	*1987*	*1988*	*1983–88*
1 Retained profits	2.75	29.08	35.57	46.18	48.93	53.85	70.06	283.67
2 Key construction fund as 10% of retained profit	–	4.91	6.74	9.27	10.69	14.66	15.13[b]	61.40
3 Government bond purchasing[a]	–	1.06	1.22	1.09	1.14	1.13	1.74	7.38
4 = (1) – (2)-(3)	2.75	23.11	27.61	35.82	37.10	38.06	53.19	214.89
5 Production fund as 60% of (4)	1.38	13.87	16.57	21.49	22.26	22.84	22.07	128.93
6 Working capital fund as 10% of production fund	0.14	1.39	1.66	2.15	2.23	2.28	2.21	12.89[c]

Note: [a] Estimated as 50 per cent of the 'units' purchasing. [b] Estimated as the same proportion as 1987. Total fund collected by the Ministry of Finance was ¥18.59 billion in 1988 (SSB, 1990: 232). [c] It is larger than the sum of each year because of rounding.

Source: General Planning Department of the MOF (1989: 47, 145, 52).

trial output in 1990) (SSB, 1991a: 397). If total industrial output is used against the available data on fixed capital stock, measurement of capital productivity would suffer from upward bias.

A.2 SCALE OF MISBEHAVIOUR IN WORKING CAPITAL SUPPLEMENTATION

To measure the relevance of this misbehaviour to expansion of bank working capital loans, one can estimate how much working capital provision is 'saved' by violating the related regulations:

(i) use 60 per cent of the retained profits as production fund;
(ii) utilise 10 per cent of the production fund as working capital;
(iii) provide 30 per cent of the quota working capital required by the 'self-financed' fixed investment.

It can be done by estimating the difference between the required and the actual supplementation of working capital, and comparing this difference to the increment in bank working capital loans.

Table A2.1 is an estimation of the required supplementation of working capital regarding the regulations (i) and (ii).

Table A2.1 suggests that through violating the regulation of 'working capital supplementation', enterprises 'saved' at most about ¥13 billion between 1983

Table A2.2 Estimation of 'saved' working capital provision by SOEs (1983–8; ¥ bn)

	1983	*1984*	*1985*	*1986*	*1987*	*1988*	*1983–88*
1 Increment of net fixed assets	39.5	35.7	40.6	76.7	84.3	109.3	386.1
2 Fixed assets investment	95.2	118.5	168.0	197.9	229.8	271.3	1080.7
3 Fixed assets formulation ratio [(1)/(2)]	0.41	0.30	0.24	0.39	0.37	0.40	0.36
4 Fixed investment by self-raised fund[2] and non-distinguishable sources	41.4	51.5	80.2	96.2	109.3	141.5	520.1
5 = (4) × (3) × 0.65 × 30%[a]	3.3	3.0	3.8	7.3	7.9	11.0	36.5

Note: [a]0.65 is the ratio of incremental quota working capital to incremental net fixed assets of the SOEs during 1983–8 (For quota working capital, see General Planning Department of the MOF (1989: 126–9)).

Source: (1) and (2): General Planning Department of the MOF (1989: 120–3, 178). (4): SSB (1987b: 14; 1989d: 18; 1990a: 158).

Table A2.3 Required and actual supplementation of working capital (1983–8; ¥ bn)

1 Required supplementation	49.39
2 Actual supplementation	10.386[a]
3 = (1) – (2)	39.004
4 Increments of working capital loans	547.90
5 Planned increment of total bank loans	532.00
6 Actual increment of loans	777.56
7 = (3)/(4) (%)	8.45
8 = (3)/(5) (%)	7.46
9 = (3)/(6) (%)	5.29

Note and Source:[a] ¥3.00 billion is estimated for 1988 (0.291, 0.555, 1.356, 2.317 and 2.866 were used for working capital from the 'extra-budget fund') see General Planning Department of the MOF (1989: 112). Other sources: (1): 49.39 = 12.89 + 36.50 (Table A2.1, A2.2). (4): *Almanac of China's Finance and Banking* (1990: 53). (5) and (6): Table 2.11.

and 1988. This is equivalent to about 5.9 per cent of the unplanned bank working capital loans to state industry and commerce during the same period. Obviously, this can hardly be regarded as one of the main causes of expansion of bank working capital loans.

Furthermore, the fact that the self-owned working capital of the SOEs was slightly reduced between 1983 (¥125.9 bn) and 1988 (¥124.4 bn) cannot simply be regarded as a result of the failure of the SOEs to provide any fund for working capital. According to one source, ¥20.8 billion 'self-owned' working capital of the SOEs was written off by the government (central and local) to cover the loss made by the SOEs during 1983 and 1985 (Yu, R., 1987: 102). This implies that the SOEs did use some of the retained profits to finance working capital investment. For example, 81 city-subordinated state-owned industrial enterprises in Liuzhou city of Yunnan province in 1981–5 took 5.1 per cent (official requirement is 10 per cent) of the production fund for working capital usage (ibid.).

Now turning to the regulation that 30 per cent of 'quota working capital' must be provided by those who raise funds from outside the state budget and bank loans to invest in fixed assets, Table A2.2 gives an estimation of the funds 'saved' by absolutely violating this regulation.

Taking into account that local governments and enterprises did provide some funds for working capital investment in this period, only 7.46 per cent of the planned or 5.29 per cent of actual lending can be directly explained in this way (Table A2.3).

A.3 A BRIEF CHRONOLOGICAL REVIEW OF CREDIT MANAGEMENT IN CHINA (1952–78)[3]

Centralised Management (1952–5)

The period 1953–5 in general characterised bank credit management by so-called 'unified collection and unified lending' (*Tongcun Tongdai*), which meant that almost all deposits of local bank branches were transferred to the PBC head office which made the decisions of credit allocation. More precisely, three rules applied:

1. Local bank branches were allowed to provide loans to fully support agricultural products procurement by state-owned commercial enterprises. If the loan needed was more than the planned quota, bank branches could make loans provided that they ask for supplementary quota grants. However, surpluses of planned credit quota were not transferable (to finance other economic activities).
2. SOEs were divided into two groups (the central-government-run SOEs and those run by local governments) and four sectors (the local-government-run enterprises were one sector, the other three were industry, domestic commerce and foreign trade). The bank loans to these four sectors and the cooperative sector were separately planned by the head office of the PBC. The local bank branches were allowed to lend part of the credit quota of one sector to another temporarily for up to three months, but the 'borrowed' credit quota had to be repaid within the following three months.
3. Bank credit quotas to agriculture, handicraft, private- and joint-owned industries were separately planned. The quotas could not be borrowed or adjusted.

Modified Centralised Control (1956–7)

The main modifications are:

(i) Provincial bank branches, subject to the annual plan quotas, were allowed to make their own quarterly plan for locally-run state-owned industries, the state-private joint enterprises and handicraft. Moreover, these quotas could be combined.
(ii) Provincial branches were allowed to use part of the credit quota reserve.
(iii) Increased urban household savings, above the planned quota (target), could be added to credit quotas for the sectors in the case (i).

Decentralisation Drive (1958–60)

Provincial branches were allowed to use 20 per cent of increased urban household saving deposits over the period July 1957 to June 1958 as credit to local industry, and 20 per cent of the total amount of rural deposits in June 1957 for additional agricultural credit.

Credit control loosened further in 1959. The measure was summarised as 'a transference in bank management to lower-level government, differential contracts of deposit-lending, and unified regulation' (*Cundai Xiafang, Jihua Baogan, Chae Guangli, Tongyi Diaodu*). It implied that:

(i) The PBC head office only managed the budget deposit and bank loans to the centrally-run SOEs.
(ii) Other banking businesses were under the direct management of provincial bank branches subject to deposit-lending differentials which were contracted between the head office and provincial branches.
(iii) The 'centrally planned deposit surplus' of local bank branches must be remitted to the head office, and the 'centrally planned deposit shortage' (meaning the centrally planned deposit was less than the centrally planned lending) must be covered by funding from the head office. The bank branches were allowed to lend out increased deposits above the centrally planned deposit quota.

In rural areas, People's Communes were empowered to make credit plans for a local bank branch subject to approved deposit-lending differentials which were negotiated twice a year.

Cease in Decentralisation (1961–3)

Beginning in 1961, in order to stop the decentralisation drive, a severe overall policy adjustment was adopted. In March 1962, the Chinese Communist Party Central Committee and the State Council issued 'The Decision to Centralise and Unify Bank Management In Real Earnest, and to Stringently Control Currency Issuance'. Almost all decentralisation measures in credit planning management ceased and economic management of 'combined vertical and horizontal management, with the former a dominance' (*Tiaokuai Jiehe, Yitiao Weizhu*) was restored. In credit formulation, 'two-line credit planning management' was tried. This means that centrally-run SOEs and local economic bureaus (which run local SOEs) draw up credit plans, report to managing ministries and meanwhile send a duplicate to the area bank branch. The latter checks the plan and reports to its higher office and so on until it reaches the head office, who work out the final credit plan for each reporter together with the ministries.

Fine-tuning (1964–5)

This period was characterised by the fine-tuning of monetary policy. The key changes were two-tiered. First, the bank head office, provincial branches and county branches made credit plans for the ministry, provincial-bureau-, and county-bureau-run SOEs respectively. Second, local bank branches had to get approval from head office for each quarter credit quota they proposed, but they were usually not rejected or changed. Therefore, the degree of centralisation in this period was lower than that of the first Five-Year-Plan period.

The Period of Disorder and Decentralisation (1966–76)

During this decade-long political turmoil known as the 'Cultural Revolution', money, monetary exchange and credit were considered alien to the socialist economic system. Even careful planning was under attack. In fact, there was no economic planning from 1967 to 1968. In October 1969 the PBC lost its position as a government department with ministerial rank. It was merged with the Ministry of Finance as a secondary level agent.

Beginning in 1971, another wave of decentralisation supported by Mao was initiated. Parallel to the massive management transformation of the SOEs from ministries to local governments, the banks extensively simplified their lending procedures and their operation became more dependent on local governments' decisions.

Order Restored (1977–8)

In credit planning, these two years were marked by 'restoring order', and the PBC's head office was separated from the Ministry of Finance and officially promoted to ministry status. The bank as the 'centre of credit, cash and clearing' was reaffirmed. The conventional banking rules and regulations including statistical system, clearing system, cash payment control, etc., were re-issued.

A.4 MATHEMATICAL DEDUCTION OF OPTIMAL INVESTMENT

$$\text{Max } R_L = (K_{1C} + K_{1L})^{\alpha} (K_{2C} + K_{2L})^{\beta}, \quad \text{S.T. } K_{1L} + K_{2L} \leq K_L \qquad [A4.1]$$

let $K_{1L} + K_{2L} = K_L$, then (A4.1) can be transformed into

$$\text{Max } R_L = (K_{1C} + K_{1L})^{\alpha} (K_{2C} + K_L - K_{1L})^{\beta} \qquad [A4.2]$$

and

$$\text{Max } R_L = (K_{1C} + K_L - K_{2L})^{\alpha} (K_{2C} + K_{2L})^{\beta} \qquad [A4.3]$$

The first order condition yields

$$dR_L/dK_{1L} = -\alpha(K_{1C} + K_{1L})^{\alpha-1} (K_{2C} + K_L - K_{1L})^{\beta} + (K_{1C} + K_{1L})^{\alpha} \beta(K_{2C} + K_L - K_{1L})^{\beta-1} = 0 \quad [A4.4]$$

and

$$dR_L/dK_{2L} = -\alpha(K_{1C} + K_L - K_{2L})^{\alpha-1} (K_{2C} + K_{2L})^{\beta} + (K_{1C} + K_L - K_{2L})^{\alpha} \beta(K_{2C} + K_{2L})^{\beta-1} = 0 \quad [A4.5]$$

(A4.4) can be rearranged as

$$=> \alpha(K_{1C} + K_{1L})^{\alpha-1} (K_{2C} + K_L - K_{1L})^{\beta} = (K_{1C} + K_{1L})^{\alpha} \beta(K_{2C} + K_L - K_{1L})^{\beta-1}$$

$$=> \alpha(K_{1C} + K_{1L})^{-1} = \beta(K_{2C} + K_L - K_{1L})^{-1}$$

$$=> \alpha(K_{2C} + K_L - K_{1L}) = \beta(K_{1C} + K_{1L})$$

$$=> (\alpha+\beta)K_{1L} = \alpha K_L + \alpha K_{2C} - \beta K_{1C}$$

$$\begin{aligned} => K_{1L}^* &= [1/(\alpha+\beta)](\alpha K_L + \alpha K_{2C} - \beta K_{1C}) \\ &= [1/(\alpha+\beta)](\alpha K_L + \alpha K_C - \alpha K_{1C} - \beta K_{1C}) \\ &= [1/(\alpha+\beta)][\alpha K_L + \alpha K_C - (\alpha+\beta)K_{1C}] \\ &= [\alpha/(\alpha+\beta)]K_L + [\alpha/(\alpha+\beta)]K_C - K_{1C} \\ &= [\alpha/(\alpha+\beta)]K_L + [\alpha/(\alpha+\beta)]K_C - [(\alpha+\beta)/(\alpha+\beta)](K_C - K_{2C}) \\ &= [\alpha/(\alpha+\beta)]K_L - [\beta/(\alpha+\beta)]K_C + K_{2C} \end{aligned}$$

For (A4.5)

$$=> \alpha(K_{1C} + K_L - K_{2L})^{\alpha-1} (K_{2C} + K_{2L})^{\beta}$$

$$= \beta(K_{1C} + K_L - K_{2L})^{\alpha} (K_{2C} + K_{2L})^{\beta-1}$$

$$=> \alpha(K_{1C} + K_L - K_{2L})^{-1} = \beta(K_{2C} + K_{2L})^{-1}$$

$$=> \alpha(K_{2C} + K_{2L}) = \beta(K_L + K_{1C} - K_{2L})$$

$$=> (\alpha+\beta)K_{2L} = \beta K_L + \beta K_{1C} - \alpha K_{2C}$$

$$\begin{aligned} => K_{2L}^* &= [1/(\alpha+\beta)](\beta K_L + \beta K_{1C} - \alpha K_{2C}) \\ &= [1/(\alpha+\beta)](\beta K_L + \beta K_C - \beta K_{2C} - \alpha K_{2C}) \\ &= [1/(\alpha+\beta)][\beta K_L + \beta K_C - (\alpha+\beta)K_{2C}] \\ &= [\beta/(\alpha+\beta)]K_L + [\beta/(\alpha+\beta)]K_C - K_{2C} \\ &= [\beta/(\alpha+\beta)]K_L + [\beta/(\alpha+\beta)]K_C - [(\alpha+\beta)/(\alpha+\beta)](K_C - K_{1C}) \\ &= [\beta/(\alpha+\beta)]K_L - [\alpha/(\alpha+\beta)]K_C + K_{1C} \end{aligned}$$

Substituting $\theta = K_C/K$ and $1 - \theta = K_L/K$ into the above solution, we have

$$K_{1L}^* = [\alpha/(\alpha+\beta) - \theta]K + K_{2C} \qquad [A4.6]$$

Substituting $k_L = K_{1L}/K_L$ and $k_C = K_{1C}/K_C$, we have

$$K_L^* = [\alpha/(\alpha+\beta) - \theta k_C]/(1 - \theta). \qquad [A4.7]$$

This is (4.3), i.e.

$$k_L = \left[\frac{\alpha}{(\alpha+\beta)}\frac{1}{(1-\theta)}\right] - \frac{\theta}{1-\theta}\,k_C \qquad [4.3]$$

By a similar procedure, we can get the central government's reaction function as (4.4).

A.5 HOUSEHOLD INCOME AND SAVINGS: DATA DESCRIPTION AND SOURCES

Households' consumption expenditure (*Ch*) – the sum of retail sales of consumer goods to households (SSB, 1991a: 591), household expenses on services (SSB, 1987a: 14, 553; 1991a: 582) and other money expenses of households (1952–83: SSB, 1984b: 14–5; 1986–9: SSB, 1991a: 582; 1984–5: estimated as an even increase between 1983 and 1986).

Household saving deposits including that in UCCs (*Dh*) – *Almanac of China's Finance and Banking*, 1991: 48, 53.

Purchasing of capital goods (*PCh*) – estimated as retail sales of agricultural capital goods.

Household cash holdings (*M0h*) – 1952–83: SSB, 1984b: 16; 1984–5: *General Planning Department of PBC*, 1988: 395; 1986–89: SSB, 1991a: 582).

Households' other financial asset holdings (*OFh*) – estimated according to General Planning Department of MOF, 1989: 52; 192–5; *Almanac of China's Finance and Banking*, 1990: 71; 1991: 58).

After-tax money income or disposable money income of households (*Yh*) – sum of *Ch*, ΔDh, *PAh*, $\Delta M0h$, and ΔOFh.

Table A5.1 lists the data series.

Table A5.1 Data series of household income and savings (1978–90; ¥100 mn)

	Yh	*Ch*	*Dh*	*M0h*	*OFh*	*PAh*	*HSR*(%)
1978	1 548	1 213	211	156	0	294	2.66
1979	1 850	1 415	281	196	0	324	6.00
1980	2 251	1 727	400	256	0	346	7.90
1981	2 446	1 920	524	310	0	349	7.29
1982	2 728	2 116	675	357	25	389	8.20
1983	3 102	2 345	893	443	55	423	10.76
1984	3 925	2 877	1 215	665	82	477	14.54
1985	4 904	3 825	1 623	813	136	504	12.37
1986	5 882	4 467	2 239	972	200	750	14.26
1987	7 132	5 235	3 081	1 161	360	705	16.71
1988	9 062	6 710	3 822	1 693	534	905	15.96
1989	10 303	7 518	5 196	1 850	760	1 027	17.06
1990	11 386	7 882	7 120	2 089	1 052	1 049	21.56

Note: *Yh* = Households' money income; *Ch* = Households' expenditure on consumer goods and services; *Dh* = household saving deposits; *M0h* = household cash holdings; *OFh* = other household financial assets; *PAh* = Households' purchasing of capital goods. *HSR* = household saving ratio.

Notes

Chapter 1

1. Liu G. (1984: 23–7); Dong F. (1988: 50–8).
2. In early 1985, the beginning of 1986, the final quarter of 1987 and again in September 1988 (*Financial Encyclopedia* (I), p. 607).
3. Same source as Table 1.2.
4. Schmidt-Hebbel (1991: 12–3).
5. Inflation is politically very sensitive. Historically, hyperinflation in 1947–9 was an important factor contributing to the collapse of the rule of the Nationalist Party in Mainland China.
6. Change in price level and money[a]/GDP ratio in some reforming economies

	Price rise[b] over the period	*Change in money/GDP ratio*
Poland (1987–91)	5800%	38% -> 25%
Russia (1990–92, projected)	897%	46% -> 15%
Bulgaria (1990–91)	551%	107% -> 18%
Romania (1990–91)	185%	54% -> 30%
Hungary (1986–91)	166%	48% -> 38%
Czechoslovakia (1989–91)	76%	71% -> 65%

Note: a: Stock. b: Consumer price index.

Source: IMF and the World Bank, cited by Schmidt-Hebbel (1991: 8, 23).

7. Before 1978, money could not buy many goods without a purchasing coupon (there were 64 coupon schemes for consumer goods in 1978 (Zhong Q., 1988: 62), but the majority of the purchasing coupons disappeared in the 1980s.
8. In May 1988, 60.8 per cent of capital goods sold by the producers were at the official prices.
9. *Reference Material of Financial Studies*, no. 10, 1989, p. 3; no. 8, 1990, p. 3; no. 7, 1991, p. 2.
10. A major proportion of loss subsidies went to the mining industry, especially coal-mining, where official coal prices were kept much lower than market prices.
11. In 1990, the sum of State budget expenses on loss subsidy and price subsidy accounted for 5.4 per cent of GNP while this ratio was 2.0 per cent in 1978. Enterprise loss subsidy was ¥57.9 billion and price subsidy was ¥38.1 billion in 1990 (SSB, 1991a: 31, 212, 216); in 1978 they

were ¥1.2 and ¥1.1 billion respectively (Zhang B., 1988; General Planning Department of the MOF, 1989: 88). Data on GNP: SSB (1991a: 31).

12. The true market 'clearing' price level may be significantly lower than the market price level under the two-track price system because the latter is effectively of marginal price.
13. It needs to be noted that, in the policy debate about monetary expansion during reform, it is not always clear what concept (M0, M1 or M2) is used. The ambiguity is of courses not surprising because theoretically there is no unique way to express quantity of money. The unsettled issue is what financial assets should and should not be included in money (Friedman, M., 1987). In other words, what financial assets have monetary status? Or, should different assets be weighted in terms of their moneyness to obtain an aggregate sum of 'money'? In the developed market economies, the difference between different financial assets in terms of 'moneyness' became further blurred in the 1980s when financial liberalisation and deregulation occurred.
14. See Kornai (1980).
15. In fact, policy swings were often associated with a change in personnel in top political leadership. The latest case was when the former premier and the Party's general secretary Zhao Ziyang was driven out of office in 1989.
16. The questions he raised are: (i) in inflation avoidable during the economic 'taking-off'? (ii) what fiscal and monetary systems should be developed in China and is the growing state budget deficit inevitable? (iii) what are the criteria by which balance of aggregate supply and aggregate demand can be judged? (iv) how great is the bank's potential in extending loans without causing danger, and what ought be the main channel of mobilisation of financial resources? and (v) what are the objectives and approach of financial reform? (*People's Daily* (Overseas Edition), 12 August 1992).
17. Stackelberg (1905–46) considered oligopoly as a market form without equilibrium. In the case of duopoly, one firm takes a dependent or follower position (i.e. takes the actual price or production of the other firm as given) and the other firm an independent or leader position (i.e knows this behaviour and fixed its price or production accordingly so that it maximises its profits or other utility indices).

Chapter 2

1. At that time, China was one of the least developed economies dominated by traditional agriculture and handicraft. The gross value of modern industrial output accounted for only about 20 per cent of the gross value of agricultural output. Even during the middle 1930s when most historical records of industrial output were made (i.e. before the War of Resistance against Japanese Aggression, 1937–45), modern industry contributed merely 10 per cent of the Gross National Product (Liang W., 1984: 131).
2. For a discussion of the relation between economic development strategy and the economic system, see Brus and Laski (1989).
3. Estimated according to data from SSB (1985: 76; 88–9)
4. For a historical perspective, see Maitra R. (1989) 'The Sun Yat-sen Pro-

gramme and China's Development Today', *Executive Intelligence Review* (EIR) vol. 16, no. 35, 26–35.

5. The survey sample covered 88 000 urban households located in 16 provinces, municipalities (directly under the central government) and autonomous regions. Those with an income per month of less than ¥20 accounted for 39 per cent of the sample, while the minimum requirement for each person was ¥24.0 per month in Beijing and ¥22.7 in Wuhan.
6. Hu Yaobang (1982: 5).
7. Li Xiannian at a meeting of the State Council (September 1978), who at that time was in charge of economic work in the Party, emphasised that enterprises must be given necessary independence in economic management (Xu J. *et al.*, 1984). See also Hu Qiaomu (1978) and Liu Guoguang (1979). Hu was the Party's leading theorist and Liu was a leading economist.
8. The 'Decision of the Central Committee of the Communist Party of China on Reform of The Economic Structure' adopted by the 12th Central Committee at its Third Plenary Session on 20 October 1984.
9. This former prime minister, in a speech presented to the Party's National Conference on 18 September 1985 also described the reforms as 'an all-sided reform with the focus on cities', as part of the Seventh Five-Year Plan (1986–90) (CEM: 608).
10. The financial reforms failed in their objectives: turning – said Deng Xiaoping – the existing banks into **genuine** banks (see Liu H., 1987: 13–4).
11. For a summary of China's reforms, see the World Bank (1990b; 1992), Blejer *et al.* (1991).
12. Financial resources possessed by the whole state sector are controlled by the state budget and the state extra-budget. The latter comprises the self-collected and self-disposed funds by the state sector (SOEs and their supervisory bodies, treasuries of the local governments and other institutions of the government sector), not included in the state budget. The main sources of the state extra-budgetary revenues include depreciation funds (part or full), funds for heavy repair, retained profits, etc.
13. Composing agriculture, industry, commerce, construction and transportation and communication.
14. The non-state sector's share in total material output in 1990 is estimated as 55 per cent (or ¥2088 billion; agriculture: 700; industry: 1034; commerce: 128; construction: 207 and transportation: 19) (SSB, 1991a: 26, 47, 541, 394).
15. *Reference Materials of Financial Studies*, 1992, nos 13–15, p. 11.
16. For a detailed study of China's GDP and its distribution, see Guo and Han (1991).
17. *The Economist*, 28 November – 4 December, 1992.
18. The effective control over population growth also contributed to the improvement in living standards. Growth of total population slowed down from 2.0 per cent in 1953–78 to 1.4 per cent in 1979–90 (SSB, 1991a: 79).
19. For the latest assessment see, e.g. Schmidt-Hebbel (1991), the World Bank (1992).
20. *People's Daily* (Overseas Edition), 14, 24 November 1990; 16 September 1991.
21. GNP figures are reconstructed according to the Standard National

Accounting recommended by the UN (Guo and Han, 1991: 290). Using official figures which usually underestimate the real scale of China's economy, exports as a proportion of GNP were 12.3 per cent in 1989 (SSB, 1991a: 31, 615).

22. For instance, it was from −0.2 to 1.0 per cent of GDP in OECD countries in 1960–90 (OECD, 1992: 16–17). In South Korea, over the period 1986–91, it was from 0.7 to 2.9 per cent (The Bank of Korea, 1992: 58–9).
23. This survey covered 10 categories of consumer goods in 10 major cities, *Chinese Women*, 27 January 1992.
24. This survey was conducted by the State Bureau of Technical Supervision covering 1761 products for domestic sale made by 1158 firms, *Economic Daily*, 14 February, 1989.
25. *People's Daily* (Overseas Edition) 5 October 1992.
26. Ibid, 7 May 1992.
27. Ibid, 2 January 1991.
28. The low quality of bank credit in China is well-known. According to the report of the 'Credit Examination' during October 1988–January 1989, 'Our incomplete data suggests that . . . overdue loans and non-performing loans amounted to ¥93.88 billion, or 8.9 per cent of total loans at the end of 1988' (*Almanac of China's Finance and Banking*, 1989: 205). Many officials of PBC suggest that non-performing loans account for over 10 per cent of total loans outstanding.
29. The obvious differences in approach and performance between China and that of the reforming economies in the CEE have aroused a debate over the merits/demerits of the 'Big Bang' versus gradualistic strategy in the transition to a market economy (See Singh (1991) 'Is There Schizophrenia about Socialist Reform Theory?' and the followed discussion by Bogetic (1991) and Klans (1991). See *Transition*, vol. 2: no. 7, p. 1–4; no. 8, pp. 6–7; no. 9, pp. 8–9).

Chapter 3

1. The formula (3.1) is derived from three identities:

$$\Delta D = \Delta BLp + \Delta BLg - \Delta NDL \quad (1)$$
$$\Delta M = \Delta D + \Delta C \quad (2)$$
$$PSBR = \Delta Gp + \Delta C - \Delta Ext + \Delta BLg \quad (3)$$

where D = banks' deposits; BLg = banks' lending to the government; C = currency held at the non-bank private sector (for an introduction, see Cuthbertson, 1985: 171–4).

2. Alternatively, the formula can be written as

$$M = H \cdot [(1 + C/D) / (R/D + C/D)]$$

3. Even if there were no such reserve requirements imposed by the central banks, the banks would have to maintain certain prudential reserves.
4. Household cash holding over total currency in circulation (SSB, 1991a: 642; Table A5.1, Appendix 5).

5. Using the revised GNP data by Guo and Han (1991: 94). For 1990, GNP figure is estimated as 117.5 per cent of the official figure.
6. Bonus and allowances as a proportion to total wage payment of staffs and workers in the state sector increased from 8.8% to 38.7% between 1978 and 1990 (SSB, 1991a: 125).
7. Because of reform, the government lost its dominance in national savings and the case in China was no longer different from that of its Asian neighbours. On average, the contribution of government saving to national saving in nine Asian economies was under 10 per cent in 1976 and less than 20 per cent in 1981 (Fry, 1988: 136).
8. Household saving as percentage of GNP over domestic saving as percentage of GDP (The UN, 1984: 134, 141, 157).
9. 43 per cent, 41 per cent, 36 per cent, 46 per cent and 45 per cent in 1970, 1975, 1980, 1985 and 1988 respectively (Table 4.8 in Chiu, 1992).
10. Yusuf, S. and Peters, R. K. (1984: 4).
11. In fact, most shares were preference shares because their returns were fixed – even guaranteed.
12. Source: Household net savings: Guo and Han (1991: Table 7.9). The household income calculation is income-based. Increments in household cash-holding and bank deposit: Appendix 3. The household income calculation is expenditure-based.
13. The central bank was established in 1983 and began to function in 1984. The data for the period 1984ml–85m5 is not available.
14. Consider two time series $\{y_t\}$ and $\{x_t\}$: the series x_t fails to 'cause' y_t if in a regression of y_t on lagged y's and lagged x's, the coefficients of the latter are zero (Granger, 1969).
15. Deposits exclude the State budget deposits and the institutional deposits held in the PBC. Lending excludes the PBC's direct lending to non-financial institutions (Source: the PBC).
16. It might be hypothesised that this was due to the still-limited demand for credit. The reality was that the demand was strong. In fact, in order to limit the credit expansion, the State Council announced in 'The Decision to Conscientiously Strengthen Credit Management and Strictly Control Currency Issuance' (issued in January 1981) that ceilings of credit extension and currency issuance must not be exceeded (Yang, Z. *et al.*, 1985: 57).
17. The SBs keep the official reserves required as well as additional deposits (which were not officially required) in the PBC. The magnitude of the latter was significant, see Table 3.1.
18. *Bulletin of the State Council of the People's Republic of China*, no. 10, 1984, in the Financial Management Department of PBC (ed), 1986a: 91–103.
19. The fixed investment which is financed other than by the State budget and bank loans.
20. The PBC, 5 May 1983, 'Request to change the present practice into the unified management of circulating fund of SOEs by PBC' (*Guanyu Guoyan Qiyie Liudong Zijin Gaiyou Renmin Yinhang Tongyi Guanli De Baogao*), in the Financial Management Department of PBC, (ed), 1986b: 47–55. This request was approved by the State Council.
21. For instance, in the 1960s, the People's Construction Bank of China began

to extend a very limited amount of loans for the technical improvement of the medium- and small-scale industrial enterprises in a few provinces. The maximum amount of each loan was ¥30 000. This business stopped after only a few years, but was restored in 1975 (Wang, F. and Ku, J. 1989: 35–6).

22. See The Fund Management Department of PBC (1990: 15) and SSB (1991a: 642).
23. Estimated as a quotient of working capital stock (sum of the self-owned working capital and bank working capital loans to the SOEs) over stock of fixed assets of the SOEs (net book value). Bank working capital loans are estimated as the sum of loans to productive industrial enterprises, to material supply and marketing enterprises, to commercial enterprises and to construction enterprises (Source: For 'self-owned' working capital of the SOEs: General Planning Department of the MOF, 1989: 130–2; for net fixed assets of the SOEs: ibid, 120–2; Bank working capital loans to the SOEs: *Almanac of China's Finance and Banking*, 1990: 52–3).
24. E.g. the Fund Management Department of PBC (1987a), *Analysis on Receipt and Payment of Money in 1986*.

Chapter 4

1. For instance, within State sector during 1981–5, 'local projects' accounted for 44 per cent of capital construction investment and 75 per cent of technical updating and transformation investment. At national level, 'central projects' accounted for 29 per cent of total fixed assets investment or 36 per cent if households' investment (primarily housing) is excluded (SSB, 1987b: 6, 64, 218).
2. *Yearbook of the Encyclopedia of China* (1983: 296–7); SSB (1991a: 147).
3. There were 6 148 100 self-employment industrial enterprises in 1988 (SSB, 1990c: 23).
4. For the ownership pattern of the industrial enterprises, see Chapter 5, Table 5.1.
5. Hainan is treated as part of Guangdong province; it was separated only in 1988.
6. *China Investment and Construction*, no. 5, 1992, p. 44.
7. The relative strength is defined as the difference between two national output shares of a province.
8. Bank loans to the State budget are excluded because they were used for fixed assets investment. More details are to be discussed later.
9. The stock of bank fixed investment loans in 1979 was ¥1.59 billion, or 0.8 per cent of total bank credit stock (Liu Z. and Liu R. 1989). Between 1980 and 1983, 360 000 technical updating projects, financed partially or fully by bank technical updating loans, amounted to ¥23 billion, of which ¥9.5 billion was repaid. More than 40 000 projects were completed, resulting in (as claimed) an increase in the gross industrial product of ¥59.6 billion (Liu, H. 1987: 15).
10. Absolutely dominated by bank loans, the other was mainly trade credit.
11. The priority was given to the 'quick return' projects. The maximum amount of each loan was set at ¥200 000 (Wang, F. and Xu, J. 1989: 36).

12. E.g. Federal Reserve in the USA.
13. The solution to the problem of inflation, according to this extremist view of the New Right, is very simple. That is: the denationalisation of money and introduction of free issues of private currency (Hayek, 1978; Dowd, 1988).
14. We assume that local governments' investment allocation decisions are identical; in other words, they can be represented by a representative local government. The local government and local government are substitutable in this section.
15. For mathematical deduction see Appendix 4.
16. State Planning Commission, *Provisions about Stopping Myopic and Duplicated Construction*, March, 1981.
17. *Investment and Construction*, no. 5, 1992, p. 44.
18. For example, in 1986, 216 of the 312 technical updating projects in Henan province were partly financed by banks. 72 of the 112 key projects in Hubei were also partly financed by bank loans, the latter contributed about two-thirds of the total investment (Deng, Y. *et al.*, 1990: 148–9).
19. Household consumption expenditure accounts for about 90 per cent of the total consumption expenditure in China and this proportion is reasonably stable the rest is the social consumption expenditure).
20. i.e gross saving less direct investment. It is estimated as sum of increments in household cash holding, bank deposits and holding of other financial assets.
21. See OECD, Economic Outlook, *Historical Statistics 1960–90*, p. 67.
22. *National Income of the Republic of China: National Accounts in Taiwan for 1951–1980*, p. 172–5; *Statistical Yearbook of the Republic of China* (1991: 106–7).
23. Concerning the effect of deposit rates on savings, the 'two-handed' view is all too well-known. A rise in interest rate makes savings more attractive but less necessary for saving a certain amount as originally planned at a lower interest rate. Findings of empirical studies about the relationship between savings and changes in real interest rates are mixed. One well-known study (Boskin, 1978) finds positive interest-rate effects. More recently, Blinder and Deaton (1985) find slightly negative effects of interest rates on consumption – thus positive effects on savings – but cannot reject the hypothesis of no effect. Typically, empirical research suggests the effects of interest rates on savings are small and hard to find. The developing economies are not unusual. Giovannini (1985) finds no significant relation between saving and real interest rate for Asian economies. Fry (1988: 131–43) reports a significant real deposit rate effect on savings in a cross-section time-series regression of 14 Asian economies (excluding China) over the period 1961–83, but quantitatively, the effect is unimportant. It takes an 8 to 25 percentage point increase in the real deposit rate, depending on the estimates, to raise the national savings rate by only 1 percentage point.

Chapter 5

1. 'Local government' refers to every tier of the government excluding the central one. Specifically, it includes government at provincial, prefectural,

county, township and village levels.

2. Incentive failure is generally recognised as a feature associated with the central planning (e.g. Yerrow, 1988).
3. China's tax system is a unitary one. Taxes and tax rates are determined by the central government; there are no independent taxing authorities other than the central government (The World Bank, 1988b: 387).
4. This view is echoed in an interesting paper by Dr Xu Chengang, titled 'M-form hierarchy and Chinese economic reform' at the Fourth Annual Conference of Chinese Economic Association (UK) at the School of Oriental and African Studies in London, 14–15 December, 1992.
5. See, for instance, Wu, D. (1987: 56).
6. For a review, see Wu, D. 1987; Teng, W. and Zhou, X., 1987; Guo, Y. 1988.
7. Theoretically speaking, 'public goods' have two salient characteristics: 'joiness' of supply and the impossibility of inefficiency by excluding others from its consumption, once it has been supplied to members of the community (Musgrave, 1959:9–12, 86; Head, 1962). A classic example is the lighthouse.
8. It is difficult to categorise the Chinese system as either a unitary state or a decentralised federal state in a conventional way. Using social and political judgement, China is clearly an unitary state, since a unitary state can be defined in terms of the constitutional sovereignty of the central government or parliament over local government or local assemblies (Wilson, 1984). Economically, the nature of the Chinese system becomes equivocal. According to Hughes (1987), a unitary state is one in which expectations of uniform national standards of service and taxation are dominant, whereas a decentralised federal state is one in which a high degree of local autonomy determines the nature and level of local government activities, even when this is at the expense of national economic and social objectives. On one hand, since the uniform national standards of taxation, government services and even of wage payment were dominant, China was a unitary economy. On the other hand, since the autonomy of local government could be exercised against the interest of the centre (e.g. against the new economic development strategy), China was closer to a decentralised federal state. Noting that the provinces possess a high measure of autonomy and have sizeable financial means at their disposal, Plasschaert (1989) argues that one could speak of a *de facto* federation in China.
9. Views shared even by Mr Chen Yun, a leading 'conservative', against the prototype Soviet model. See Chen's speech in the First Personnel Conference of the Chinese Communist Party, CEM, p. 20.
10. *The Economist*, 1 August 1987, p. 15.
11. *Selected Works of Mao Zedong*, vol. 5, p. 275.
12. The cyclic movement of centralisation–decentralisation (Lin, 1990).
13. The economic system under Nikita Khrushchev's reforms in the former USSR in 1957 had some analogy to the decentralisation in China. He replaced 23 ministries at the USSR level and 113 ministries at republic level with 105 economic administrative committees (Wu, J. and Liu, J, 1991: 159).

14. Although they are often mistakenly called enterprises, they are actually closer to a *workshop* of an enterprise in the industrialised market economies. All managerial functions are exercised by different government departments in charge of production, printing, human resources, material supply, development planning, etc. (see Figure 4.1).
15. For a well-documented survey and assessment, see Byrd (1991).
16. About three-quarters of the investment projects in technical updating in China were 'local projects' (*Difang Xiangmu*), defined as the projects in which planning, investment financing and the supply of physical resources were all managed by the local governments (SSB, 1987b: 429).
17. See, for example, Lange, O. and Taylor, F. (1964).
18. The employment pressure on the Chinese regional governments was greater because of the strict control over population mobility. The control was based on the household register system. Simply speaking, one may not migrate from one place to another without permission from the government.
19. It is very doubtful that the answer to the following could be in the positive: 'Can the motives of the managers (or provincial administrators, party functionaries) with rather short horizons (tenures) be consistent with the requirements of long-term efficiency in the economy?' (Yenal, 1989: 13).
20. General Planning Department of MOF (1989: 17, 37, 41).
21. SSB (1990c: 182–361).
22. *The Economist*, 'A survey of China's Economy', 1 August 1987, pp. 3–22.
23. In former West Germany, and also to a certain extent in Belgium, the system consists of 'shared' revenue from nationally-set taxes between the provinces and the Centre (Plasschaert, 1989).
24. The profits retained by small enterprises may be mobilised by the local government through their unofficial collection called *Tang Pai*.
25. Only 252 bankruptcy cases had been accepted and heard by courts by the end of 1991 (*Abstract of Newspapers and Magazines* (*Baokan Wenzhai*) 24 March 1992.

Chapter 6

1. A huge number of the Rural Credit Cooperatives existed throughout the period handling rural banking business (60 000 by 1979, under which there were 22 000 branches and 328 000 offices) (Yang, P., 1984, 430). Although they assumed sole responsibility for their profits and losses, they were restrictively under the leadership of the Agricultural Bank when the latter existed, thus indirectly controlled by the PBC. Or, directly controlled by the PBC when the Agricultural Bank was abolished. They implement the country's 'unified' monetary policy.
2. Rural Credit Cooperatives transferred about 72.1 per cent of the deposits collected by them to the State bank during 1953–78 (The PBC).
3. The state-owned enterprises (SOEs) were divided into two groups, the central-government-run SOEs and the local-government-run ones, and four sectors. The other three were industry, domestic commerce and foreign trade.
4. See Liu, R. *et al.* (1989: 222–35).
5. Figures of the PBC branches from Yang P. (1984: 427) and division of

administrative regions is 1983 figure (SSB, 1984a: 1).
6. *Almanac of China's Finance and Banking* (1990: 49).
7. *Almanac of China's Finance and Banking* (1990: 53, 65–6, 84–6).
8. In Hong, Y. and Xu, S. (ed.) (1989: 58).
9. 'The State Council's Decision Concerning Transforming PBC into the Central Bank' (17 September 1983) in the Financial Management Department of PBC (1986b: 30–3).
10. The Financial Management Department of PBC (1986a: 3).
11. Ibid (1986a: 25–6).
12. *The Financial Encyclopedia (I)*, p. 659.
13. Bank Branches in Fuzhou, Sanmenxia, Pingdingshan and Yueyang, in *China Finance*, no. 1, 1990, 52–9; no. 2, 1990, 53–6; no. 1, 1991, 54–8; no. 3, 1991, 51–7.
14. 14 in 1990.
15. Chen, W. *et al.* (1989: 86–7).
16. *Tongyi Jihua*, *Fengji Guanli*, *Cundai Guagou*, *Chae Kongzhi* (*Baogan*).
17. This policy, as some analysts argued, may cause credit expansion through the multiplier effect. However, since credit-ceiling control was still in effect, bank credit expansion was restricted (see Chapter 3).
18. The arrangement was named *Tongyi Jihua*, *Huafeng Zijin*, *Shicun Shidai*, *Xianghu Rongtong*.
19. For details of 1985's credit fund management reform, see the PBC *et al.*, 1984.
20. Normally, less than a quarter.
21. For details of 1987's reform, see the Fund Management Department of PBC, 1987.
22. Yin Zhihai (1984), summary speech on ICBC Section of the Conference of the Reform of Bank Credit and Fund Management System, October 17, 1984, in PBC *et al.* (ed.), *Document Collection of the Conference of Bank Credit and Fund Management System*, China Financial Press, 1984, 128–38.
23. Industrial and Commercial Bank of China (1990: 15).
24. Wang, L. (1989: 298).
25. For the investment exceeding ¥200 million.
26. Chen, W. *et al.* (1989: 137–8).
27. The Financial Management Department of PBC (1986a: 75).
28. Hong, Y, and Xu, S, (1989: 90).
29. The Financial Management Department of PBC (1986a: 91; 1986b: 53).
30. Ibid (1986b: 41–5).
31. Ibid (1986b: 44).
32. Ibid (1986b: 546–5).
33. As regards corporate control, Corbett and Mayer (1991) argue that bank ownership of equity is not necessarily crucial for distinguishing financial systems. They classify financial systems into the outsider systems and the insider systems, instead of the bank-based and the market-based systems. According to them, the most important feature of a financial system is whether ownership and control are dispersed or concentrated.
34. For instance, banks held 18 per cent of corporate equity in Japan (in 1985) and half of the listed firms had one or more representatives from their main bank on their boards in 1980 (Sheard, 1985).

35. The Financial Management Department of PBC (1986a: 99).
36. For industrial firms, the proportion was 70 per cent; for capital goods suppliers, 50 per cent; for wholesale commercial firms, 20 per cent; for retail sale commercial firms, 50 per cent (The Financial Management Departent of PBC, 1986a: 94).
37. Huashang Shibao (16 May, 1992).
38. ICBC (1990: 21).
39. For a detailed policy review of 'paying the loan before taxation' and 'paying the loan with taxes', see He, Y., 1987.
40. As mentioned in Chapter 3, the government guaranteed immediate cashing of household bank deposits and responsibility of cash management was exclusively under the central bank.
41. E.g. *The State Council's Decision on Strengthening Credit Management and Controlling Issue of Money*, 29 January 1981.
42. See The State Council's Circular on *Strengthening Management Working of Bank and Credit*, 27 June 1985, in The Financial Management Department of PBC (1986b: 69–70) and *The State Council's Decision on Further Control Money and Stabilize Finance*, 27 September 1988, in General Office of PBC *et al.* (1988a: 31–3).

Chapter 7

1. Planned at the beginning of the year, not revised during the year.
2. See Prime Minister Li Peng's speech, *Almanac of China's Finance and Banking* (1989: 10–14).
3. *Almanac of China's Finance and Banking* (1990: 9); *Economic Studies*, no. 5, 1990: 63.
4. See *Almanac of China's Finance and Banking* (1989: 19–21).
5. Total funds for fixed assets investment provided by the State banks was ¥59.5 billion in 1988, including the PBC's specially approved loans ¥19.5 billion, the SBs' loans for capital construction and technical updating, and the capital construction bonds bought by them totalling ¥40.0 billion. For 1989, bank fixed investment loans was ¥34.3 billion, also including the use of funds for fixed investment but not computed into the item of 'fixed investment loans' (The Fund Management Department of PBC (1988; 1990).
6. For instance, the Capital Iron & Steel Company received ¥227 million (in forms of compensating trade funds) for fixed assets investment from 45 investors, of which 84.6 per cent came from bank working capital loans (Financial Study Group of the State Planning Commission, 1988: 3).
7. The usual practice in monetary management is through the policy document issued to the provincial branches of the PBC and headquarters of the SBs by the Head Office of the PBC with (if very important) or without approvement of the State Council.
8. For reference, the total number of inspectors of the PBC was 4470.
9. *Almanac of China's Finance and Banking* (1989: 201–5).
10. Appointments and removals of governors and vice-governors of the provincial branches (including the autonomous region, the municipality directly

under the central government) are to be initiated by the Head Office of the PBC. Its nomination will then be submitted to the Ministry of Personnel for examination, and the Ministry will in turn submit its proposals to the State Council for final approval.

11. *Almanac of the China's Finance and Banking* (1990: 201).
12. The difference between lending rate of working capital loans and retail price index. The lending rates of fixed investment loans varied. Generally, lending rates for the fixed investment loans with 1–3 years duration are 0.7–1.4 percentage higher than that of working capital loans.
13. The loans were specified in terms of receiver SOEs, amount, usage and duration.
14. *Almanac of China's Finance and Banking* (1990: 204–5).
15. Ibid. (1990: 223).
16. Ibid. (1990: 210).
17. The average deposit in 1989 was estimated as ¥447.42 billion [(380.15 + 514.69)/2] (SSB, 1991a: 44).
18. Total interest payment in 1989 was nearly ¥60 billion (*Reference Material of Financial Studies*, no. 24, 1990, p. 4) while according to the average deposit and the average deposit rate, only ¥50.7 billion was needed (447.42 x 11.34%). The difference was about ¥9 billion.
19. GNP deflator and retail price index are used to transfer fixed investment and retail sales into real terms respectively (SSB, 1990a: 19, 5, 90, 249).
20. Monthly price index for industrial goods is not available.
21. Monthly data of the fixed investment of the non-State sector is not available.
22. There was no significant change to the credit ceilings *per se*. For instance, they were all in the range of a 15–17 percentage growth over the previous year.
23. *China Commercial Daily*, 22 February 1990.
24. Xinghua News Agency, 4 February 1990.
25. SSB (1990c: 6); *People's Daily* (*Overseas Edition*), 25 November 1991.
26. General Planning Department of the MOF (1989: 17, 146).
27. Of which 23.9 per cent was related to the fact that costs of stocks are larger than their prices, 25.4 per cent of less or non-reduction of selling expenses off 'profits', and 50.7 per cent mainly to suspension of shortage in physical inventory and bad debts.
28. *Economic Daily*, 14 February 1989.
29. Bank loans include that of the RCCs and UCCs (*Almanac of China's Finance and Banking*, 1990: 52, 65; 1991: 41, 53, 239).
30. The General Planning Department of MOF (1989: 138, 141–2); SSB (1991b: 81).
31. *Economic Daily*, 9 March 1990.
32. One source of the PBC estimates that non-operating loans accounted for about 13 per cent of total bank loans (Dai, G., 1992).
33. *People's Daily* (*Overseas Edition*), 19 March 1992.

Chapter 8

1. Viewing passively the role of macro policy in China's economic man-

agement, Yusuf, the leading economist of the World Bank, in the China Department, remarks 'In my view, there is little which macro policies can do in the existing context, to enhance productivity, minimise the severity of business cycles or lessen the risk of inflation. At best, they can, at considerable cost, bring inflation to a halt' (Yusuf, 1990).

2. See, e.g. Caprio and Levine (1992).
3. Jeffrey Sachs, a 'big-bang' proponent from Harvard and adviser to the Polish and Russian governments said that without wholesale privatisation the Chinese economy would grind to a halt (*The Economist*, 'A Survey of China', 28 Nov. – 4 Dec. 1992).
4. Whatever the choice between shock therapy and more gradualist strategies in ownership reform might be made, the considerably long period of transition during which local government continues to be the dominant owner seems unavoidable.
5. This situation is analogous to IMF membership: a country could gain full membership of IMF by making its currency convertible for current account transactions while at the same time not being required to liberalise capital account transactions (Giovannini and Mayer, 1991).
6. United Study Group (1987).
7. It is analogous to suggestions to decentralise planning at the intermediate levels through economic organisations (Spulber, 1971; Brus, 1972; Tardos, 1982, Schüler 1988, Singh, 1989).
8. Facing problems caused by the high level of debt financing in the British nationalised industries in the 1960s, Exchequer Dividend Capital, subsequently named Public Dividend Capital (PDC) was introduced in 1966, allowing certain industries (Airways, Steel, Giro, Aerospace and Shipbuilders) to engage in variable return borrowing. PDC is a form of debt-funding analogous to the equity capital of the private sector. By issuing PDC, the British government expects that over the period of the business cycle, the average return of PDC would be at least equal to the interest payments on a loan from the National Loans Fund. In fact, however, dividends paid have been low and certainly less than the cost of debt capital. Apart from easing the problem of high gearing, PDC permits a low payment or no payment for the poor performers. For good performers, they have no formal duty to return a dividend greater than the cost of its loan capital. Thus the government loses out all round (Taylor, 1989): 168–9, 177).
9. In Japan, the outstanding stock of government debt amounted to nearly 50 per cent of the GNP in the early 1980s.
10. The need for a complete recapitalisation of the existing State banking system, before normal lending on commercial terms can begin, is stressed by Brainard (1990).
11. On one hand, coordination among institutionally separated owners would be necessary; on the other hand, mistrust among several players might arise and agency problems might not be controllable at a low enough cost. When the costs of joint action are high enough, joint monitoring fails (Roe, 1990).
12. On the issue of why institutions (they are themselves corporations with dispersed owners or creditors) should do better in corporate control, see

Roe (1990). He argues that as long as their agency difficulties do not correlate with those afflicting industrial companies in which they own stock, beneficial monitoring could occur. Three potentially beneficial forms of monitoring are identified: hierarchical, collegial, and probabilistic. Hierarchical monitoring could occur if financial institutions have industry expertise. Collegial monitoring seems to occur in Japanese conglomerates, where banks and industrial companies own one another and meet regularly to exchange ideas to reach consensus. Probabilistic monitoring is generally non-intrusive. It occurs only when poor performance is faced and intervention is thought necessary.

13. Debt-for-equity swaps have been employed with some success as a vehicle for debt reduction and foreign investment promotion in countries such as Chile and Argentina.
14. The number of competitors was reduced initially then stabilised. For example, there were over 50 competitors in the Japanese motorcycle industry in the early 1950s. This number was reduced to 30 by 1960 and to 8 by 1965. By 1969, there were only 4 producers left (Honda, Yamaha, Suzuki, and Kawasaki), and the composition of the Japanese motorcycle, industry has remained unchanged since then (Abegglen and Kaisha (1985: 43–44).

Appendices

1. Data for originally valued fixed capital of the State-owned industry: SSB (1989b: 51).
2. Defined as funds which are not from the State budget, domestic banks, foreign investors and other sources.
3. If not specified, the review draws on Yang, Z. *et al.* (ed.) (1985) *Theory and Practice of the Credit Planning*, China Financial Press, The PBC Administration Office *et al.* (ed.) *Selection of the Financial Regulations, 1987, 1988*, China Financial Press.

Bibliography

PRINTED WORKS IN CHINESE

Abstract of Newspapers and Magazines (*Baokan Wenzhai*) 24 March 1992.

Almanac of China's Finance and Banking (1989, 1990, 1991).

Cao, Fenge (1988) *Retrospect of Fund Management in 1987 and Tasks of Fund Management in 1988* (*1987 Zijin Guanli Huigu He 1988 Zijin Guanli Renwu*) January 1988.

CE: The *Chronicle of Events in the Economy of the People's Republic of China*, Fang, Weizhong *et al.* (ed.) (1984) China Social Science Press.

CEM: The *Chronicle of Events in the Economic Management of the People's Republic of China*, Editing Board of Economic Management in Contemporary China (ed.) (1986) China Economic Press.

Chen, Shengchang and Li, Yue (1981) 'Structure of Enterprises' Scale', in Ma H. (ed.) (1981) 688–715.

Chen, Wanghe *et al.* (1989) *Management of Credit for Fixed Assets Investment*, China Financial and Economic Press.

Chen, Yue (1988) 'On Economic Cycles in China', in Zhang, F. (ed.) (1988) 64–91.

China Commercial Daily (1990).

China Economic Reform Institute (1987) *Report Series of Economic Reform*, no. 35, 10 November 1987.

China Finance, various issues of 1990, 1991.

China Investment & Construction, various issues.

China Social Survey Institute (1990) *Report on China's Conditions* (*Zhongguo Guoqing Baogao*), Liaoning People's Press.

Dai, Gengyou (1992) 'Analysis of the Present Financial Situation and an Outlook', *Reference Material of Financial Studies*, no. 1, 1992, 1–4.

Data of 1985 Industrial Census in China (*Zhonghua Renmin Gonghe Guo 1985 Nian Gongye Pucha Ziliao*), vol. 13, no. 1 (light industry), China Statistical Press, 1988.

Deng, Yingtao (1987) 'Material Constraint in China's Economic Growth and Long-Term Prospect of Development Pattern', in Gao S. (ed.) (1987b) 400–10.

Deng, Yingtao *et al.*, (1990) *Analysis of the 'Extra Budget Funds' in China*, People's University Press.

Dong, Fureng (1988) *Study on Economic Development Strategy*, Economic Science Press.

Du, Shuyong and Zheng, Xiangyang (1990) 'Market Slacks and the Choices of Savings Policy', *Reference Material of Financial Studies*, no. 24, 1990, 1–5.

Economic Studies, no. 5, 1990.

Financial Encyclopedia (I) and (II) The China Development Press, 1990.

Financial Management Department of PBC (1986a) *Handbook of Financial Laws and Regulations (I)* China Financial Press.

Financial Management Department of PBC (1986b) *Handbook of Financial Laws and Regulations (II)* China Financial Press.

Financial Statistics and Analysis (1989, 1990).

Financial Study Group of the State Planning Commission (1988) *Financial System Reform and Macroeconomic Management*, Economic Science Press, 1988.

Fixed Assets Investment Department of SSB (1987) *Statistical Working Handbook of Fixed Assets Investment*, China Statistical Press.

Fujian Statistical Bureau (1989) 'Initial Analysis of the Change in Industrial Structure in Fujian during the Past 8 Years and the Structural Improvement', in Industrial and Transportation Department of SSB (ed.) (1989) *Selected Reports of Industrial Statistical Analyses 1988*, 168–81.

Fund Management Department of PBC (1987a) *Analysis of Receipts and Payments of Money in 1986*, 26 January 1987.

Fund Management Department of PBC (1987b) *Collection of the Documents on Improvement of the Credit Management System (Wanshang Xingdai Zijin Guanli Tizhi De Wenjian Huibian)* China Financial Press.

Fund Management Department of PBC (1988) *Viewing Macro Financial Control and Adjustment in 1988.*

Fund Management Department of PBC (1990) *Analysis of Money and Credit in 1989.*

Gao, Shanquan (ed.) (1987a) *China: Development and Reform 1984–85*, China Party's History Press.

Gao, Shanquan (ed.) (1987b) *China: Development and Reform*, vol. 2, Sichuan People's Press.

Gao, Shanquan (1991) *China's Economic System Restructuring*, People's Press.

General Office of the PBC *et al.* (1988a) *Selection of Financial Regulations and Rules (I)*, China Financial Press.

General Planning Department of the MOF (1989) *China Finance Statistics (1950–88)*, China Financial and Economic Press.

General Planning Department of PBC (1988) *National Surveys on Allocation of Cash Holding (1979–86)*, China Financial Press.

Guo, Shuqing (1991) 'Analysis of Usage of National Income in China during Reform', in *Yanjiushen Xuebao of the Chinese Academy of Social Sciences*, no. 3, 1991, 9–24.

Guo, Shuqing and Han, Wenxiu (1991) *Distribution and Utilisation of GNP in China*, Beijing: People's University Press, 1991.

Guo, Shuqing *et al.* (1991) 'The Strategic Choices on How to Extricate from Economic Dilemma', *Economic Studies*, no. 5, 1991, 5–12.

Guo, Yahong (1988) 'Fiscal Structure and Policy', in Zhang F. (ed.) (1988) 146–86.

He, Yan (1987) 'Strong and Weak Points of "Paying the Loans Before Taxation"', *China: Development and Reform*, no. 10, 1987, 28–32.

Hong, Yunchen and Xu, Shuxing (eds) (1989) *Carrying Out the Policy of Stabilisation and Reform, and Improving the Financial Work*, Financial Press.

Hu, Liwen (1988) 'Unifying Enterprise Income Tax Rates for an Equalized Tax Burden', *Jianghuai Tribune*, no. 6, 1988, 13–17.

Hu, Qiaomu (1978) 'Speeding up Four Modernizations According to the

Objective Economic Laws', *People's Daily*, 6 October 1978.

Hu, Yaobang (1982) Speech at the Party's Twelfth Congress, *Yearbook of Encyclopedia of China 1983.*

Huang, Xue (1988) 'Analysis on the Supply of, and Demand for, Money', in Zhang, Fengbo (ed.) (1988) 187–224.

Industrial and Commercial Bank of China (July 21, 1987) *Provision of the Experiment on Management Targeting Responsibility Scheme.*

Industrial and Commercial Bank of China (1990) *Handbook of Industrial Credit (Gongye Xindai Gongzuo Guicheng).*

Investment & Construction, various issues, 1992.

Jiang, Xiaojuan (1991) 'On Effects of the Industrial Structural Policy and Change of the Adjustment Mechanism', *Economic Studies*, no. 2, 1991, 27–34.

Liang, Wenshen (1984) 'Issues of China's Approach to Industrialization and Strategy', in Liu, Guoguang (ed.) (1984) 129–45.

Liu, Guoguang (1979) 'A View on Several Important Issues in the Economic System Restructuring', *Economic Management*, no. 11, 1979.

Liu, Guoguang (ed.) (1984) *Studies of Chinese Economic Development Strategy*, Shanghai People's Press.

Liu, Hongru (1987) *Studies on China's Reform of Financial System*, China Financial Press.

Liu, Hui *et al.* (1981) 'Redirecting Capital Construction Investment and Promoting Rationalisation of Economic Structure', in Ma, H. (ed.) (1981) 411–36.

Liu, Rui *et al.* (1989) *Financial Reform and Innovation in the East and the West*, China Financial Press.

Liu, Zhiqiang and Liu, Renhui (1989) 'Doing What One is Capable in Banks' Lending for Fixed Asset Investment' (*Guding Zican Daikuan Bixu Liangli Erxing*) *Reference Material of Financial Studies*, no. 15–16, 1989, 1–5.

Ma, Hong (ed.) (1981) *Studies on China's Economic Structure*, People's Press.

Ma, Yukang (1983) 'On Dual Objectives of Monetary Policy', in the Institute of Finance, Trade and Material of the Chinese Academy of Social Sciences (1983) *Issues of Monetary Circulation in the New Era*, China's Financial Press, 36–47.

Management Department of PBC (ed.) (1986) *Handbook of Financial Regulations I* (*Jinrong Fagui Shouce I*) China Financial Press.

Niu, Renliang *et al.* (1990) 'Analysis of the Total Effect of Retrenchment Policy since 1988' *Economic Studies*, no. 5, 1990, 13–22.

PBC (1985–90) *Monthly Report of the Banks and the Rural Credit Cooperatives.*

PBC (1988) *Bank Deposit and Lending Rates*, China Financial Press.

PBC (1989–92) *Reference Material of Financial Studies*, various issues.

PBC (1990) *An Opinion about Circulating Fund*, a document issued on PBC's Provincial Governors' meeting.

PBC *et al.* (eds) (1984) *Collection of the Documents on the Symposium of the Reform of Bank Credit Fund Management System*, China Financial Press.

People's Daily (1988–92).

People's Daily (Overseas Edition) (1989–92).

Planning Department of PBC (1988) *Survey of Distribution of Cash Circulation in the National Market (1979–1986)*, Financial Press.

Qian, Jiaju (1989) 'Comment on Financial System Reform', *Finance and Economy*, Nanchang, no. 3, 1989, 6–7.

Qiu, Jingji and Huang, Juefei (1981) 'Structure of Machinery Industry', in Ma, H. (ed.) (1981) 317–45.

Reference Material of Financial Studies (1989–92).

Rong, Donggu and Huang, Rongsheng (1984) 'The Issue of Energy in China's Economic Development', in Liu, G. (ed.) (1984) 175–97.

Rong, Fenge *et al.* (1990) 'Deepening Reforms and Establishing the Socialist Credit Management System with Chinese Characteristics', in Hong, Y. and Xu, S. (eds) (1990) 146–58.

Shao, Qiuming (1989) 'Retrospect of 10 Years Financial Reforms', *Jiangxi City Finance*, November 1989, 5–7.

SSB (China State Statistical Bureau) (1984a) *China Statistical Yearbook 1984*, China Statistical Press.

SSB (1984b) *China's Statistical Data of Trade and Price 1952–1983*, China Statistical Press.

SSB (1985) *China's Industrial Statistical Data 1949–1984*, China Statistical Press.

SSB (1987a) *China Statistical Yearbook 1987*, China Statistical Press.

SSB (1987b) *China's Statistical Data of Fixed Investment 1950–1985*, China Statistical Press.

SSB (1988a) *Statistical Yearbook 1988*, China Statistical Press.

SSB (1988b) *Statistical Yearbook of China's Industrial Economy 1988*, China Statistical Press.

SSB (1989a) *Forty Years in Advance*, China Statistical Press.

SSB (1989b) *A Statistical Survey of China*, China Statistical Press.

SSB (1989c) *Statistical Yearbook of China's Industrial Economy 1989*, China Statistical Press.

SSB (1989d) *Statistics on investment in fixed assets of China (1986–87)*, China Statistical Press.

SSB (1989e) *China Statistical Yearbook 1989*, China Statistical Press.

SSB (1990a) *China Statistical Yearbook 1990*, China Statistical Press.

SSB (1990b) *A Statistical Survey of China 1990*, China Statistical Press.

SSB (1990c) *Statistical Yearbook of China's Industrial Economy 1990*, China Statistical Press.

SSB (1990d) *Historical Statistics of Provinces, Autonomous Regions and the Municipalities under the State Council (1949–89)*, China Statistical Press.

SSB (1991a) *China Statistical Yearbook 1990*, China Statistical Press.

SSB (1991b) *A Statistical Survey of China 1991*, China Statistical Press.

The State Council (1977) *'The Decision of Cash Management' (Guanyu Xianjin Guanli De Jueding*), in Financial Management Department of PBC, 1986, Handbook of Financial Regulations, vol. 2, 34–5.

State Planning Commission (1981) *Provisions of Stopping Myopic and Duplicated Construction*.

Statistical Monthly various issues, published by SSB.

Sun, Xuewen and Ding, Jilong (1984) 'Reform of the Management System of Machinery Industry', in Zhou T. (ed.) (1984) *The Restructuring of the*

Economic System in Modern China, China's Social Science Press, 287–318.

Tang, Zongji *et al.* (1987) *Comments after 10 Years: Collection of the Studies on the 'Cultural Revolution'*, Reference Publishing House of the History of the Chinese Communist Party.

Teng, Weiming and Zhou, Xingxin (1987) 'History, Present and Reforms of the Multi-Level Budget Management in China', *Management World*, no. 5, 1987, 47–56.

United Study Group (1987) 'Views of Expertise of the World Bank about China's Enterprise Reforms', *China: Development and Reform*, no. 10, 1987, 39–43.

Wang, Derong *et al.* (1984) 'Strategic Issues of China's Transportation and Communications', in Liu G. (ed.) (1984) 198–216.

Wang, Deyan (1990) 'The Main Tasks of the Bank of China in Improvement and Rectification of Economy and Deepening Reforms', in Hong, Y. and Xu, S. (eds) (1990) 76–87.

Wang, Fuxiang and Xu, Jianzhong (1989) *Fixed Investment Loans ABC*, China Financial Press.

Wang, Lan (1989) *Practical Lending Handbook*, China Financial and Economic Press.

Wei, Ruilang *et al.* (1981) 'The Structure of Chemical Industry', in Ma, H. (ed.) (1981) 346–82.

Wu, Deming (1987) *Introduction to State Budget Management System*, China Financial and Economic Press.

Wu, Jinglian (ed.) (1989a) *A Positive Analysis of China's Economy 1986*, China Social Sciences Press.

Wu, Jinglian (1989b) *A Positive Analysis of China's Economy 1987*, China Social Sciences Press.

Wu, Jinglian and Liu, Jirei (1991) *On Competitive Market Systems*, China Financial and Economic Press.

Xu, Jian (1989) 'On Monetary and Fiscal Policies under Tight Control', *Economic Daily*, 12 May 1989, p. 3.

Xu, Jingan *et al.* (1984) 'The New Phase of the Economic Restructuring', in Zhou, T. (ed.) (1984) 159–209.

Xu, Xiaobo (1988) 'The Behaviour of Fixed-Assets-Investing Bodies in China', *China: Development and Reform*, no. 11, 1988, 23–30.

Yang, Peixing (1990) 'Study on Current Situation and Countermeasure', *Economic Studies*, no. 7, 1990, 38–45.

Yang, Pengzhang (1989) 'A Thought about Assets-Liability Management of the Specialised Banks', *Economic Studies,* no. 8, 1989, 68–70.

Yang, Zhesheng *et al.* (1985) *The Theory And Practice of Credit Planning*, China Financial Press.

Yearbook of the Encyclopedia of China (1983).

Yin, Zhihai (1984) 'Summary Speech on ICBC Section of the Conference of the Reform of Bank Credit and Fund Management System', 17 October 1984, in the PBC *et al.* (eds) (1984) 128–38.

Yu, Luming *et al.* (1989) 'On Dilemma of the Central Bank and its Restructuring', *Hangzhou University Journal (Social Sciences)* February 1989, 16–22.

Yu, Reixiang (1987) *Study of Financial Issues in Contemporary China*, China's Financial Press.

Yu, Reixiang (1989) 'A Brief Comment on Overcoming Inflation', Kunming: *Yunnan Caimao Xuebao*, February 1989, 7–10.

Yuan, Baohua (1992) 'Enterprises Must Face Market', *Seeking the Truth (Qiu Shi)*, no. 16, 2–5.

Zhang, Bo (1988) 'The Cause of Long-Term Loss-Making: Rigidity of Capital Stock', *Management World*, no. 4, 1988, 74–85.

Zhang, Bo and Zuo, Yi (1987) 'Objective Structure, Budget Constraint and Firm Behaviour: A Case Study', in Gao, S. (ed.) (1987b) 247–59.

Zhang, Da (1985) *Principle of Money and Credit*, China's Financial Press.

Zhang, Fengbo (ed.) (1988) *Macroeconomic Structure and Policy in China*, China Financial and Economic Press.

Zhang, Shaojie *et al.* (1987a) 'Investment: Initial Changes in Mechanism and Clues to the Economic Reforms', in Gao, S. (ed.) (1987b) 321–33.

Zhang, Shaojie *et al.* (1987b) The Practical Financing Mechanism and its Reforms in China', *Economic Research*, no. 11, 1987, 10–20.

Zhong, Qirui (1988) *Structural Analysis of Money*, Beijing: Financial Press, 1988.

Zhou, Jun (1984) *Socialist Money and Banking*, China's Financial Press 2nd edition.

Zhou, Taihe (ed.) (1984) *The Restructuring of the Economic System in Temporary China*, China's Social Science Press.

Zhu, Guanxin and Zhang, Qizuo (1989a) 'Retrospect and Perspective of the Financial Reforms in the past 10 Years (I)', *Study of Technical Economy and Management*, Taiyuan, no. 2, 1989, 18–21.

Zhu, G. and Zhang, Q. (1989b) 'Retrospect and Perspective of the Financial Reforms in the past 10 Years (II)', ibid, no. 3, 1989, 15–20.

PRINTED WORKS IN ENGLISH

Abegglen, J. C. and Kaisha, G. S. (1985) *The Japanese Corporation*, New York: Basic Books.

Alesina, A. (1988) 'Macroeconomics and Politics', in National Bureau of Economic Research (1988) *Macroeconomic Annual*, Cambridge: MIT Press, April, 13–52.

Backus, D. and Driffill, J. (1985) 'Inflation and Reputation', *American Economic Review* **75**, 530–38.

Bade, R. and Parkin, M. (1980) *Central Bank Laws and Monetary Policy*, mimeo, Department of Economics, University of Western Ontario.

Balassa, B. (1982) 'Economic Reforms in China', *BNL Quarterly Review* **142**, 307–33.

Balow, J. and Jhoven, J. (1978) 'The Bankruptcy Decision', *Bell Journal of Economics* **9**, 437–56.

Bank of Korea (1978) *National Income in Korea.*

Bank of Korea (1992) *Annual Report.*

Barro, R. J. (1983) 'Inflation Finance under Discretion and Rules', *Canadian Journal of Economics* **16**, 1–16.

Barro, R. J. (1986) 'Reputation in A Model of Monetary Policy with Incomplete Information', *Journal of Monetary Economics* **17**, 3–20.

Barro, R. J. and Gordon, D. B. (1983a) 'A Positive Theory of Monetary Policy in a Natural Rate Model', *Journal of Political Economy* **91**, 589–610.

Barro, R. J. and Gordon, D. B. (1983b) 'Rules, Discretion, and Reputation in a Model of Monetary Policy', *Journal of Monetary Economics* **12**, 101–21.

Baumol, W. J. (1952) 'The Transaction Demand for Cash: An Inventory Theoretic Approach', *Quarterly Journal of Economics* **66**, November, 545–56.

Bayliss, B. and Butt Philip, A. (1980) *Capital Markets and Industrial Investment in Germany and France*, Fanborough, Saxon House.

Bewley, R. A. (1981) 'The Portfolio Behaviour of the London Clearing Banks 1963–71', *Manchester School* **49**, 191–210.

Blejer, M. *et al.* (1991) China: Economic Reform and Macroeconomic Management, IMF Occasional Paper No. 76.

Blejer, M. and Szapary, G. (1990) 'The Changing Role of Macroeconomic Policies in China', *Finance and Development*, June, 1990, 32–5.

Blinder, A. S. and Deaton, A. (1985) 'The Time Series Consumption Function Revisited', *Brookings Paper on Economic Activity*, vol. 2, 1985, 465–511.

Blundell, R. (1988) 'Consumption Behaviour: Theory and Empirical Evidence – A Survey', *The Economic Journal*, **98**, March 1988, 16–65.

Bodart, V. (1990) *Central Bank Independence and the Effectiveness of Monetary Policy: A Comprehensive Analysis*, mimeo, IMF paper.

Boskin, M. (1978) 'Taxation, Saving, and the Rate of Interest', *Journal of Political Economy*, April 1978.

Bowles, P. and White, G. (1989) 'Contradictions in China's Financial Reforms: The Relationship Between Banks and Enterprises', *Cambridge Journal of Economics*, vol. 13, no. 4, 481–95.

Brainard, L. J. (1990) 'Reform in Eastern Europe: Creating a Capital Market', *The AMEX Bank Review: Special Paper, 18*, November, 1990.

Breton, A. (1985) Supplementary Statement in *Report of the Royal Commission on the Economic Union and Development Prospects for Canada*, Ottawa: Minister of Supply and Service.

Brick, A. B. (1991) 'The Relationship Between Free Market Economics and Free Market Politics', *Transition* (The newsletter about reforming economies published by the World Bank), vol. 3, no. 2, p.7.

Brunner, K. (1987) 'Money supply', in Eatwell J. *et al.* (eds) (1987) 263–67.

Bruno, M. (1992) *Stabilization and Reform in Eastern Europe: A Preliminary Evaluation*, IMF Working Paper, WP/92/30.

Brus, W. (1972) *The Market in A Socialist Economy*, London and Boston: Routledge & Kegan Paul.

Brus, W. and Laski, K. (1989) *From Marx to Market: Socialism in Search of an Economic System*, Oxford: Clarendon Press.

Bulow, J., Geanakoplos, J. and Klemperer, P., 1985, 'Multimarket Ologopoly: Strategic Substitutes and Complements', *Journal of Political Economy* **93**, 488–511.

Burdekin and Willett, (1990) cited in Lin, C.Z. (1991) *Central Banking and Financial Market Reform in China: Principles and Prototypes from Western Theory and Evidence*, A background paper prepared for the State Commission for Restructuring the Economic System, Beijing, China.

Byrd, W. (1983) *China's Financial System: The Changing Role of Banks*, Boulder, Colorado: Westview Press.

Byrd, W. (1991) 'The Contractual Responsibility System in Chinese State-Owned Industry: A Preliminary Assessment', *Advances in Chinese Industrial Studies*, **2**, 7–35.

Calvo, G. (1978) 'Optimal Seigniorage From Money Creation', *Journal of Monetary Economics* **4**, 503–17.

Caprio, G. Jr. and Levine, R. (1992) 'Reforming Finance in Transitional Socialist Economies: Avoiding the Path From Shell Money to Shell Games', *The World Bank Policy Research Working Paper*, WPS 898.

Carter, H. and Partington, I. (1984) *Applied Economics in Banking and Finance*, 3rd edition, Oxford University Press.

Chen, K. *et al.* (1988a) 'New Estimates of Fixed Investment and Capital Stock for Chinese State Industry', *China Quarterly* **114**, 243–66.

Chen, K. *et al.* (1988b) 'Productivity Change in Chinese Industry: 1953–85', *Journal of Comparative Economics* **12**, 570–91.

Chenery, H. and Srinivasan, T. N. (eds) (1988) *Handbook of Development Economics*, Amsterdam: North-Holland.

China Statistical Information and Consultation Centre, University of Illinois at Chicago, *China Statistical Monthly*, various issues.

Chiu, P. C. H. (1992) 'Money and Financial Markets: The Domestic Perspective', in Ranis, G. (ed.) (1992) *Taiwan: From Developing to Mature Economy*, Westview Press, 121–94.

Cho, Y. J. (1989) 'Finance and Development: The Korean Approach', *Oxford Review of Economic Policy*, vol. 5, no. 4, 88–102.

Chow, G. C. (1985) 'A Model of Chinese National Income Determination', *Journal of Political Economy* vol. 93, no. 4, 782–92.

Collier, P. and Mayer, C. (1989) 'The Assessment: Financial Liberalization: Financial Systems, and Economic Growth', *Oxford Review of Economic Policy*, vol. 5, no. 4, 1989, 1–12.

Corbett, J. (1987) 'International Perspectives on Financing: Evidence From Japan', *Oxford Review of Economic Policy*, vol. 3, no. 4, 30–55.

Corbett, J. and Mayer, C. (1991) 'Financial Reform in Eastern Europe: Progress with the Wrong Model', *Oxford Review of Economic Policy*, vol. 7, no. 4, 57–75.

Council for Economic Planning and Development, Republic of China (1987) *Taiwan Statistical Data Book.*

Courakis, A. S. (1974) 'Clearing Bank Asset Choice Behaviour: A Mean Variance Treatment', *Oxford Bulletin of Economics and Statistics* **36**, 173–201.

Cox, D. (1989) *Success in Elements of Banking*, 5th edition, London: John Murray.

Cuthbertson, K. (1985) *The Supply of Demand for Money*, Oxford: Basil Blackwell.

Day, A. C. L. (1957) *Outline of Monetary Economics*, Oxford: Clarendon Press.

Diamond, D. W. (1989) *Monitoring and Reputation: the Choice between Bank Loans and Directly Placed Debt*, mimeo.

Diamond, D. W. and Dybvig, P. H. (1983) 'Bank Runs, Deposit Insurance, and Liquidity', *Journal of Political Economy* **91**, 401–19.

Dickey, D. A. and Fuller, W. A. (1981) 'The Likelihood Ratio Statistics for Autoregressive Time Series with a Unit Root', *Econometrica* **49**, 1057–72.

Donnithorne, A. (1967) *China's Economic System*, New York: Praeger.

Donnithorne, A. (1972) 'China's Cellular Economy: Some Trends Since the Cultural Revolution', *China Quarterly*, October/December 1972, **52**, 605–19.

Dow, J. C. R. and Saville, I. D. (1988) *A Critique of Monetary Policy*, Oxford: Oxford University Press.

Dowd, K. (1988) *Private Money: The Path to Monetary Stability*, Hobart Paper, no. 112, London: Institute of Economic Affairs.

Eatwell, J. *et al.* (eds) (1987) *The New Palgrave: Money*, Basingstoke: Macmillan.

Eatwell, J. *et al.* (1989) *Allocation, Information and Markets*, Basingstoke: Macmillan.

Economic Commission for Europe (1991) *Economic Survey of Europe in 1990–1991*, New York: United Nations.

Ellman, M. (1992) 'Money in the 1980s', in Ellman, M. and Kontorovich, V. (eds) (1992) *The Disintegration of the Soviet Economic System*, London: Routledge, 106–36.

Engle, R. F. and Granger, C. W. J. (1987) 'Cointegration and Error Correction: Representation, Estimation and Testing', *Econometrica*, vol. 55, no. 2, 251–76.

Eshag, E. (1971) 'The Relative Efficiency of Monetary Policy in Selected Industrial and Less-Developed Countries', *The Economic Journal* **81**, June, 1971, 294–305.

Feltenstein, A. *et al.* (1986) 'Savings, Commodity Market and the Real Rate of Interest in China', *Country Policy Department Discussion Paper*, no. 27, World Bank.

Feltenstein, A. and Farhadian, Z. (1987) 'Fiscal Policy, Monetary Targets and the Price Level in a Centrally Planned Economy: An Application to the Case of China', *Journal of Money, Credit and Banking* **19**, 137–56.

Feltenstein, A. and Ha, J. (1989) *Measurement of Repressed Inflation in China: The Lack of Coordination between Monetary Policy and Price Control*, Working Paper, Department of Economics, University of Kansas.

Fisher, I. (1911) *The Purchasing Power of Money*, 2nd revised edition, 1926, reprinted in New York, by Kelley, 1963.

Fisher, I. (1930) *The Theory of Interest*, New York: Macmillan.

Friedman, B. (1981) *The Roles of Money and Credit in Economic Analysis*, Working Paper **831**, National Bureau of Economic Research.

Friedman, L. S. (1985) *Microeconomic Policy Analysis*, International student edition, New York: McGraw-Hill Book Company.

Friedman, M. (1957) *A Theory of the Consumption Function*, Princeton, New Jersey: Princeton University Press.

Friedman, M. (1987) 'Quantity Theory of Money', in Eatwell J. *et al.* (eds) (1987) 1–40.

Fry, M.J. (1988) *Money, Interest, and Banking in Economic Development*, Baltimore and London: The Johns Hopkins Press.

Gardener, E. P. M. and Molyneux, P. (1991) *Changes in Western European Banking: An International Bankers Guide*, London: Unwin Hyman.

Gerlach (1987) *Alliances and the Social Organization of Business*, Working Paper, University of California, Berkeley, Cal.

Gertner, R. and Scharfstein, D. (1989) *A Theory of Workouts and the Effects of Reorganization Law*, Working Paper, University of Chicago, Chicago, Ill.

Giovannini, A. and Mayer, C.P. (1991) *European Financial Integration*, Cambridge: Cambridge University Press.

Goodhart, C. A. E. (1973) 'Analysis of the Determination of the Stock of Money', in Parkin, J. M. and Nobay, A. R. (eds) (1973) *Essays in Modern Economics*, London: Longman, reprinted in Goodhart, C. A. E. (1984) *Monetary Theory and Practice*, Basingstoke: Macmillan Press, 182–99.

Goodhart, C. A. E. (1987) 'Monetary Base', in Eatwell J. *et al.* (eds) (1987) 206–11.

Granger, C. W. J. (1969) 'Investigating Causal Relations by Econometric Methods and Cross-Spectral Methods', *Econometrica* **37**, 24–36.

Granger, C. W. J. (1981) 'Some Properties of Time Series Data and Their Use in Econometric Model Specification', *Journal of Econometrics*, 121–30.

Granick, D. (1990) *Chinese State Enterprises: A Regional Property Rights Analysis*, Chicago and London: University of Chicago Press.

Greenwald, B. and Stiglitz, J. (1986a) 'Money, Imperfect Information, and Economic Fluctuations', *Symposium on Monetary Theory*, The Institute of Economics, Academia Sinica, Taipei, Taiwan.

Greenwald, B. and Stiglitz, J. (1986b) 'Externalities in Economies with Imperfect Information and Incomplete Market', *Quarterly Journal of Economics*, **101**, 229–64.

Grossman, H. I. and Van Huyck, J. B. (1986) 'Seigniorage, Inflation and Reputation', *Journal of Monetary Economics* **18**, 21–31.

Gurley, J. G. and Shaw, E. S. (1960) *Money in a Theory of Finance*, Washington, D.C.: Brookings Institute.

Haberler, G. (1941) *Prosperity and Depression*, London: Allen & Unwin, (reprinted 1964).

Hahn, F. H. (1982) *Money and Inflation*, Oxford: Blackwell.

Hall, R. E. (1978) 'Stochastic Implications of the Lifecycle-Permanent Income Hypothesis: Theory and Evidence', *Journal of Political Economy*, **86**, 971–88.

Hawtrey, R. G. (1919) *Currency and Credit*, London: Longman, Green & Co.

Hayek, F. A. (ed.) (1935) *Collectivist Economic Planning*, London: Routledge.

Hayek, F. A. (1978) *Denationalization of Money: The Argument Refined*, Hobart Paper 'Special', no. 70, 2nd edition, London: Institute of Economic Affairs.

Head, J. G. (1962) 'Public Goods and Public Policy', *Public finance* **17**, 197–221.

Helm, P. and Smith. S. (1987) 'The Assessment: Decentralization and the Economics of Local Government', *Oxford Review of Economic Policy*, vol. 3, no. 2, i–xxi.

Hendry, D., Engle, R. and Richard, J. L. (1983) 'Exogeneity', *Econometrica*, vol. 51, no. 2, March, 227–304.

Hester, D. D. and Tobin, J. (1967) *Financial Markets and Economic Activity*, New York: Wiley.

Hetzel, R. L. (1986) 'A Congressional Mandate for Monetary Policy', *Cato Journal* **5**, 797–820.

Hicks, J. R. (1935) 'A Suggestion for Simplifying the Theory of Money', *Economica* **2**, 1–19.

Hirschman, A. O. (1958) *The Strategy of Economic Development*, New Haven, Conn.: Yale University Press.

Hodgman, D. (1960) 'Credit Risk and Credit Rationing', *Quarterly Journal of Economics* **74**, May, 258–78.

Hodgman, D. R. (1962) 'Soviet Monetary Controls Through the Banking System', in Franklyn, D. H. (ed.) (1962) *Readings on the Soviet Economy*, Chicago: Rand McNally & Co., 581–602.

Holmstrom, B. and Myerson, R. B. (1983) 'Efficient and Durable Decision Rules with Incomplete Information', *Econometrica* **51**, 790–819.

Hsiao, K. H. (1971) *Money and Monetary Policy in Communist China*, New York and London: Columbia University Press.

Hsiao, K. H. (1982) 'Money and Banking in the People's Republic of China: Recent Developments', *China Quarterly* **91**, Sept. 1982, 462–77.

Hughes, G. A. (1987) 'Fiscal Federalism in the UK', *Oxford Review of Economic Policy*, vol. 3, no. 2, 1–23.

Hughes, G. A. and Smith, S. (1991) 'Economic Aspects of Decentralized Government: Structure, Functions and Finance', *Economic Policy* **13**, 425–59.

Hurwicz, L. (1972) 'On Informationally Decentralized Systems', in Radner, R. and McGuire, C. B. (eds) (1972) *Decision and Organization: A Volume in Honour of Jacob Marschak*, Amsterdam: North-Holland, 297–336.

IMF, *International Financial Statistics,* various issues.

Jaffee, D. (1987) 'Credit Rationing', in Eatwell J. *et al.* (eds) (1987) 103–8.

Jaffee, D. and Russell, T. (1976) 'Imperfect Information, Uncertainty, and Credit Rationing', *Quarterly Journal of Economics*, vol. 90, no. 4, November, 651–66.

Jefferson, G. H. *et al.* (1992) 'Growth Efficiency and Convergence in China's State and Collective Industry', *Economic Development and Cultural Change*, 239–66.

Johnson, H. G. *et al.* (1972) *Readings in British Monetary Economics*, Oxford: Oxford University Press.

Jorgenson, D. W. (1965) 'Anticipations and Investment Behaviour', in Duesenberry, J. (ed.) (1965) *The Brookings Quarterly Econometric Model of the United States*, Amsterdam: North-Holland.

Jorgenson, D. W. (1967) 'The Theory of Investment Behaviour', in Ferber, R. (ed.) (1967) *Determination of Investment Behaviour*, New York: National Bureau of Economic Research, 129–55.

Kahn, A. E. and Peck, M. J. (1991) 'Price Deregulation, Corporatization, Competition', in Peck, M. J. and Richardson, T. J. (eds) (1991) *What Is To Be Done?*, New Haven and London: Yale University Press, 38–82.

Kane, E. J. (1982) 'External Pressure and the Operations of the Fed.', in

Lombra, R. E. and Witte, W. E. (eds) (1982) *Political Economy of International and Domestic Monetary Relations*, Ames: Iowa State University Press.

Kaser, M. and Allsopp, C. (1992) 'Macroeconomics of Transition in Eastern Europe 1989–91', *Oxford Review of Economic Policy*, vol. 8, no. 1, 1–13.

Keynes, J. M. (1936) *The General Theory of Employment, Interest and Money*, London: Macmillan.

Khanin, G. (1992) 'Economic Growth in the 1980s', in Ellman, M. and Kontorovich, V. (eds) (1992) *The Disintegration of the Soviet Economic System*, London: Routledge, 73–85.

Kim, I. Z. (1990) *'Over-Investment in China: Sources and Processes', 1979–88*, D. Phil. thesis, University of Oxford.

Kornai, J. (1980) *Economics of Shortage*, Amsterdam, New York, Oxford: North-Holland Publishing Company.

Kydland, F. E. and Prescott, E. S. (1977) 'Rules Rather than Discretion: The Inconsistency of Optimal Plans', *Journal of Political Economy* **85**, 473–91.

Lange, O. and Taylor, F. (1964) *On the Economic Theory of Socialism*, New York: McGraw-Hill.

Lau, K. T. and Brada, J. C. (1990) 'Technological Progress and Technical Efficiency in Chinese Industrial Growth: A Frontier Production Function Approach', *China Economic Review*, vol. 1, no. 2, 113–24.

Lavington, F. (1921) *The English Capital Market*, London: Methuen.

Ledyard, J. O. (1989) 'Incentive Compatibility', in Eatwell J. *et al.* (eds) (1989) 141–51.

Lieberthal, K. and Oksenberg, M. (1988) *Policy Making in China: Leaders, Structures, and Processes*, Princeton, New Jersey: Princeton University Press.

Lin, C. Z. (1990) *Marxian Economic Categories and Problems of Centralised and Decentralised Planning in China*, D. Phil. thesis, University of Oxford.

Lombra, R. and Moran, M. (1980) 'Policy Advice and Policy Making at the Federal Reserve', *Carnegie–Rochester Conference Series on Public Policy* **13**, 9–68.

Lyons, T. P. (1987) *Economic Integration and Planning in Maoist China*, New York: Columbia University Press.

Maitra, R. (1989) 'The Sun Yat-sen Programme and China's Development Today', *Executive Intelligence Review* (EIR), vol. 16, no. 35.

Marschak, T. (1989) 'Organisation Theory', in Eatwell J. *et al.* (eds) (1989) 223–30.

Masera, R. S. and Portes, R. (1991) 'Foreword', in Giovannini, A. and Mayer, C. (eds) (1991) *European Financial Integration*, Cambridge University Press.

Mayer, C. (1987) 'The Assessment: Financial Systems and Corporate Investment', *Oxford Review of Economic Policy*, vol. 3, no. 4, i–xvi.

McCallum, B. T. (1990) 'Inflation: Theory and Evidence', in Friedman and Hahn (eds) (1990) *Handbook of Monetary Economics*, vol. I, 357–98.

McCallum, B. T. and Goodfriend, M. (1987) 'Demand for Money: Theoretical Studies', in Eatwell J. *et al.* (eds) (1987) 117–43.

McGuckin, R. H. *et al.* (1989) 'Multifactor Productivity in Chinese Industry', Washington, D.C., mimeo.

McKinnon, R. I. (1973) *Money and Capital in Economic Development*, Washington, D.C.: Brookings Institution.

McKinnon, R. I. (1989) 'Financial Liberalization and Economic Development: A Reassessment of Interest-rate Policies in Asia and Latin America', *Oxford Review of Economic Policy*, vol. 5, no. 4, 29–54.

McKinnon, R. I. (1991) *The Order of Economic Liberalization: Financial Control in the Transition to a Market Economy*, Johns Hopkins University Press, 1991.

Meyer, J. and Kuh, E. (1957) *The Investment Decision*, Cambridge, Mass.: Harvard University Press.

Modigliani, F. and Brumberg, R. (1954) 'Utility Analysis and the Consumption Function: An Interpretation of Cross-Section Data', in Kurihara, K. K. (ed.) (1955) *Post-Keynesian Economics*, New Brunswick: Rutgers University Press, 388–436.

Moore, B. J. and Threadgold, A. R. (1980) *Bank Lending and the Money Supply*, Discussion Paper **10**, Bank of England.

Moore, B. J. and Threadgold, A. R. (1985) 'Corporate Bank Borrowing in the UK, 1965–81', *Economica* **52**, 65–78.

Mueller, D. C. (1989) *Public Choice II*, Cambridge: Cambridge University Press.

Musgrave, R. A. (1959) *The Theory of Public Finance*, New York: McGraw-Hill.

Myerson, R. B. (1989) 'Mechanism Design', in Eatwell J. *et al.* (1989) 191–206.

National Income of the Republic of China: National Accounts in Taiwan for 1951–1980.

Newcomb, S. (1885) *Principles of Political Economy*, New York: Harper & Brothers.

Newlyn, W. T. (1962) *Theory of Money*, 1st edition, Oxford: Clarendon Press.

Newlyn, W. T. (1971) *Theory of Money*, 2nd edition, Oxford: Clarendon Press.

Nove, A. (1968) *The Soviet Economy: An Introduction*, 3rd edition, Chapter 6.

Oates, W. E. (1972) *Fiscal Federalism*, New York: Harcourt Brace Jovanovich.

OECD (1987) *OECD Historical Statistics 1960–1985.*

OECD (1992) *OECD Historical Statistics 1960–1990.*

OECD (1992) *National Accounts: Main Aggregates, 1960–90.*

Parkin, J. M. (1970) 'The Portfolio Behaviour of Commercial Banks', in Hiton, K. and Heathfield, D. F. (eds) (1970) *The Econometric Study of the United Kingdom*, Basingstoke: Macmillan.

Patinkin, D. (1965) *Money, Interest and Prices*, 2nd edition, New York: Harper & Row.

Pigou, A. C. (1941) *Employment and Equilibrium*, London: Macmillan.

Pigou, A. C. (1943) 'The Classical Stationary State', *Economic Journal* **53**, 343–51.

Pigou, A. C. (1947) 'Economic Progress in a Stable Environment', *Economica* **14**, 180–8.

Plasschaert, S. (1989) *China, A Quasi-Federal State?*, paper presented in Dutch at the session of the Class for Moral and Political Sciences, which was held in Antwerp University, Belgium on 16 May 1989.

Portes, R. (1991) *The Path of Reform in Central and Eastern Europe: An Introduction*, the special issue of the EC publication, *European Economy*, June 1991.

Portes, R. and Santorum, A. (1987) 'Money and Consumption Goods Market in China', *Journal of Comparative Economy* **11**, 3, 354–71.

Qian, Y. Y. (1988) 'Urban and Rural Household Saving in China', *International Monetary Fund Staff Papers* **35**, 4, 592–627.

Qin, D. (1991) 'Aggregate Consumption and Income in China', *Journal of Comparative Economics* **15**, 132–41.

Radcliffe Committee Report (1959) *Report of the Committee on the Working of the Monetary System*, London: HMSO.

Radner, R. (1989) 'Teams', in Eatwell J. *et al.* (eds) (1989) 295–304.

Ray, G. F. (1991) 'Innovation and Productivity in Eastern Europe: An International Comparison', *National Institute Economic Review*, **138**, November, 75–83.

Riedel, J. (1988) 'Economic Development in East Asia: Doing What Comes Naturally?' in Hughes, H. (ed.) (1988) *Achieving Industrialization in East Asia*, Cambridge: Cambridge University Press, 1–38.

Roe, A. and Popiel, P. A. (1990) *The Restructuring of Financial Systems in Latin America*, An EDI Policy Seminar Report, no. **25**, The World Bank.

Roe, M. J. (1990) 'Political and Legal Restrictions on Ownership and Control of Public Companies', *Journal of Financial Economics*, vol. 27, no. 1, 7–41.

Rogoff, K. (1987) 'Reputational Constraints on Monetary Policy', *Carnegie-Rochester Conference Series on Public Policy* **26**, 141–82.

Roosa, R. V. (1951) 'Interest Rates and the Central Bank', in Waitzman, H. L. (ed.) (1951) *Money, Trade, and Economic Growth: Essays in Honour of John H. Williams*, New York: Macmillan.

Rostowski, J. and Auerbach, P. (1988) 'Intra-Year Fluctuations in Production and Sales: East and West', in Wiles, P. (ed.) (1988) *The Soviet Economy on the Brink of Reform*, Boston, London, Sydney and Wellington: Unwin Hyman, 82–111.

Santorum, A. (1989) *The Control of Money Supply in Developing Countries: China, 1949–1988*, London: Overseas Development Institute, Working Paper **29**.

Sayers, R. S. (1964) *Modern Banking*, 6th edition, Oxford: Clarendon Press.

Schleifer, M. (1985) 'A Theory of Yardstick Competition', *Rand Journal of Economics*, vol. 16, 319–27.

Schmidt-Hebbel, K. (1991) *Market Reforms, Inflation and Growth in China*, Country Economics Department, Macroeconomic Adjustment and Growth Division, the World Bank, mimeo.

Schüller, A. (1988) *Does Market Socialism Work?*, London: The Centre for Research into Communist Economies.

Shaw, E. S. (1973) *Financial Developing in Economic Development*, New York: Oxford University Press, 1973.

Sheard, P. (1985) 'Main Banks and Structural Adjustment in Japan', *Pacific Economic Papers*, **129**, 1–93, Australia-Japan Research Centre.

Shmelev, N. and Popov, V. (1990) *The Turning Point: Revitalizing the Soviet Economy*, London: I.B. Tauris.

Singh, A. (1989) *The Institution of a Stock Market In a Socialist Economy: Notes on the Chinese Economic Reform*, mimeo.

Song, H. K. (1991) 'Who Benefits from Industrial Restructuring?: Reflections on the South Korea Experience in the 1980s', *Korea Journal*, vol. 31, no. 3.

Spancer, P. D. (1986) *Financial Innovation, Efficiency and Disequilibrium*, Oxford: Clarendon Press.

Spulber, N. (1971) *Socialist Management and Planning: Topics in Comparative Socialist Economies*, Bloomington and London: Indiana University Press.

Statistical Yearbook of the Republic of China, 1991.

Stevenson, A., Muscatelli, V. and Gregory, M. (1988) *Macroeconomic Theory and Stabilisation Policy*, Oxford: Phillip Allan.

Stiglitz, J. E. (1989a) 'Financial Markets and Development', *Oxford Review of Economic Policy*, vol. 5, no. 4, 55–68.

Stiglitz, J. E. (1989b) *Money, Credit, and Business Fluctuations*, National Bureau of Economic Research Working Paper, No. **2823**.

Stiglitz, J. E. and Weiss, A. (1981) 'Credit Rationing in Markets with Imperfect Information', *American Economic Review*, vol. 71, no. 3, 393–410.

Svejnar, J. (1991) 'Microeconomic Issues in the Transition to a Market Economy', *Journal of Economic Perspectives*, vol. 5, no. 4, 123–38.

Taiwan Monthly Statistics, 1991.

Tam, O. (1986) 'Reform of China's Banking System', *The World Economy*, vol. 9, no. 4, 427–40.

Tardos, M. (1982) 'Developing Programme for Economic Control and Organization in Hungary', *Aeta Oecon.*

Tang, Zongkun (1992) 'The Transfer of Profits in the State-Owned Enterprises and the Vitality of These Enterprises', Discussion Paper, mimeo.

Taylor, T. W. (1989) *The Financing of Industry and Commerce*, London: Heinemann.

Teibout, C. M. (1956) 'A Pure Theory of Local Government Expenditures', *Journal of Political Economy* **64**, 416–24.

Tidrick, G. (1986) *Productivity Growth and Technological Change in Chinese Industry*, World Bank Staff Working Paper **761**, Washington, DC.

Tietmeyer, H. (1990) *The Role of an Independent Central Bank in Europe*, paper presented to the IMF Seminar on Central Banking, IMF.

Tobin, J. (1958) 'Liquidity Preference as Behaviour Towards Risk', *Review of Economic Studies* **25**, February, 65–86.

Tobin, J. (1963) 'Commercial Banks as Creators of "Money"', in Carson, D. (ed.) (1963) *Banking and Monetary Studies*, Homewood, Irwin, reprinted in Hester, D. D. and Tobin, J. (1967) *Financial Markets and Economic Activity*, New York: Wiley, 1–11.

Tobin, J. (1969) 'A General Equilibrium Approach to Monetary Theory', *Journal of Money, Credit, and Banking* **1**, 15–29.

Topham, N. (1983) 'Local Government Economics', in Millward, R. (1983) *Public Sector Economics*, London: Longman, 129–98.

Transition (The News Letter about the Reforming Economies), published by the World Bank, various issues.

United Nations (1985) *Economic and Social Survey of Asia and Pacific 1984*.

Uno, K. (1991) 'Privatization and Creation of Commercial Banking Systems', in Peck, M. J. and Richardson, T. J. (eds) (1991) *What Is To Be Done?* New Haven and London: Yale University Press, 149–78.

US Department of Commerce (1960) *Historical Statistics of the United States: Colonial Times to 1957*, Washington, DC.

US Department of Commerce (1975) *Historical Statistics of the United States: Colonial Times to 1970*, Washington, DC.

Walras, L. (1886) *Théorie de La Monnaie*, Lausanne: Corbaz. See Walras L. in Eatwell J. *et al.* (eds) *The New Palgrave: A Dictionary of Economics*, vol. 4, (1987) Basingstoke: Macmillan.

Wang, Yijiang (1990) 'Decentralization, Resource Misallocation and Inflation: a Behaviourial Model Based on the Chinese Experience', in the Chinese Young Economist Society (ed.) (1990) *Proceedings of the Symposium on Economic Reforms in China*, pA1–40.

Wang, Yijiang (1991) 'Economic Reform, Fixed Capital Investment Expansion, and Inflation: Behavioral Model based on the Chinese Experience', *Chinese Economic Review*, vol. 2, no. 1, 3–27.

White, G. and Bowles P. (1988) 'China's Banking Reforms: Aims, Methods and Problems', *National Westminster Bank Review*, November 1988, 28–37.

White, G. R. (1975) 'Some Econometric Models of Deposit Bank Portfolio Behaviour in the UK, 1963–70', in Renton, G. A. (ed.) (1975) *Modelling the Economy*, London: Heinemann, 457–99.

Wilson, T. (1984) 'Matters of Public Policy', in Wilson, T. (1984) *Fiscal Decentralisation*, London: Anglo-German Foundation, 1–52.

Wolf, T. A. (1990) 'Reform, Inflation, and Adjustment in Planned Economies', *Finance and Development*, March 1990, 2–5.

Wong, C. P. W. (1985) 'Material Allocation and Decentralisation: Impact of the Local Sector on Industrial Reform', in Perry E. J. and Wong C. (eds) (1985) *The Political Economy of Reform in Post-Mao China*, Cambridge, Mass.: Harvard University Press.

Wong, C. P. W. (1987) 'Between Plan and Market: The Role of the Local Sector in Post-Mao China', *Journal of Comparative Economics*, vol. 11, no. 3, September 1987, 385–98.

Wood, A. (1975) *A Theory of Profits*, Cambridge: Cambridge University Press.

Wood, A. (1991) *China's Economic System: A Brief Description, with Some Suggestions for Further Reform*, CP, no. 12, The Development Economics Research Programme, London School of Economics.

Wood, G. (1991) *Independent Central Banks from Historical Perspectives*, paper presented in the seminar in Brasenose College, the University of Oxford, 26 November 1991.

World Bank (1985a) *China: Economic Structure in International Perspective*.

World Bank (1985b) *China: Economic Structure in International Perspective, Annex 5 to China: Long-term Development, Issues and Options*.

World Bank (1985c) *China: Long-Term Development Issues and Options*, Baltimore: Johns Hopkins University Press.

World Bank (1988a) *World Development Report 1988*.

World Bank (1988b) *China: Finance and Investment*, A World Bank Country Study.

World Bank (1989) *World Development Report 1989: Financial Systems and Development*, New York: Oxford University Press.

World Bank (1990a) *China: Macroeconomic Stability and Industrial Growth under Decentralised Socialism.*

World Bank (1990b) *China: Country Economic Memorandum: Between Plan and Market.*

World Bank (1991) *World Development Report 1991.*

World Bank (1992) *China: Reform and the Role of the Plan in the 1990s.*

World Bank (1993) *The East Asian Miracle: Economic Growth and Public Policy*, Oxford: Oxford University Press.

Wulf, L. D. and Goldsbrough, D. (1986) 'The Role of Monetary Policy in China', *International Monetary Fund Staff Papers*, vol. **33**, 209–42.

Yang, Peixin (1984) 'Banking', in Yu, Guanyuan (ed.) (1984) *China's Socialist Modernization*, Beijing: Foreign Language Press, 405–36.

Yenal, O. (1989) *Chinese Reforms, Inflation and the Allocation of Investment in a Socialist Economy*, Internal Discussion Paper, Asia Regional Series, no. 52, the World Bank.

Yerrow, G. (1988) 'Comment on Perestroika: Transition from Central Planning to Market Socialism', by Nuti, D. M. (1988) in *Economic Policy: A European Forum* **7**, October 1988, 386–8.

Yi, Gang (1991) 'The Monetization Process in China during the Economic Reform', *China Economic Review*, vol. 2, no. 1, 75–96.

Yi, Gang (1992) *Toward Estimating the Demand for Money in China*, mimeo.

Yoshitomi, M. (1991) 'Country Study: Japan', in Marer, P. and Zecchini, S. (eds) (1991) *The Transition to a Market Economy*, vol. 1, OECD, 140–50.

Yule, G. (1926) 'Why Do We Sometimes Get Nonsense-Correlations Between Time Series?' *Journal of Royal Statistics Society*, vol. 89, no. 1, 1–64.

Yung, Chul Park (1991) 'Country Study: South Korea', in Marer, P. and Zecchini, S. (eds) (1991) *The Transition to a Market Economy*, vol. 1, OECD, 150–2.

Yusuf, S. (1990) *Macroeconomic Development and Policies in China: Remarks*, mimeo.

Yusuf, S. and Peters, R. K. (1984) 'Saving Behaviour and its Implications for Domestic Resource Mobilization: The Case of the Republic of Korea', *The World Bank Staff Working Paper*, no. **628**.

Index